CO-OPERATIVES FOR RURAL DEVELOPMENT

Co-operatives for Rural Development

Edited by :

Dr. S.N. Tripathy

Deptt. of Econoics
Aska Science College
Aska—761 111 (Orissa)

DISCOVERY PUBLISHING HOUSE
NEW DELHI – 110 002

Published by :

Discovery Publishing House
4831/24, Ansari Road, Prahlad Street
Darya Ganj, New Delhi–110 002 (INDIA)
Phone : 327 9245
Fax : 91–11–3253475

First Published—1998
Reprint : 2012

ISBN 81–7141–428–1

Laser Typeset by :

Allied Computers,
Karnal (Haryana)

Printed at Dynamic Printers

Preface

The Co-operative movement was introduced in India in the early years of 20th century with the main object of relieving the peasantry's burden of debt and for providing credit through a local agency on the principles of thrift, self-help and mutual aid.

Till the publication of the All India Rural Credit Survey Committee Report (1954), Co-operative as an effective channel of agricultural credit was not recognised. Later on, co-operative credit as an integral part of the successive Five Year plans was accorded priority resulting in phenomenal expansion of co-operative movement. During 1969, it was felt that due to financial and manegerial weaknesses, co-operative by themselves may not be able to meet the fast growing credit needs of the agricultural sector, and commercial banks were assigned the role in the field of rural credit.

Today the Indian co-operative movement is one of the biggest in the world; encompassing agricultural credit, marketing, handlooms, fisheries, food-processing, house-building, milk production and a number of other spheres.

Originally, it was envisaged that commercial banks would supplement the efforts of the co-operative societies till that period when the co-operatives become strong enough to undertake the responsibility of meeting the whole co-operate needs. However, the situation subsequently demanded for a multi-agency approach. The primary purpose of the multi-agency approach is to facilitate greater effectiveness of all the agencies involved in rural credit—commercial banks, regional rural banks and co-operative banks, and widening of the total availability of institutional finance to the rural sector. Strengthening of industrial co-operatives is a better solution to meet the challenges of the growing rural unemployment. The industrial co-operatives not only ensure employment to the rural masses, but also help in many other ways in ameliorating their living conditions. Without affecting their main sources of employment—agriculture, the industrial co-operatives effectively cater to the varying employment needs of the rural landless labour and artisans. Without any strict adherence to the number of working hours, depending on their workneeds, the industrial co-operatives provide employment opportunities as and when they are required. Thus, the solution to the problem of growing rural employment in India lies in the organisation of rural industries and agricultural allied activities in the co-operative form otherwise known as 'Industrial Co-operatives'.

Co-operative forming, in spite of a large number of problems was the only strucutre which could ensure active participation of small, marginal producers and landless labourers in the growth process.

It is imperative to evolve a total integration of specialised co-operative functioning in rural areas to make co-operatives indispensable agencies in economic development. The officials of the co-operative department have to review their functioning as well as schemes, and devote greater attention with sincerity for perspective planning. High default rates, leading to increase in the quantum of overdues has been the factor crippling the strength and viability of the co-operative credit institutions.

Planned efforts for accelerating the recovery of overdues, reducing the transaction cost, and cost of management are needed.

Exclusive dependence on outside borrowings should be controlled. Borrowers affected by repeated natural calamities should adopt crop insurance scheme to mitigate their problems through risk cover. This will also bring stability to the rural credit institutions.

The co-operative banks should be resource based, self-supporting, strong and financially viable institutions capable of providing cost effective credit and banking services to the farmers.

"Co-operatives for Rural Development"—contains 16 contributions of eminent economists. This volume examines the entire gamut of issues relating to co-operative sector and its role in developing the rural sector; covering development, problems and prospects.

This volume could not have been brought to light without the contribution of papers by the eminent authors. The editor expresses his deepest gratitute to all the contributors whose papers have enriched this volume.

S. N. Tripathy

Contents

Preface V

1. New Economic Policy and Co-operatives : Problem and Prospects 1
—Dr. M.S. Subramaniam

2. What Ails Co-operative Societies in India 8
—Dr. I. Satya Sundaram

3. Co-operative Sugar Mills in Tamil Nadu 19
—Dr. V. Rangaswami
Dr. K.A. Alagar
Prof. Raghuraman Narayanan

4. Towards Alleviation of Poverty : Co-operatives and Dairy Development 37
—Sri Chitaranjan Dash

5. Natural Resources and Co-operation 54
—Prof. Raghuraman Narayan

6. Marketing Co-operatives in India 79
—Dr. S. N. Tripathy

7. Strengthening Co-operatives in Tribal Areas 85
—Dr. Kulwant Pathania
Mr. Yoginder Singh Thakur
Miss Anita Pathania

8. Role and Performance of Dairy Co-operatives in Rural Development 100
—Dr. Surendranath Behera

9. **Fisheries Co-operatives in Orissa : A Case Study of Financing Beach Landing Crafts in Ganjam District (Orissa)** 113

—Mr. P. Sahu
Dr. N.B. Pradhan

10. **Women Co-operation and Rural Enterprise Development** 125

—Dr. M. Sundarapandian

11. **Problems and Prospects of Primary Handloom Weavers' Co-operative Societies in Orissa** 142

—Sri Radhakrishna Panda

12. **Issues and Problems of Co-operatives in India** 164

—Dr. Sudhakar Patra

13. **Agricultural Financing and Problems of Overdues** 184

—Dr. Rabi Narayan Mishra

14. **Co-operative Movement in India** 205

—Dr. (Major) G.P. Mahapatra

15. **Rural Development Through Dairy Co-operatives** 225

—Dr. S. N. Tripathy

16. **Housing Finance in India** 229

—Dr. Bhagabat Patra

1

New Economic Policy and Co-operatives : Problems and Prospects

Dr. M.S. Subramanian*

Co-operatives are voluntary, people-oriented and self-help organisations. They aim at meeting the human needs through collective action without any exploitation. Co-operative sector in India presently comprises more than 3,53,000 co-operative societies with a membership of 164 millions and working capital of Rs. 71,000 crore. In various sectors of our economy, co-operatives have made impressive contribution - in agricultural credit 43.3 percent, fertilizer distributed 34 percent, sugar produced 62.4 per cent, splindledge 11 per cent, yarn production 16.4 per cent, cotton-ginning and pressing units 12 per cent, cotton yarn exported 11 per cent, handloom co-operatives 58 per cent, wheat procurement 30 per cent, jute procurement 21 per cent, fishermen co-operatives 11 per cent, powerloom co-operatives 5 per cent and rural fair price shops 26 per cent. Co-operatives, thus have reached the remotest villages in the country and contributed to the growth of the rural economy.

Historical Perspective

In India co-operatives were first started in 1904 as an extension of government activities and worked as a department of the

* Professor, Department of Agricultural Economics, School of Economics, Madurai Kamaraj University, Madurai— 625 021, Tamil Nadu.

government for distributing loans to agriculturists. Our planned economic development from 1951 onwards has boosted co-operatives in India. Since independence co-operation has been recognised as one of the important segments of our economy. Our first seven Five Year Plans have incorporated specific guidelines for setting out policy for the development of co-operatives.

The First Five Year Plan recognised the importance of co-operatives as an instrument of economic planning. The Second Five Year Plan emphasised the building up of a strong co-operative sector as an important part of national policy. The diversification of co-operative activities took place during the Third Five Year Plan.

During the Fourth Five Year Plan multi-agency approach was introduced in co-operation and weaker sections were given importance. The Fifth Five Year Plan recognised co-operatives as an institutional agency for the development of weaker sections and as an important organisational mechanism to implement Public Distribution System. Sixth Five Year Plan gave importance to strengthening of primary co-operative societies and co-operative federal organisations and development of professional manpower in co-operatives. The Seventh Five Year Plan emphasised the strengthening of institutional structure of co-operatives at all levels and democratisation of professional management. Thus the Indian co-operatives have grown more and more and have tremendous reach throughout length and breadth of the country by way of their vast network.

New Economic Policy

In post-independent India, although planned economic development helped the country in attaining self-sufficiency in food-grains, a strong industrial infrastructure and a number of milestones in the field of social development, a deepening of economic crisis characterised by Balance of Payment problems, disrupted industrial production, shortage of Foreign Exchange, budgetary deficits combined with accelerated inflationary trends prompted the government to initiate economic policies for stabilisation and structural reforms in national economy. The new economic policy represents a fundamental departure, market orientation, privatisation and globalisation. Liberalisation amounted to (i) dismantling the control regime, (ii) delicensing and decontrolling the industries and trade, (iii) reformation of fiscal and financial sectors, (iv) encouraging direct foreign investment and (v) opening up economy. Market orientation aims at minimising the role and involvement of government in influencing market mechanism and promoting competition. Privatisation implied diversifying the government ownership of economic enterprises and encouraging promotion of private sector enterprises. Globalisation aims at (i) encouraging free flow of foreign capital and technology, (ii) encouraging and establishment of internal joint ventures and (iii) dismantling restrictive trade regime permitting entry of multinational corporations.

Challenges

In the wake of above new economic policy package measures, co-operatives will be facing the challenges of increasing competition, emerging opportunities and withdrawal of government support. There is a fear that co-operatives will not be able to face competition from the private sector. This fear is largely unfounded because of various reasons. Co-operatives have already a handlong advantage in terms of their reach and vast infrastructure. The area of co-operative business is such that in most cases private entrepreneurship shy away from investing. Co-operatives have the inherent strength of developing intimate relations with its customers. It is this strength on which it has to build upon. There is no need to abandon their social objectives in the changed scenario.

The Anand experiment has already shown the power and potential of the co-operative sector. The Gujarat Co-operative Milk Federation, Indian Farmers Fertilizers Co-operative, Pravara Co-operative Complex at Maharashtra and Krishak Bharati Co-operatives etc. have performed admirably. If the right options are placed at their disposal, they can face competition from any quarters. It is high time, the co-operative sector is restructured, revitalised and reorganised. There is little logic in insulating the co-operative sector from the winds of change blowing in the economic arena in the form of new economic policy.

Sugar Sector

Among the most successful sectors of the co-operative movement in India is one comprising co-operative sugar mills. New economic policy has created many problems to sugar industry. The co-operative sector as a whole is strongly opposed to any move to delicense the sugar industry. While a private sugar factory can bring financial resources from anywhere, the co-operatives have to mobilise resources from its own members. This will make them less effective in a competitive situation. The existing co-operative sugar mills are already facing shortages of cane. The delicensing will aggravate the problem of lack of enough raw material supply and will enhance their costs. Co-operative sugar factories will be ruined if any one opens factory without considering raw materials supply. Private sugar mills are unlikely to make investments on irrigation like co-operatives. Amidst these problems, the market value of sugar co-operative shares will also decline.

Marketing Co-operatives

Liberalisation has exposed marketing co-operatives to competition from national and multi-national giants. It has also opened up vast opportunities to marketing co-operatives for growth and expansion. Now they can sell their products in America, Europe, Middle East and East Asia and obtain higher prices. But the present Co-operative Act does not permit them to function with freedom. While marketing co-operatives are subject to audit and supervision by the Registrar of Co-operative Societies and required to pay sales tax, entry tax and octroi, AMPC fee and all other kinds of duties and taxes, private traders are able to evade most of these taxes. This has put marketing co-operatives at a disadvantageous position. Marketing co-operatives are now compelled to pay income tax. Their bank accounts are being frozen and so they are left with little surplus. They are likely to suffer heavily from this situation.

Co-operative Credit

As a part of new economic policy and many financial reform measures are implemented in the banking sector. As far as co-operative banks are concerned, these reform measures include capital adequacy norms, establishment of separate rural banks, 10 per cent of the net credit for export purposes, 2 to 6 per cent concessional interest rate for agricultural credit etc. At present co-operative banks are under considerable pressure causing decline in productivity and efficiency, low profitability, unremunerative direct investment, deterioration in the quality of portfolio, inadequacy of capital, inadequacy of loan provision, large scale loan waiver, duplication of infrastructure, over staffing, management weakness etc. These constraints may considerably influence institutional finance for priority sector in the long run. These banking sector reforms have led to the following challenges to co-operative banks:

(a) Though in theory, the management of a co-operative bank is to be vested in a democratically elected board, in practice, it is managed by government appointed boards or administrators. Therefore, political interference is inevitable.

(b) The deregulation of interest rate may affect the financial viability of co-operative banks.

(c) Co-operative banks are expected to be self-reliant but in practice they depend heavily on financial support of the Government.

(d) Many co-operative banks have remained inefficient and non-viable. In the case of Primary Agricultural Co-operative Societies financial costs are observed to be higher.

(e) The loan portfolios of co-operative banks do not show any trend of diversification. Co-operative banks could not settle their interest rates at realistic levels.

Dairy Industry

In dairy industry co-operatives have been instrumental in improving the availability of cattle feed and fodder and improving the management capability of milk producers. Co-operative dairies are controlled under co-operative law. On the contrary the private dairy enterprises are guided by the company law. Co-operatives are at present facing working capital problems. At the same time nationalised banks do not treat them on par with big business houses. At one hand, GATT agreements impose a renewed thrust for the development of strong international co-operation in the dairy sector. On the other hand, the delicensing of dairy industry seems to have put paid to all the efforts make over the past 25 years to nurture a modern viable co-operative dairy industry in India. The major consequence of delicensing in dairy industry is that the efforts and investments of the dairy co-operatives to increase milk production is now benefitting the private dairies. The new private dairies are not looking for easy pickings in those very areas where the co-operative ventures are well established and they have already spent substantial resources to enhance milk production. The mushrooming of new private dairies is leading to a run on the raw material - milk - that is available in the milk sheds. The resulting unhealthy competition has eroded the ability of dairy co-operatives to repay their loans and in turn place co-operative funding agencies in an awkward position to fulfill their onward obligations to the government and international agencies.

Strategies for Revitalisation

The Central issue of co-operatives at this point of time is to reorient and readapt their structure, functioning and management. There should be a well conceived action programme which should provide specific guide points to co-operatives in the areas of professionalism and efficiency, induction of modern technology, systematic training through effective interplay of inter co-operative relationship, mobilisation of resources and enhancing participation of members in decision making process and reducing dependence on government assistance. Following are the specific strategies to be adopted to revitalise co-operatives:

(a) Co-operatives who have lost relevance to their members and have no potential to plan concrete actions in this regard should be amalgamated and wound up.

(b) A new law should be enacted to end undue political and bureaucratic interventions in international affairs of co-operatives and law should be strictly enforced.

(c) The co-operative societies should formulate norms for minimum member economic participation in the business of co-operatives. The members who do not fulfill these norms should be disqualified to exercise their right of membership and for occupying the positions in co-operatives.

(d) Co-operatives must improve their marketing methods and practices.

(e) They must be financially strong. Basic level co-operative institutions must be strengthened.

(f) They must adopt innovative methods, practices and product mix using the most modern technologies available.

(g) They must be sensitive to market signals and be able to adjust their operating policies to cater to the changing demands of their clients.

(h) They must ensure and maintain high quality of their products and services and establish their credibility and image by proving good value for the money spent by their clients.

(i) They should hereafter be cost-conscious, honest and committed to the attainment of their objectives.

(j) They must enjoy full autonomy to determine the prices of their products and services and follow democratic practices in the decision making and election.

(k) The co-operatives have to develop their own management system, including information technology, to face the emerging competitive environment. They should enter into new areas like electrification, tourism, agro exports, textile mills and flouri-culture.

(l) The government must prepare a new national policy on co-operatives with the help of academicians and thinkers.

Conclusion

No doubt, co-operatives will strive even under the changing scenario. Implementation of new economic policy should not be treated as a threat for the survival of co-operatives. In fact it should be treated as an incumbent action on the part of the Government and law to redeem co-operatives of its interference and control. This in turn calls for co-operatives to stand on their feet as strong, efficient and member responsive enterprises.

References

1. Katar Singh, "Co-operatives in Rural Economy", (Rapporteur's Report), *Indian Journal of Agricultural Economic*, Vol. 52, No. 1, January-March, 1997.
2. Venkatappiah, "Co-operation and Rural Development", *National Bank Review*, April 1997.
3. B.D. Sharma, "Economic Reforms and Inevitability of Coops", *The co-operator*, January 1995.
4. A. Ravi Shankar, "Co-operatives and Liberalistion: Challenges and Opportunities,", *The Co-operator*, May 1996.

2

What Ails Credit Co-operatives in India ?

Dr. I. Satya Sundaram*

Providing an ideal credit system for the rural poor is no easy task. The rural poor are vast in size and they take up diverse occupations. Most of them work in the unorganised sector. Moreover, the power structure in rural India is unfavourable for the poor. The rural credit system must be accessible to the poor.

I

Rationale and Progress of Credit Co-operatives

The co-operative structure is based on the concept of self-help and people's active participation in the management of institutions. Basically, the co-operatives are thrift promoting organisations. Members' participation is the essence of co-operative democracy.

The co-operative structure in India is not only old, but also a very large one. There are various types of co-operatives like agricultural co-operatives, handloom weavers' co-operatives, fishery, dairy and industrial and housing co-operatives. Yet, the co-operative sector is not receiving the attention which it deserves.

The success of credit orient development projects largely depends on the soundness of the credit structure and the credit system.[1] Co-operatives are the ideal institutions to serve the rural poor as they are very close to the people they serve.

* Research Director, Post-Graduate Department of Economics, The Hindu College, Machilipatnam, Andhra Pradesh.

There is nothing wrong with the concept of co-operation. If the performance of co-operative institutions is not up to the mark, it is because of the absence of the pre-conditions for their success. About co-operative movement, it has been rightly observed, "Since co-operation is a voluntary, people's movement, honesty, transparency of co-operation, ideological commitment and self-discipline are essential for it to succeed. It is bound to derail, if any one of the factors is lacking or deficient.[2]

The co-operatives possess some unique and welcome features: non-exploitative character, voluntary membership, the principle of one-man-vote, decentralised decision-making and self-imposed curbs on profits.

Co-operative development in India can be traced to the enactment of the first co-operative legislation in 1904 which provided for the establishment of agricultural co-operative credit societies with unlimited liability. Under the Act of 1904, a number of co-operative credit societies came into existence and the co-operative credit movement recorded considerable progress. The cooperative legislation became inevitable because of high incidence of agricultural indebtedness.

The co-operative credit institutions made considerable progress. Their share has gone up from 3.0 per cent in 1951-52 to 29 per cent in 1981 in the total outstanding debt of the farmers and they provided, by 1990, about 60 per cent of the total institutional finance for agriculture.

There are about 3.53 lakh co-operative societies bringing within their fold a membership of 17.51 crores and employing a working capital of over Rs. 76,000 crores, enveloping almost every conceivable economic activity. Almost all the villages in the country have been covered by 95,200 Primary Agricultural Cooperative Societies (PACT) with about 67 per cent coverage of rural households.[3]

Production credit from co-operative banks moved up from Rs. 4403 crore in 1991-92 to Rs. 9750 crore in 1996-97 while medium and long-term credit rose from Rs. 1397 crore to Rs. 2729 crore in the same period.

Co-operatives continue to be the major source of institutional credit for agriculture. During 1993–94, a sum of Rs. 8500 crore was provided to the farmers as short, medium and long term credit by the co-operatives whereas the commercial banks and regional rural banks together provided only Rs. 6600 crore. The co-operative share of the institutional credit thus stood at 56 per cent.[4]

The progress of PACS is impressive in regard to their advances. Short term loans issued by them increased from Rs. 305 crore in 1965-66 to Rs. 2746 crore in 1985-86. During this period, term loans issued increased from Rs. 37 crore to Rs. 334 crore. Their total loans and advances outstanding increased from Rs. 1299 crore in 1975-76 to Rs. 4313 crore in 1985-86

The amount of loans advanced by PACS was Rs. 23 crore in 1950-51 which increased to Rs. 4200 crore in 1988-89. By 1989, the outstanding advances of PACS stood at Rs. 840 crore, covering 65 per cent of rural population. As a result of reorganisation, the number of PACS came down from 1,60,000 in 1969 to 92,000 in 1988. The percentage of borrowing members to the total membership has shown a steady decline from 54.8 per cent in 1960-61 to 24 per cent in 1987-88. In Assam it was only 13.61 per cent and in Punjab it was 14.38 per cent.[5]

Table 2.1 : Progress of Cooperatives in India (Number and Deposits) during 1960–61 to 1990–91

(Rs. in Crores)

	Co-operative Year, July–June			
	1960–61	1970–71	1980–81	1990–91
State Coop. Banks				
Number	25	25	27	28
Deposits	72	279	1675	6128
Central Coop. Banks				
Number	340	341	337	356
Deposits	112	439	2419	10251
State/Central Land Development Banks				
Number	19	19	19	19
Deposits	6	7	29	NS
Primary Agri. Credit Societies				
Number (000's)	212	161	95	88
Deposits	15	69	289	1349

NA = Not Available

Table 2.2 : Recovery Performance of Cooperatives during 1988–89 and 1989–90 (July–June)

	Percentage of Overdues to			
	Loans Outstanding		Demand	
	1960–61	1970–71	1980–81	1990–91
State Coop. Banks	10.2	13.7	13.7	17.7
Central Coop. Banks	24.2	33.0	36.7	51.7
State/Central Land Development Banks	19.8	22.1	55.9	66.8
Primary Agri. Credit Societies	38.6	38.9	42.6	48.8

NA = Not Available

The Seventh Plan (1985-90) target for co-operative credit has been fixed at Rs. 7090 crore for short, medium and long-term loans.

However, the co-operative are plagued with poor deposit mobilisation and mounting overdue. The share of co-operatives in total farm lending has come down to 36.6 per cent in 1991-92-decline of more than 26 per cent in a decade.

The co-operatives' share in total lending was 62.7 per cent in 1980-81. The recovery position of short-term credit is also on the decline. From 59.8 per cent in June 1988, it had fallen to 57.5 per cent a year later.

The share of co-operative in agricultural credit (short term) has come down from 78 per cent in 1974-75 to about 45 per cent in 1988-89.

II

Problems of Credit Co-operative

The credit co-operatives are suffering from staggering overdues, poor recoveries, too much of unwarranted government and political interference and the obnoxious practice of nominations on the managements of co-operative societies by the Government. The accounts remain unaudited for years together. Also, the elections to even apex co-operative institutions are not held regularly. No wonder, some of the District Cooperative Banks become ineligible for NABARD refinance. Misallocation and misutilisation of co-operative loans is very common.

For various reasons, the co-operative movement has lost not only its teeth, but its true character as well. It has been pertinently pointed out by the eminent co-operative leader, Dr. V. Kurien. "The unfortunate fact of the matter is that today our co-operative movement is neither co-operative, nor a movement. It has become a department of the Government rather several departments."[6]

Over a period, the spirit of cooperation has been slowly eliminated. The laudable objective of democratic self-management has been jettisoned. What we actually see today in the co-operatives is the vested interests working against genuine democracy.

The PACS are expected to inculcate the saving habits in the members and attract those savings in the form of deposits to the society. However, most PACS are not even conscious of their role as promoters of thrift and have made no efforts for deposit mobilisation.

In 1982-83, only 56.5 per cent of PACS were earning profit. The tendency of the states of write-off the co-operative dues is a matter of extreme concern as it hampers recovery of dues from the farmers and affects the recycling funds and credit expansion.[7]

The PACS remain unviable because of their poor performance on the credit front. At the national level the loans advanced per PACS were Rs. 4.09 lakh in 1987-88. The Agricultural Credit Review Committee (1989) had suggested that a PACS, in order to be viable, must disburse at least Rs. 10 lakh as agricultural credit.

About 9000 PACS are dormant. A large number of PACS do only token business and therefore are not economically viable. The situation is the direct product of inefficient management, inadequate supervision, high incidence of leakages and poor financial position. The N.R. Mirdha Committee has rightly observed, "a genuine, self-reliant cooperative movement cannot grow until and unless this extensive problem of dormancy affecting the viability of the primary credit structure is satisfactorily tackled."

Lack of member's involvement has made the performance of PACS very poor. The percentage of borrowing members to the total membership has declined from 54.8 per cent in 1960-61 to 24.0

per cent in 1987-88. This reveals the organisational weakness of the PACS. In some states, the percentage is very low - 13.61 per cent in Assam and 14.38 per cent in Punjab in 1992. The success of PACS depends on its ability to involve its large number of inactive members in the organisation.[8]

The PACS are facing a number of problems and therefore they remain weak. By June 1986, the over dues of PACS amounted to Rs. 1807 crore (41 per cent of the demand). More than 51 per cent of the overdues of the PACS were more than three years old, indicating their sticky nature. The margin of PACS per Rs. 100 of agricultural loans was negative at Rs. 3.21. This would be definitely more if the costs of over dues and bad debts are taken into account.

The co-operatives which are expected to serve the target groups, have indeed become conduits of cheap popularity in the hands of politicians. It has been rightly observed by Prof. A.M. Khusro, "The co-operative sector is being totally neglected, in fact, throttled by too much intervention. It is a case of killing with kindness, through over-regulation official diktat and curbing of freedom to perform."[9]

State government interference in their day-to-day operations is not the only problem. An antiquated management structure too has rendered most co-operatives unviable and uncompetitive compared with other competing sectors and enterprises.[10]

The limited success of co-operative institutions is mainly due to mismanagement. There is need for professionalisation of management. It has been rightly pointed out, "The government should desist from populist schemes such as loan melas and debt relief since they do more harm than good and weaken the credit system. Finally, a human resource development strategy should be adopted by the co-operative institutions. It involves two activities to begin with, co-operative entrepreneurship development programme and training for business development planning and improving management skill and operational efficiency of the societies' managers/secretaries and member of the managing committees.[11]

The bureaucratic approach and outdated laws are the bane of co-operative movement. The co-operative law, inherited from the colonial masters, was based on mistrust of people. As rightly observed by Dr. Kurien, "It created a registrar, the friend, philosopher and guide to make certain the natives did not pocket the co-operative funds. It vested the registrar with the powers of God, and allowed him to exercise those powers with virtually no accountability to anyone other than his own conscience."

Absence of accountability is the main problem facing the co-operative structure. As observed by Dr. Kurien, "And so we saw a situation arise where the co-operatives, owned and supported by the labour and individual enterprise of our farmers, become top heavy superstructures managed, and often led, by bureaucrats accountable to government or, in other words, to themselves."

The recovery performance of co-operatives in the case of term loans which has slided to 39.7 per cent in June, 1989, has further come down to about 20 per cent during 1990-91.

In the case of co-operatives, of the 369 District Central Co-operative Banks (DCBs) only about 170 were generating profits: the overdues constituted 33 per cent of demand. Similarly, only 60 per cent of the 70, 783 PACs were viable: overdues constituted about 38 per cent of loans.[12]

Not a few factors have contributed to the worsening problem of overdues. Agricultural credit is being used to achieve short-term populist objectives. Government measures such as waiving of agricultural dues, concessions/reliefs announced by political functionaries from public platforms, stay orders on legal processes of recovery, disbursement of loans/assets at the hands of political dignitaries in loan *melas* etc. have vitiated the recovery climate.[13]

III
Measures to Strengthen Credit Co-operatives

Every effort should be made to see that the PACS become economically viable. No PACS should remain economically unviable for long. The state government's share capital should be gradually reduced. With this, the tendency to prop up weak and unviable societies with government share capital will come to an end and those which are commercially unviable will have a natural eclipse.[14]

The Seventh Five Year Plan (1985-90) aimed at :[15]

i) comprehensive development of primary agricultural credit societies to function as multi-purpose viable units;

ii) realignment of the policies and procedures of co-operatives to expand the flow of credit and ensure supply of inputs and services particularly to the weaker sections;

iii) taking up of special co-operative programmes for implementation in the underdeveloped states specifically in the North Eastern Region, and

iv) promoting professional management and strengthening of effective training facilities for improving the operational efficiency.

In 1985, the Government constituted a committee headed by K.N. Ardhanareeswaran, then additional secretary in the Department of Agriculture and Co-operatives. The Committee submitted its report in 1987. It made some radical recommendations as far as the state government's role was concerned.

In March, 1990, the Planning Commission itself set up a committee under the chairmanship of Chaudhary Brahma Prakash, a veteran co-operative leader. The Committee, drafted a model co-operative societies Bill which it submitted to the Government in November 1990. The intention was to minimise government control and interference and develop self-reliance and self-confidence within these bodies. Some states did raise objections to the suggestions made by the committee.

The model law has recommended new norms of membership, suggesting that entry into a co-operative society should be voluntary and available to all without any artificial restriction.

The simplified registration procedure as outlined in the model bill grants registration to any society within 60 days of application. This is of course undermines the role of the registrar, a state representative. This is not liked by most state governments. Under the model Bill, a formal declaration on the part of an applicant society expressing its willingness to abide by the co-operatives objective will suffice. The state governments feel that this 'liberalisation' w[illegible] be misused.

The model bill [illegible]tates that any federal co-operative may be formed with the signature of authorised representatives of at least two primary cooperatives.

The model bill makes a provision where a co-operative society can acquire a holding company status. It is said that any financial help from the government should henceforth come in the form of grant or loan.[16]

In 1994, the RBI freed deposit and lending rates to make the co-operative banks viable, but the measure failed to deliver the goods. There is need for the Government to come to the rescue as it is not a majority stake-holder in the co-operative banks. Co-operative banks have little freedom with rural interests and registrar refusing permission to co-operative banks to change market rates.[17]

The quantum of resources required to cleanse the balance sheets of the co-operative institutions, other than short-term and long-term structures has been tentatively estimated to be of the order of Rs. 6600 crore.

On August 8, 1997, the Minister of State for Agriculture, announced in the Rajya Sabha a Rs. 6600 crore write-off to clean up the balance sheets of co-operative credit institutions.

Toning up management practices in co-operatives is most essential. It is said[18]:

> The decision making in a co-operative must ultimately lie with the general body, which shall also elect an executive or governing body. The one-man-one-vote principle may have to be amended in the interest of cooperative management. A more appropriate basis of voting should be the patronage (i.e. the extent of user-participation) by the members.

We must think of preparing a workable plan for the gradual withdrawal of the government presence from the affairs of the co-operatives.[19]

Of course, the co-operatives should not confine themselves to meeting the credit needs. Indeed, credit may not be of much help, if other inputs are not available. The Committee to Review Arrangements for the Institutional Credit for Agriculture and Rural Development (CRAFICARD) has rightly observed:

in planning the future of reorganised societies the aim should be to transform them into a single contact point in the village for all types of credit and not merely for agriculture in the narrow sense. In other words, they should also have the capacity to serve other rural procedures such as artisans, craftsmen and agricultural labourers in respect of their economic activities. They must offer a package of services of the clientele, for example, input supplies and marketing help. They have to be servicing agencies either by directly undertaking the services required by the producers or by forging effective links with other agencies such as marketing societies and fertiliser suppliers who render such services.

The co-operatives should decide the strategy to be followed by them. The co-operative system should not continue as a government or Five-Year plan programme. The plan should only aim at a package of financial and other incentives/disincentives and public investment for building up of rural infrastructure which helps to boost the co-operative system.[20]

It is necessary to ensure flow of adequate co-operative credit to the weaker sections, particularly the Scheduled Castes and Scheduled Tribes. Membership should be open to these classes. To meet specific requirements, like those of the tribals, large sized multi-purpose societies should be organised. The linkage between PACS and the commercial banks should be strengthened. The commercial banks can assist PACS in the proper maintenance of books of accounts, accounting procedures etc. The PACS are close to the local people. They can assist commercial banks branches in the identification of eligible borrowers and recovery of loans.

References

1. A.S. Kahlon and Karam Singh: *Managing Agricultural Finance*. Allied Publishers Private Ltd., New Delhi. 1984 p.107.
2. S.K. Ramno: 'Sad State of Rural Credit Cooperatives', *The Hindu*, April 16, 1993.
3. U.M. Shah: 'Cooperative Development—Progress and Trends', *Kurukshetrra*, November 1995, p.3.

4. J.P. Singh: 'Cooperatives: Continued Relevance to Farming', *The Hindu Survey of Indian Agriculture 1995.* p. 161.

5. M.B. Patil: 'PACS: Why They Need a Shake-Up', *Yojana*, December 31, 1992, p.6.

6. *The Financial Express*, April 12, 1993.

7. C.M. Choudhary: 'Making PACS Economically Viable', *Kuruskshetra*, July 1992, p.14.

8. M.B. Patil: 'Who can Save Primary Agricultural Co-operative Societies (PACS)? ', *Southern Economist*, November 1, 1992, p. 21.

9. *Indian Expess*, May 14, 1992.

10. Ratna Ganguli : 'Co-operatives: Stating the Case', *The Economic Times*, May 20, 1991.

11. J. N.L. Srivastava : 'Primacy for Co-operatives', *The Hindu Survey of Indian Agriculture* 1991. p. 169.

12. N.A. Majumdar: 'Rural Credit Delivery: Innovative Linkages, the Answer', *The Hindu, Business Line*, September, 17, 1997.

13. D. Ramachandra Reddy: 'Financing Agriculture by Formal Agencies: A Study with Special Reference to Co-operatives', *Kurukshetra*, November 1995, p. 50.

14. P.Satish: 'Commercialising Cooperatives', *The Economic Times*, June 24, 1995.

15. Planning Commission, Government of India (1985): *The Seventh Five Year Plan 1985-90.* Vol II. p. 26.

16. Nilakantha Rath: 'Restructuring the Co-operatives', *The Economic Times*, September 13, 1994.

17. P. Devarajan: ' Rural Credit Delivery; Freeing the Co-operative Banks', *The Hindu Business Line*, September 2, 1997, p.24

18. Nilakantha Rath: op. cit.

19. K.K. Taimino : 'Co-ops and Structural Adjustment', *The Economic Times*, April 26, 1993.

20. H.B Shivamaggi: 'Future Strategy for Development of Co-operatives', *Economic and Political Weekly*, March 18, 1996, p. 1188.

3

Co-operative Sugar Mills in Tamil Nadu

Dr. V. Rengaswamy*
Dr. K. Alagar**
Prof. Raguraman Narayanan***

Introduction

The sugar industry is the second largest agro-based industry in India next only to textiles. India today has the pride of place on the world sugar map as the world's largest producer of cane sugar. "As on 31st March, 1994, there are 394 sugar factories in operation in India, out of which 222 are in the co-operative sector. The co-operative sugar factories are responsible for 56 per cent of the national production.[1]

Although the co-operative movement in India had its beginning in 1904, only four co-operative sugar factories were set-up in the pre-independence era. "The growth of the co-operative sector of the sugar industry is a post-independence phenomenon."[2]

The sugar co-operatives have brought about significant socio-economic development in their areas. They have not only modernized agriculture in sugar-cane growing areas and changed

---

* Professor of Commerce, Madurai Kamaraj University, Madurai—625 021
** Senior Lecurer in Commerce, Yadava College, Madurai—625 014
*** Department of Economics. Madurai College, Madurai—625 011

it from being a mere means of subsistence to a commercial proposition, but have also brought about a far-reaching social, economic and political transformation in the rural areas. All co-operative sugar factories have been mostly a nucleus for the development of rural areas around them. "Because of the help given by the co-operative sugar factories by way of advice, better seeds and training, the farmers have improved their yield and are obtaining better return for their produce."[3]

The sugar co-operatives have also reduced unemployment significantly. The cultivation of sugar-cane itself requires labour throughout the year. Besides, the sugar factories provide direct and indirect employment to several thousands of people. The ancillary industries which have come up around the co-operative sugar factory areas also provide employment to people living there.

In spite of the significant role played by the sugar co-operatives in India's development and growth, they stand today at cross roads. Under the new economic policy, they are facing some problems.

Sugar Industry in Tamil Nadu

Origin and Growth

Sugar industry plays a vital role in the development of the rural economy in Tamil Nadu. It serves as one of the important agencies to bring about rural development. It is a major industry which directly helps to improve the economic conditions of farmers in the rural areas. It has helped in the development of a network of good roads in rural areas.

The State of Tamil Nadu is one of the leading sugar producers in India. The sugar produced by the Tamil Nadu sugar mills is about 10 per cent of India's total sugar production. In Tamil Nadu the income generated from sugar-cane sales exceeds Rs. 1000 crores per year.[4]

EID Parry's sugar mill, at Nellikuppam, in South Arcot district, started in 1897, is the oldest sugar mill in Tamil Nadu. As on 31st March, 1994 there were 32 sugar mills in Tamil nadu, of which 15 were in the co-operative sector, three in the public sector and 14 in the private sector.

Objectives

The main objectives of the co-operative sugar mills are[5] :

1. To help the farmers to get fair price on their products.
2. To carry on the manufacture of sugar from sugarcane and sell the sugar and its by-products to the best advantage of members.
3. To undertake and assist in establishing industries associated with such by-products.
4. To arrange for marketing of sugarcane produced by the members.
5. To undertake co-generation of power.
6. To aid, develop, and maintain sugar and sugar related organisations.

Common Features of Co-operative Sugar Mills in Tamil Nadu

Management

Upto 1977, Co-operative Sugar Mills in Tamil Nadu had a Board of Directors elected by the members at the general body meeting. Since 1977, there has been no elected Board and the co-operative sugar mills are managed by a Special Officer for each mill appointed by the Government of Tamil Nadu.

Organisational Structure

The organisational structure of a co-operative sugar mill in Tamil Nadu is shown in Chart 1.

For each co-operative sugar mill in Tamil Nadu, there is a Special Officer appointed by the Government of Tamil Nadu. He is the administrative head, administering the day-to-day affairs of the mill. In the day to-day management the Special Officer is assisted by a Chief Engineer, a Chief Cane Officer, a Chief Chemist and a Chief Accountant.

The Chief Engineer is in charge of machinery operating in the sugar mill. In the maintenance of machines, he is assisted by a Deputy Engineer and skilled and unskilled workers.

The Chief Cane Officer is in charge of the cane procured by the mills. In this connection, he registers the farmers who have

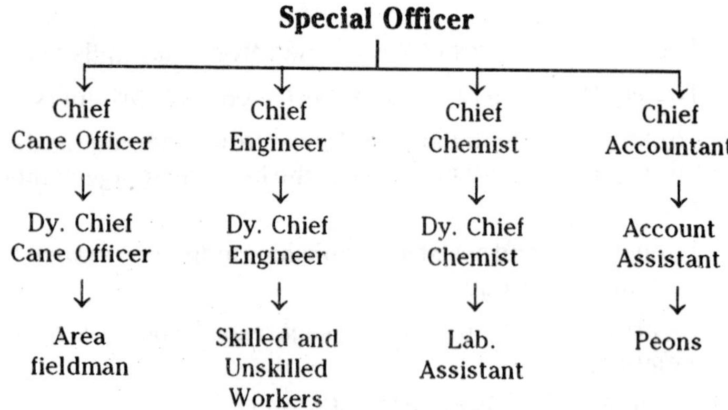

Chart 1 : Organisational Structure of the Co-operative Sugar Mills in Tamil Nadu

agreed to supply the sugar-cane. He makes field visits when the sugar-cane is grown. He suggests new techniques of cultivation to the farmers and decides on the date for cutting the sugar-cane. In the discharge of his duties, the Chief Cane Officer is assisted by a Deputy Cane Officer and area fieldmen.

The sugar production performance of a mill depends on the quality of the sugar-cane supplied. The Chief Chemist of the mill is in charge of testing the quality of sugar-cane supplied by the members and the sugar recovery rate. This helps to determine the approximate quality of sugar that will be produced from a particular lot supplied by the farmers. In the discharge of his duties, the Chief Chemist is assisted by a Deputy Chief Chemist and a laboratory assistant.

In the daily administration, the Chief Accountant is assisted by accounts assistance, clerks and peons.

Sector-wise Distribution of Sugar Mills in Tamil Nadu

The sector-wise distribution of sugar mills in Tamil Nadu during the period 1982-83 to 1993–94 is given in Table 3.1.

It is observed from Table that the number of sugar mills in the co-operative sector in Tamil Nadu which stood at 10 in 1982-83 has steadily increased to 15 in 1993-94. The number of sugar mills in the other sectors in Tamil Nadu which stood at 11 in 1982-83 has increased to 17 in 1993-94. The share of co-operative varied

Table 3.1 : Sector-wise Distribution of Sugar Mills in Tamil Nadu

Sl. No.	*Year*	*Co-operative Sugar Mills*	*Other Mills*	*Total*
1.	1982–83	10 (47.61)	11 (52.39)	21 (100)
2.	1983–84	11 (47.82)	12 (52.18)	23 (100)
3.	1984–85	11 (47.82)	12 (52.18)	23 (100)
4.	1985–86	11 (45.83)	13 (54.17)	24 (100)
5.	1986–87	12 (48.00)	13 (52.00)	25 (100)
6.	1987–89	12 (44.44)	15 (55.56)	27 (100)
7.	1989–90	13 (44.33)	17 (55.67)	30 (100)
8.	1990–91	14 (45.16)	17 (54.84)	31 (100)
9.	1991–92	14 (45.16)	17 (54.84)	31 (100)
10.	1992–93	15 (46.87)	17 (53.13)	32 (100)
11.	1993–94	15 (46.87)	17 (53.13)	32 (100)

Source : National Federation of Co-operative Sugar Factories Limited, *Co-operative Sugar*, Vol. 25, No. 5 & 6, January–February, 1994, p. 227.

Note : Figures in brackets denote percentage to total.

between 44.33 per cent and 48.00 per cent during the period under study.

Sector-Wise Sugar Production in Tamil Nadu

The sector-wise sugar production in Tamil Nadu during the period under study is given in Table 3.2.

It is clear from the Table that the sugar production in Tamil Nadu has been fluctuating between 4.24 lakh tonnes and 12.64 lakh

Table 3.2 : Sector-wise Production in Tamil Nadu

Sl. No.	Year	Co-operative Sugar Mills	Other Mills	Total
1.	1982–83	2.84 (43.60)	3.67 (56.40)	6.51 (100)
2.	1983–84	1.76 (41.51)	2.48 (58.49)	4.24 (100)
3.	1984–85	2.59 (43.17)	3.41 (56.83)	6.00 (100)
4.	1985–86	3.49 (43.03)	4.62 (56.27)	8.11 (100)
5.	1986–87	3.56 (43.73)	4.58 (56.97)	8.14 (100)
6.	1987–89	4.51 (44.90)	5.53 (55.10)	10.04 (100)
7.	1989–90	3.57 (40.16)	5.32 (59.84)	8.89 (100)
8.	1990–91	4.63 (39.14)	7.20 (60.86)	11.83 (100)
9.	1991–92	4.95 (39.14)	7.69 (60.84)	12.64 (100)
10.	1992–93	4.39 (44.97)	5.37 (55.03)	9.76 (100)
11.	1993–94	4.44 (40.88)	6.42 (59.12)	10.86 (100)

Source : National Federation of Co-operative Sugar Factories Limited, *Co-operative Sugar*, Vol. 25, No. 5 & 6, January–February, 1994, p. 220.

Note : Figures in brackets denote percentage to total.

tonnes. The production was maximum in the year 1991-92 with 12.64 lakhs tonnes. The lowest production was the in 1983-84 with 4.24 lakh tonnes.

The sugar production in the co-operative sugar mills in Tamil Nadu has been fluctuating from 1.76 lakh tonnes to 4.95 lakh tonnes. The highest production was in the year 1991-92 with 4.95 lakh tonnes. The lowest production was in the year 1983-84 with 1.76 lakh tonnes. The share of co-operative sugar mills varied from

39.14 per cent to 44.97 per cent during the period under study.

The sugar production in private and public sector sugar mills in Tamil Nadu varied from 2.48 lakh tonnes to 7.69 tonnes during the period under study.

Growth of Co-operative Sugar Mills

The growth of co-operative sugar mills in Tamil Nadu is given in Table 3.3.

Table 3.3 : Growth Co-operative of Sugar Mills in Tamil Nadu

Sl. No.	*Year*	Co-operative Sugar Mills
1.	1982–83	10
2.	1983–84	11
3.	1984–85	11
4.	1985–86	12
5.	1986–87	12
6.	1987–89	13
7.	1989–90	14
8.	1990–91	14
9.	1991–92	15
10.	1992–93	15
11.	1993–94	15

Source : National Federation of Co-operative Sugar Factories Limited, *Co-operative Sugar*, Vol. 25, No. 5 & 6, January–February, 1994, p. 227.

District-Wise Classification of Co-operative Sugar Mills

The district-wise classification of co-operative sugar mills in Tamil Nadu as on 31st March 1994 is shown in Table 3.4.

Table 3.4 indicates that the North Arcot Ambedkar and Tanjore districts have the maximum of three sugar mills each followed by South Arcot Vallalar district with two sugar mills. The Chengalpattu M.G.R. district, Coimbatore district, Dharmapuri district, Madurai district, Salem district, Vallumpuram Ramasamy Padayatchi district and Pudukkottai district have one co-operative sugar mill each.

Table 3.4 : District-wise Classification of Co-operative Sugar Mills in Tamil Nadu

Sl. No.	*Name of the District*	*No. of Co-operative Sugar Mills*
1.	Chengalpattu M.G.R.	1
2.	Coimbatore	1
3.	Dharmapuri	1
4.	Madurai	1
5.	North Arctor Ambedkar	3
6.	Salem	1
7.	South Arcot Vallalar	2
8.	Tanjore	3
9.	Villapuram Ramasamy Padaiyatchi	1
10.	Pudukottai	1
	Total	**15**

Source: Compiled from the Annual Reports on the Co-operative Sugar Mills in Tamil Nadu.

Production

The sugar production by the co-operative sugar mills in Tamil Nadu during the period under study is given in Table 3.5.

It is clear from Table 3.5 that the quantity of sugar produced by the co-operative sugar mills in Tamil Nadu during the period under study shows a fluctuating trend. The quantity of sugar produced varied between 1.76 lakh tonnes and 4.95 lakh tonnes. This fluctuation in production is due to the fluctuation in the area under sugar-cane cultivation based on the sugar-cane price.

Sugar Sales

The value of sugar sold by the co-operative sugar mills in Tamil Nadu during the period under study is given in Table 3.6.

It is inferred from Table 3.6 that there is a steady increase in the value of sugar sold by the co-operative sugar mills in Tamil Nadu during the period under study, except during the year 1984-85, 1989-90 and 1990-91. The value of sugar sold by all the co-

Table 3.5 : Sugar Production by the Co-operative Sugar Mills in Tamil Nadu

(In Lakh Tonnes)

Sl. No.	*Year*	Quantity of Sugar Production
1.	1982–83	2.84
2.	1983–84	1.76
3.	1984–85	2.59
4.	1985–86	3.49
5.	1986–87	3.56
6.	1987–89	4.24
7.	1989–90	3.57
8.	1990–91	4.63
9.	1991–92	4.95
10.	1992–93	4.39
11.	1993–94	4.44

Source : National Federation of Co-operative Sugar Factories Limited, *Co-operative Sugar*, Vol. 25, No. 5 & 6, January–February, 1994, p. 220.

Table 3.6 : Sugar Sales by the Co-operative Sugar Mills in Tamil Nadu

Sl. No.	*Year*	Sales value
1.	1982–83	8,304.60
2.	1983–84	9,558.99
3.	1984–85	8,802.12
4.	1985–86	13,139.05
5.	1986–87	16,166.95
6.	1987–89	22,877.19
7.	1989–90	22,849.53
8.	1990–91	16,199.11
9.	1991–92	22,185.74
10.	1992–93	23,190.37
11.	1993–94	31.058.03

Source : Compiled from the Annual Reports of the Co-operative Sugar Mills in Tamil Nadu.

operative sugar mills in Tamil Nadu which stood at Rs. 8,304.60 lakhs in 1982-83 has increased to Rs. 31,058.03 lakhs in 1993-94. During the year 1993-94, there is more than a three-fold increase in the value of sugar sold when compared to 1982-83. In the year 1984-85 and 1990-91, the decline in sugar sales has been due to the accumulation of sugar stock. The decline in the value of sugar sold during the year 1989-90 has been due to decline in the quantity produced (vide Table 3.8).

Number of Employees

The number of persons employed in the co-operative sugar mills in Tamil Nadu during the period under study is given in Table 3.7.

It is inferred from Table 3.7 that the total number of persons employed in the co-operative sugar mills in Tamil Nadu which stood at 10,371 has steadily increased to 14,103 in 1993-94, resulting in 43.7 per cent increase.

Table 3.7 : Number of Persons Employed in the Co-operative Sugar Mills in Tamil Nadu

Sl. No.	*Year*	Number of Persons Employed
1.	1982–83	10,371
2.	1983–84	10,948
3.	1984–85	10,908
4.	1985–86	10,810
5.	1986–87	11,610
6.	1987–89	11,605
7.	1989–90	12,524
8.	1990–91	13,368
9.	1991–92	13,376
10.	1992–93	14,093
11.	1993–94	14,103

Source : National Federation of Co-operative Sugar Factories Limited, *Co-operative Sugar*, Vol. 25, No. 5 & 6, p. 227.

Membership

The membershipof the co-operative sugar mills consist of 'A' and 'B' class members. 'A' class members are farmers who own lands or cultivate sugar-cane in the area of operation of a sugar mill. 'B' class members are Government of Tamil Nadu, National Co-operative Union of India and National Federation of Co-operative Sugar Factories Limited. Table 3.8 shows the Individual Membership position of co-operative sugar mills in Tamil Nadu during the period under study.

It is observed from Table 3.8 that the individual members in co-operative sugar mills in Tamil Nadu during the period under study which stood at 1,55,127 in 1982-83 has steadily increased to 2,10,759 in 1993-94 representing a 35 per cent increase.

Table 3.8 : Membership of Co-operative Sugar Mills in Tamil Nadu

Sl. No.	*Year*	Number of Grower Members
1.	1982–83	1,55,127
2.	1983–84	1,56,752
3.	1984–85	1,60,780
4.	1985–86	1,63,838
5.	1986–87	1,64,652
6.	1987–89	1,66,654
7.	1989–90	1,67,253
8.	1990–91	1,68,568
9.	1991–92	1,76,474
10.	1992–93	1,76,846
11.	1993–94	2,10,759

Source : Compiled from the Annual Reports of the Co-operative Sugar Mills in Tamil Nadu.

Resources

The resources of the co-operative sugar mills consist of owned funds and borrowed funds. The owned funds are

1. Share Capital,
2. Reserve Fund and
3. Entrance Fee.

The borrowed funds are

1. Deposits from member and non-members.
2. Loans from District Central Co-operative Banks.
3. Loans from Tamil Nadu Government.
4. Loans from Tamil Nadu State Apex Co-operative bank.
5. Loans from National Federation of Co-operative Sugar Factories Limited and
6. Loans from Financial Institutions such as Industrial Development Bank of India and Industrial Financial Corporation of India.

Share Capital

Share Capital plays an important role in the resources of co-operative sugar mills. The paid-up share capital or all the ten co-operative sugar mills in Tamil Nadu during the period under study is shown in Table 3.9.

It is observed from Table 3.9 that the paid up share capital of all the ten co-operative sugar mills in Tamil Nadu has doubled in 1993-94 when compared to 1982-83.

In the total paid-up share capital of co-operative sugar mills in Tamil Nadu, the share of paid-up capital contributed by individuals members which stood at 64.43 per cent in 1982-83, has steadily increased to 74.23 per cent in 1993-94. On the other hand, the share capital contributed by the Government of Tamil Nadu which stood at 35.57 per cent in 1982-83 has gruadually declined to 25.77 per cent in 1993-94. This has been due to the steep increase in the share capital contributed by the individual members and there is no corresponding increase in the share capital contributed by the Government.

Profits of the Co-operative Sugar Mills

One of the important factors used for measuring the efficiency of an organisation is the profits earned by it. The efficiency of the co-operative sugar mills in Tamil nadu has been analysed in terms of profits earned by them. Table 3.10 shows the profits earned by the co-operative sugar mills in Tamil Nadu during the period under study.

It is observed from Table 3.10 that the profits of the all the Co-operative Sugar Mills in Tamil Nadu which stood at Rs. 24.88

Table 3.9 : Paid-up Share Capital of all the Co-operative Sugar Mills in Tamil Nadu

(In Lakh of Rupees)

Sl. No.	*Year*	*Paid-up Capital Collected from Individual Members*	*Government of Tamil Nadu*	*Total*
1.	1982–83	1,323.14 (64.43)	730.45 (35.57)	2,053.59 (100)
2.	1983–84	1,431.91 (66.22)	730.45 (33.78)	2,162.36 (100)
3.	1984–85	1,629.91 (70.24)	690.45 (29.76)	2,320.36 (100)
4.	1985–86	1,730.68 (71.48)	690.45 (28.52)	2,421.13 (100)
5.	1986–87	2,051.66 (74.82)	690.45 (25.18)	2,742.11 (100)
6.	1987–89	2,086.22 (73.50)	752.17 (26.5)	2,838.39 (100)
7.	1989–90	2,236.93 (74.84)	752.17 (25.16)	2,989.1 (100)
8.	1990–91	2,215.69 (69.62)	843.33 (30.38)	3,182.71 (100)
9.	1991–92	2,544.63 (73.10)	936.29 (26.90)	3,480.87 (100)
10.	1992–93	2,251.50 (65.68)	1,021.35 (34.32)	3,428.16 (100)
11.	1993–94	2,979.36 (74.23)	1,034.32 (25.77)	4,013.68 (100)

Source : Computed from the Annual Reports of the Co-operative Sugar Mills in Tamil Nadu.

Note : Figures in brackets denote percentage to total.

lakhs in 1982-83 has steadily increased to Rs. 1010.16 lakhs in 1993-94 except during 1987-89, 1991-92 and 1992-93. There is more than a forty-fold increase in profits during the period under study.

Table 3.10 : Profits of the Co-operative Sugar Mills in Tamil Nadu

Sl. No.	*Year*	Profit/Loss (Rs. in Lakhs)
1.	1982–83	24.88
2.	1983–84	430.05
3.	1984–85	557.16
4.	1985–86	667.06
5.	1986–87	1,035.90
6.	1987–89	621.22
7.	1989–90	1,057.49
8.	1990–91	(–) 570.73
9.	1991–92	92.39
10.	1992–93	801.53
11.	1993–94	1,010.16

Source : Compiled from the Annual Reports of the Co-operative Sugar Mills in Tamil Nadu.

During 1990-91 the Co-operative Sugar Mills in Tamil Nadu incurred a loss of Rs. 570.73 lakhs.

Comparison of Profit Performance of the Co-operative Sugar Mills in Tamil Nadu

The comparison of profit performance of the co-operative sugar mills in Tamil Nadu during the period under study is given in Table 3.11.

It is observed from Table 3.11 that the Amaravathi Co-operative Sugar Mills Limited, earned profit for all the years under study except during 1993-94. The profits of the mill had varied from Rs. 20.34 lakhs to Rs. 234.59 lakhs with an average of 97-36 lakhs. The mill incurred a loss of Rs. 33.62 lakhs. This has been due to the increase in operative costs.

Profits of the Ambur Co-operative Sugar Mill Limited show a fluctuating trend during the period under study. The profit has varied between Rs. 1.44 lakhs and Rs. 52.10 lakhs with an average of Rs. 17.31 lakhs.

In Chengalryan Co-operative Sugar Mills, the mill earned profit during the period under study, except during 1982-83, 1987-89, 1990-91 and 1991-92. The average profit earned during the period under study amounted to Rs. 16.15 lakhs.

Table 3.11 : Comparison of Profit Performance of Co-operative Sugar Mills in Tamil Nadu

(Rs. in Lakhs)

Mills	*1982–83*	*1983–84*	*1984–85*	*1985–86*	*1986–87*	*1987–89*	*1989–90*	*1990–91*	*1991-92*	*1992–93*	*1993–94*	Average
Amaravathi	78.09	151.55	114.44	234.59	134.94	122.74	122.73	79.89	20.34	45.32	–33.62	97.36
Ambur	5.83	4.04	4.46	1.44	21.36	38.10	52.10	14.81	2.16	6.11	40.01	17.31
Chengalrayan	–27.19	116.62	62.28	79.83	171.48	–682.54	273.16	–248.51	–312.16	412.63	332.06	16.15
Dharmapuri	–2.23	12.50	20.82	32.09	–101.08	215.09	62.09	–77.58	109.49	74.87	114.49	41.87
Kallakurchi	12.50	–32.59	50.09	125.94	154.96	358.14	150.58	35.45	108.51	145.92	266.74	125.11
Madurantakam	–10.03	78.17	65.43	139.66	158.91	141.71	174.62	11.16	16.64	–7.89	89.17	77.96
National	2.39	17.97	88.90	42.02	35.52	13.69	–5.39	–240.63	–130.71	–7.61	–6.04	–17.26
Salem	4.04	4.64	16.74	67.77	199.07	48.46	132.38	122.36	242.02	38.00	26.90	82.03
Tirupattur	–50.68	–84.66	45.66	–90.11	156.63	169.94	–66.94	–68.16	35.68	34.83	37.74	10.90
Vellore	12.16	161.81	88.34	33.83	104.11	195.89	161.36	–199.52	0.42	59.35	142.71	69.13

Source : Compiled from the Annual Reports of Co-operative Sugar Mills in Tamil Nadu.

The profits of the Dharmapuri Co-operative Sugar Mill Limited show a fluctuating trend during the period under study. The profit has varied from Rs. 12.50 lakhs to Rs. 215.09 lakhs. The mill incurred losses of Rs. 2.23 lakhs, Rs. 101.08 lakhs Rs. 77.58 lakhs during 1982-83, 1986-87 and 1990-91 respectively.

It is observed from Table 3.11 that the Amarvathi Co-operative Sugar Mills Limited, earned profit for all the years under study except during 1993-94. The profits of the mill had varied from Rs. 20.34 lakhs to Rs. 234.59 lakhs with an average of Rs. 97.36 lakhs. The mill incurred a loss of Rs. 33.62 lakhs. This has been due to the increase in operative costs.

Profits of the Ambur Co-operative Sugar Mill Limited show fluctuating trend during the period under study. The profit has varied between Rs. 1.44 lakhs and Rs. 52.10 lakhs with an average of Rs. 17.31 lakhs.

In Chengalrayan Co-operative Sugar Mills, the mill earned profit during the period under study, except during 1982-83, 1987-89, 1990-91 and 1991-92. The average profit earned during the period under study amounted to Rs. 16.15 lakhs.

The profits of the Dharmapuri Co-operative Sugar Mill Limited show a fluctuating trend during the period under-study. The profit has varied from Rs. 12.50 lakhs to Rs. 215.09 lakhs. The mill incurred losses of Rs. 2.23 lakhs, Rs. 101.08 lakhs, Rs. 77.58 lakhs during 1982-83, 1986-87 and 1990-91 respectively.

Kallakurchi Co-operative Sugar Mills Limited earned profit during the period under study except in 1983-84. The profit of the mill has varied from Rs. 12.50 lakhs to Rs. 358.14 lakhs with an average of Rs. 125.11 lakhs during the period during study.

Madurantakam Co-operative Sugar Mills Limited earned profits during the period under study except during 1982-83 and 1992-93. The profit of the mill has varied between Rs. 11.16 lakhs and Rs. 174.62 lakhs during the period under study.

The National Co-operative Sugar Mills Limited has earned profit from 1982-83 to 1987-89. The mill incurred losses from 1989-90 onwards. On an average, the mill incurred a loss of Rs. 17.26 lakhs during the period under study.

The profit of the Salem Co-operative Sugar Mills Limited which stood at Rs. 4.04 lakhs in 1982-83 had steadily increased to

242.02 lakhs in 1991-92 except during 1987-89 and 1990-91. During 1992-93 and 1993-94 the profits of the mill amounted to Rs. 38.00 lakhs and Rs. 26.90 lakhs respectively.

The Tirupattur Co-operative Sugar Mills Limited earned profit during 1984-85, 1986-87 1987-89, 1991-92, 1992-93 and 1993-94. The mill incurred losses during rest of the period under study. On an average, the Mill earned a profit of Rs. 10.90 lakhs during the period under study.

Vellore Co-operative Sugar Mills Limited earned profit during the entire period under study except during 1990-91. The profit of the mill has varied between Rs. 0.42 lakhs and Rs. 195.89 lakhs during the period under study. The Mill has incurred a loss of Rs. 199.52 lakhs in 1990-91.

On an average, except the National Co-operative Sugar Mills Limited, all the nine co-operative Sugar Mills had earned profit during the period under study. The highest profit of Rs. 125.11 lakhs was earned by kallakurchi Co-operative Sugar Mills Limited, followed by Amaravathi Co-operative Sugar Mills Limited with a profit of R. 97.36 lakhs and Salem Co-operative Sugar Mills Limited with a profit of Rs. 82.03 lakhs. The lowest profit was recorded in Tirupattur co-operative Sugar Mills Limited with Rs. 10.90 lakhs. The National Co-operative Sugar Mills Limited incurred a loss of Rs. 17.26 lakhs during the period under study.

Ambur and Salem Co-operative Sugar Mills are the only two Mills that have earned profit during the entire period under study.

Conclusion

North Arcot district has the largest number of co-operative sugar mills in Tamil Nadu and it is followed by South Arcot Vallalar district. The quantity of the sugar produced by the co-operative sugar mills in Tamil Nadu during the period under study shows a fluctuating trend. Ambur and Salem co-operative sugar mills are the only two co-operative sugar mills in Tamil Nadu that have earned profit during the entire period under study.

References

1. M.S. Marathee, Role of Co-operative Sugar Factories in National Development, *The Co-operator*, Vol. XXXII, No. 5, November 1994, p. 173.

2. *Ibid.*, p. 174.
3. M.S. Marathe, Role of Co-operative Sugar Factories in National Development, *The Co-operator*, Vol.XXXII, No. 5, November 1994, p. 175.
4. A Vijayakumar, A. Venkatachalam, Growth Performance of Sugar Industry in 2000 A.D., *The Tamil Nadu Journal of Co-operation*, Vol. 80, No. 11, February, 1995, p.22.
5. Government of Tamil Nadu, *The Co-operative Manual*, Madras, 1972, p.302.
6. Government of Tamil Nadu, Report on Sugar Industry in Tamil Nadu-Present Position, Government of Tamil Nadu, Madras, 1988.
7. Annaul Reports of the Co-operative Sugar Mills in Tamil Nadu.
8. National Federation of Co-operative Sugar Factories Limited, Co-operative Sugar, Various Volumes (1982-83 to 1993-94).

4

Towards Alleviation of Poverty:

Co-operatives & Dairy Development with Special Reference to The Orissa State Co-operative Milk Producers' Federation (OMFED)

Chita Rajan Dash*

In a peasant dominated state like Orissa where around 75.74 per cent of working people depend on agriculture to earn their livelihood. Out of them 31.43 per cent classified as agricultural labourers in 1991 Census. Declining death rate as a result of improvement in health measures, caused rate of growth of population to nearly double as the rate of birth remains more or less constant. The augmenting poverty and inequality due to improper concentration of income generating assets with few hands on one hand acceleration of growing unemployed entering into working groups out numbered existing number of superannuating group caused more pressure on land thereby reducing the marginal productivity of land closer to zero. The additional out-put due to a additional worker tend to negligible, due to fixed land and diminishing returns to worker, the increase in out put contributed by each additional worker is less then the contribution of the previous worker. Hence, total output of product of grains from agriculture will increase at a lower rate due to declining marginal product of labour. The same process will be reverse when labour is withdrawn from agriculture.

* Nabakrushna Choudhury Centre for Development Studies, Bhubaneswar—751013, Orissa, India

The importance of diminishing returns in agriculture stems from the fact that in a competitive market economy, the wage rate of a worker is determined by the worth of his marginal product. If economic development is to make a dent on poverty, the wage rate must rise because almost all landless workers living in lowest strata, below poverty line. The marginal product of a worker in agriculture must rise in order to have a higher wage rate. If the technology in agriculture is stagnant, the only way to translate this by labour being drawn away from agriculture to other activities. Thus, the Economic and Social Commission of the World Food Congress emphasised that: "The ultimate solution of the problem of hunger and malnutrition in the developing countries lies in increasing the purchasing power of the mass of the population through general economic development" (FAO, 1969). As most of the population derived their requirement from agriculture remain at the subsistence level. High levels of productivity in an agriculture depend increasingly upon the industrial products viz. Fertilizer, insecticide, machineries & other suitable equipments to fit the farm. The farmers ability to apply these highly productive inputs depend on a various factors. Firstly, since the physical, economic and social conditions differ sharply from one area to another, local research and experimentation are required to evolve techniques appropriate to local conditions after deep study on facility of various inputs including irrigation, infrastructure as well as to create interest among people to learn and apply it. Secondly, substantial use of purchased inputs necessitates an increase in the cash income which can only usable by increasing productivity of agriculture sector. Thirdly, any social constraints must be over come, last but not the least factor is how to make people carry out the work, to achieve the high level of income, consumption and production in a state of hunger and poverty, very often terming them poor (have-nots).

Who is Poor

Poverty has various manifestations, including lack of income and productive resources, malnutrition and hunger, illiteracy, hopelessness and inadequate housing, hazardous environment and social discrimination and exclusions.

People below the poverty line known as poor. Poverty line being defined as a minimum per capita consumption expenditure which could satisfy the basic calories needs of an individual for leading an active life. According to age, gender and occupation, separate poverty lines are estimated for persons living in the rural and urban sector. The planning commission estimates using the actual data on consumption expenditure obtained from the National Sample Survey (NSS) the persons who were unable to meet the required level of calories intake of 2400 per day in rural areas and 2100 calories intake in urban areas.

The Task Force on projection of minimum needs and effective consumption demand constituted by the planning commission, which submitted its report in 1979, estimated the cost of consumption basket in 1973-74 as monthly per capita consumption expenditure of Rs. 49.09 in rural areas and Rs. 56.64 in urban areas corresponding to the 2400 calories and 2100 calories intake per capital per day. This was called the poverty line.

The expert Group on Estimation of proportion and number of poor in 1993 has worked out statewise poverty lines after taking into account the interstate disparity in the cost of living. The expert group decided to accept the minimum living standard set out by the task force in 1979 in order to define poverty line.

The state specific poverty lines are worked out by the export group on the basis of the national poverty line using the consumption basket of such people at national level in 1973-74 as weighting diagram. The national poverty line of 1973-74 is converted into 1960-61 prices and state specific poverty line in 1960-61 is adjusted for the inter-state price differential that existed in that year. The state specific poverty lines estimated by the export Group for the periods 1977-78, 1983 and 1987-88 based on qinguinnial survey of consumption expenditure by the NSS reflect the inter-state price differential are indicative of the inter-state disparities in cost of consumption basket of the poor. The poverty line for Orissa and India indicated in Table 4.1.

In order to draw state specific poverty line the Expert Group used consumer price index of agricultural Labourers (CPIAL) to reflect the prices of goods constituting the consumption basket of the poor. The inter-state price differentials of commodities/goods constituted the consumption basket of the people around poverty line is indicative of the inter-state disparities in cost of consumption basket of the poor. The cost of basket both in Rural and Urban

Table 4.1 : Poverty Line in Rural and Urban Area in Orissa and All India

(Rs. per capita per month expenditure)

Period		*Orissa*	*All India*
1		2	3
1977–78			
	Rural	58.89	56.84
	Urban	75.00	72.50
1983			
	Rural	106.28	89.45
	Urban	127.16	117.64
1987–88			
	Rural	121.42	115.43
	Urban	170.62	165.58

Orissa is laying all times higher than national level. The cost of living of poor in Orissa is more from the average Indian poor.

Poverty Ratio

The number of poor as a percentage to total population termed as poverty ratio. The poverty ratio is Orissa and All India estimated for the year 1977-78, 1983 and 1987-88 depicted in Table

Table 4.2 : Poverty Ratio in Rural and Urban Area in Orissa and All India

(per cent)

Period		*Orissa*	*All India*
1		2	3
1977–78			
	Rural	72.38	53.07
	Urban	53.55	47.40
1983			
	Rural	67.53	45.61
	Urban	50.61	42.15
1987–88			
	Rural	59.21	39.06
	Urban	44.37	40.12

4.2.

In rural Orissa poverty ratio declined from 72.38% in 1977-78 to 67.53% in 1983 and 59.21% in 1987-88 for the corresponding periods in India average poverty line declines from 53.07% to 45.61% and 39.06 respectively. The average poverty ratio in urban areas are estimated as 47.4% in 1977-78, 42.15 in 1983 and 40.12% in 1987-88 in India whereas during the corresponding period urban poverty in Orissa decline from 53.55% to 50.61% and 44.37%.

It is clear picture depicted in above table todraw conclusion that higher proportion of poor in both rural and urban area residing in Orissa from the view point of National level.

The key to reducing poverty is at first moving labour out of agriculture into other productive activities which are having more marginal returns than agriculture. In such away workers should be distributed to all productive activities so that to equalise marginal returns from all productive activities. Secondly, diverting additional labour to such other activities which are not characterised by diminishing returns. Thirdly, effective steps may be taken to have rapid technical progress in agriculture, in other words if the people below poverty line are not to be left out from showing the fruits of economic growth by applying the technology in the agriculture and allied activities should have achieved a certain minimum level of productivity. But it should be so designed to bring the poor people to the fold of sharing benefits. For example, the introduction of High yielding varieties (HYVS) of grain, which triggered the green Revolution in the late sixties, effect of new technology felt much more in Punjab, Haryana and Western U.P. than in other states of India. The Green Revolution accompanied by the adoption of labour-displacing technology, such as use of tractors, deprived the worker from enjoying the share of benefits, even in these areas as much as they could have.

The basic reason for the failure of rural development and poverty alleviation programmes is the exclusion of the people abandonment of the institutions of domestic decentralisation of the related electoral process. The resulting alienation of the people from the most exciting task of development in post independence India, on the one hand, and the continuation of the colonial pattern of administration directed from the top and unaccountable to the local population - on the other, have serious implications for both development and democracy (Jain, 1985).

Co-operatives

To define cooperatives specifically as voluntary association by people on the basis of common economic interest. Co-operative organised by co-ordinate the activities of the group to achieve specified objective. The principle governing co-operatives (hence for Co-ops,) its aim, objective, natural and area of activity duties and responsibilities of functionaries and all other conditions required for smooth functioning of the around service encoded in the by-laws and submitted for Registration under Co-operative Societies Act. After Registration under Co-operative Societies Act the organisation comes into being. Co-operative principles envisage an economic system based upon common ownership, mutual aid and in which none would be in a position exploit the rest, in which equity, individual freedom and a strong sense of coordination conducive for all Raju (1996) explained logic of collective action as propounded by Olson in 1971 viz., (1) common fallacy or common interest (2) Individual incentives essential for collective action (3) consensus is necessary but not sufficient, (4) Initiative comes from Significant Stoke holders as well as non-economic motive of collective action initiators, (5) Collective interest and individual interest, (6) Significant initial costs deter collective Action.

However, the Co-operative Principles stressed to be organised on the basis of (1) Voluntary membership; (2) Democratic decision making, (3) Limited interest on share capital (4) equitable distribution of surplus, (5) Co-operative education and (6) mutual co-operation.

Keeping the vital role of Co-operative in mind First Five year Plan aptly remarks "in a regime of planned development, cooperation is an instrument, with which relating some of the advantages of decentralization and local initiative will serve willingly and readily the overall purposes and directives of the plan. The Co-operative form of organisation can no longer be treated as only a specie with in the private sector. It is an indispensable instrument of planned economic action in a democracy[1] (All India Rural Credit Survey - Report of the Committee of Direction, Vol. II, RBI, Bombay, 1954) recommended to have large-sized societies to ensure viability to the Society.

Co-operative Legislations

In order to encourage thrifts, self-help and co-operation amongst agriculturist, artisans and persons of limited resources the first piece of Co-operation legislation in India was the co-operative credit societies Act, 1904 with provisions only regarding primary societies and also with substantial powers vested in the register. In 1912 act with the object to promote the economic interest of its members in accordance with the principle of cooperation, provided for federal societies in addition to primary societies, but retained the power of the registrar of cooperative societies.

The Reform act 1919, for the first time, conferred law making power on provinces, by which several rule were enacted. The Government of India Act, 1935, reconfirmed the 1912 Act including the subject "Co-operation" under State list. The enactment of multi unit Societies Act, 1942, widen the scope of activities of societies beyond the provincial territory. After independence, the All India Rural credit Survey-Report of the Committee of Direction, 1954 recommended to have large sized societies to ensure viability to the society. A Committee on cooperative law constituted in 1956 with a view to prepare a Model Co-operative Bill for execution of recommendation of Rural credit Survey. In 1965, the Ram Niwas Mirdha Committee on Co-operation suggested guidelines for removal of vested interest from the co-operative system by incorporating suitable amendments. As a result more and more stringent and restrictive provisions inserted in the cooperative Acts. Multi-state co-operative societies Act 1984, the Ardhanareeswaram Committee on democratisation of co-operatives and professionalisation of management 1985, and the model Act 1991 drafted by planning commission are important milestones in the way of co-operative legislation.

Cooperative Legislation in Orissa

In Orissa, the Co-operative Societies Act 1962 was amended in 1991 extensively on the basis of guidelines circulated by the Central Government with the ostensible purpose of democratising, deofficialising and depoliticising the co-operative movement. Indian Institute of Management, Ahmedabad made a study for World Bank Comparing M.P., U.P. and Orissa Acts commented "Orissa appears to have come somewhat nearer to the Model act" in regard the enterprise related parameters, which the other two states indulged in near cosmetic changes (Rama Krishnayya, 1997).

Orissa Cooperative societies Amendment Act 1991 (1) created a separate post of Auditor General (Cooperative Audit) who should to submit Annual Report with in a month of the closure of cooperative year stating particulars of Audit Classification of societies which will be placed in state legislature, incorporating cooperative principles and raising minimum no. of members of primary cooperative 50 (Fifty) except housing society where the number should be eleven [3–4 (2)(6)]. Under Sect. 16(1) treated wife and husband as one (Joint Membership).

Introduced provisional registration for a period of 3 months in case no order issued for registering of denying registration is communicated within a period of 3 months from the date of application (5.7). Under Section 15(A) permitted partnership of Cooperatives. When two or more co-operatives by regulation passed by majority of general Body can enter into a contract of partnership for carrying out any business permissible under the bye-laws, which can be registered under our law. Sub-section (B) of the above said section provided scope for creation or subsidiary organisation by a Co-operative for the furtherance of its stated objective, by majority resolution of the General Body Meeting. There is a provision for reservation under Section 28(2) (d) of directorship one each for women, SC and ST in primary Co-operatives have been made. To make effective functioning of Co-operatives there is also a provision for disqualification for non-participation. If a Board of Director of President abstain from attending the committee meeting for a continuous period of 6 months and abstain himself from attending the Annual Special General Body over a continuous period of one year without prior intimation for every such meeting and where the committee disapproves the absentness on intimation then the Director/President will disqualify himself from continuing and becoming a director upto a period of 2 years (S. 28(3) M & O).

As per Sec. 28A, the President of the Committee of every co-operatives should be directly elected by and from among the General body and other members of the Committee by the members of the concerned constituency.

The state Government empowered to inspect, inquire and issue directions in the public interest, in the interest of securing proper linkage or co-ordination between related co-operative activities like production, marketing or credit support or implementation of co-operative production and other developmental programmes approved or undertaken by the Government or in the interest of proper management of the business of the society. Therefore under Sec. 123(A) State Government exercise power to intervene and give direction though after giving an opportunity of being heard.

Therefore, it is pertinent to note that despite the aim of depoliticising co-operative movement. In Orissa ample scopes laying for Government intervention under Section 21 and 123A to intervene unnecessarily in the function of co-operative where parties opposition members hold the key position in Cooperative General Body by winning elections.

The supervision of the Management Committees of many co-operatives by the Government of Orissa as a preparatory step for their reconstitution after fresh elections to achieve partisan ends. It is now to consider how the so-called improvement of 1991 in the co-operative law have not prevented an arbitrary supervision of the management boards of co-operatives on a massive scale in the some manner as before and what level safeguards are necessary for ensuring in future that the co-operative enterprises are true to run their affairs and stand up to competition from other forces in the economy (Rama Krishnaya, 1997).

The new direction of economic policy announced by the Rao Government in 1991 read as : "Unrestricted Capitalism will serve interests of only the rich - Stagnation in India is caused by excessive Government Control of the economy and there is an urgent need for liberalisation. - Trade with developed countries will only benefit the rich by giving them easy access to western style consumption goods and, in fact, will hurt the poor by causing.

"Neither the Sarkar not the bulk of development agencies have had any applicable measure of success in fighting poverty. However, among the economic organisations functioning in rural areas, those which sprang up by means of grass-roots efforts, and were sustained by such efforts, have had some measures of success. The milk co-operatives of western India, with a grass-roots base and with one weapon at their disposal, namely, dairying, came face to face with the resource less poor of their respective district. (Somjee and Somjee, 1989). In the present context of 'The new economic environment of the country, co-operatives may still be the only institutional structure that will protect the interest and enhance the livelihood of resource-poor rural population, particularly in under developed regions (Saha, 1995).

In the context of dairy co-operative and rural development, the National Commission on Agriculture (1972) in their interim report on milk production recommended that benefit of increasing demand of milk in large cities, towns and industrial areas should go to small and marginal farmers and landless labourers. Efforts should be made to promote as much of milk production as possible involving this segment of rural population. Landless labourers were given due importance in the Government's overall policy on dairy development (Shah, Deepak, 1997).

In order to achieve a successful diary development programme one should cast a glance to the policy and programmes undertaken to improve the quality/productivity and viability of its bovine stock. Therefore, the policy and programmes regarding development of bovine stock in Orissa laid in a brief note.

Programme and Policy to Develop Bovine Stock in Orissa

After formation of the Separate Orissa in 1st April, 1936, the provincial Government had taken as a first step in Upgrading the indigenous cattle purchased Haryana bulls and Red Sindhi bulls in 1937 for breeding of good health and big sized cows. But due to smaller cows were allowed to show high service figures, as a consequent, the big progenies could not thrive with scanty milk of mothers. In 1944 for first time Penicillin injection tried to animals and after a year i.e., 1945 first time started live stock census in Orissa. After India won her independence from the clutches of British Rule in 1947, the constitution of India come into force from 26th day of January 1950. India opt for planning development and the term province replaced 64 State. During first five year plan Key village scheme was started along with the National extension Service Blocks to improve the livestock and productivity later emerged with ICDP. During 1958 the National Rinderpest Eradication Scheme was operated in Orissa. For proper utilisation and marketing of milk the Phulnakhara Milk Pasteurization Plant was establish in the year 1960.

In order to increase milk production by improving dairy animals cross breeding with exotic bulls started in 1964 to fill up the gap of demand for milk in urban areas. In 1978, with Danish assistance use of frozen semen started from High pedigreed bulls for artificial Insemination. The latest technology for development of quality and productivity of our bovine stock is Embryo Transfer (ET), implemented by OMFED, under aegis of NDDB. In 1991-92 30 E.Ts. were made by OMFED Training and Demonstration Centre (OMFED, 11th Annual Report).

Operation Flood and Co-operative Development

The working group appointed by the Govt. of India in 1962 Stressed the need to develop dairying and animal, husbandry through co-operative effort (NCA, 1976). In pursuance with the recommendation National Dairy Development Board (NDDB) at Anand (Gujarat) was constituted in 1965; as a programme launching body and provide technical service on a non-profit basis in the field of dairy development. But as the NDDB, being a programme launching body, was not authorised to transact any financial and commercial activities, the union Government set up the Indian Dairy Cooperative (IDC) in 1970 at Baroda to execute the operation flood programme which is first of its kind in Third World Countries, with a financial grant of its kind in Third World Countries, with a financial grant of its kind in Third World Countries, with a financial grant of Rs. 95 crores (Fourth Five Year Plan). It was primarily decided by the Council of European Economic Community (EEC), Minister's meeting held on April, 1969, to include for the first time dairy products with in its food aid programme and consequently allocated during that yea 35,000 tonnes of Butter Oil (BO) and 123,000 tonnes of skimmed milk powder (SMP) to the world food programme, which channeled most of it to India's Operation Flood Programme (Dorsten, 1986). The aim of OF-1 was confined to the development of dairying in metropolitan cities, and to build a viable self-sustaining dairy development on co-operative lime which encompassed production, procurement and marketing of milk. The OF-1 launched in 1970 with the assistance of Word Food Programme (WFP), EEC countries and other International agencies in the form of food aid of 1,26,000 MT. of Skimmed Milk Powder (SMP) and 42,000 MT. of BO. Funds generated through sale of these commodities were used in the development of 27 rural milk sheds in 10 states and four metropolitan city centres to market the milk.

The successful result of OF-1 promoted the Government of India decided to carry out OF-II aimed at building a National Milk Grid drinking 136 milk sheds in 22 states and union -terrorists. OF-II inaugurated on 2nd October 1978 with a greater allocation of Rs. 485 crores (NDDB, 1979).

While, OF-I was in operative in Orissa, the OF-II programme launched in Orissa under the aegis of NDDB after the Orissa State Co-operative Milk Producers Federation (OMFED) comes into being in 1980-81. It was primarily started in four district i.e., Puri, Cuttack, Dhenkanal and Keonjhar. Of was act as an instrument for replication of Anand Pattern in Orissa named after Kheda District Co-operative Milk Producers' Union (AMUL) Dairy complex at Anand involves a three tire organisation and set of interrelated functions. Milk producers at the village level are organised into a co-operative Society. The village societies are in turn organised into a district Co-operative Milk Producers Union and about six or more district unions in a given milk shed area combined to form a marketing federation in the apex of the System, generally one in a State to link rural producers with urban buyers.

Progress of Anand Pattern DSC and Farms Members

There were only 52 functional societies with a membership of 3328 only, in its area of operation in districts of Cuttack, Puri, Dhenkanal and Keonjhar, during operation Flood-III incision of Sambalpur raised the number to 663 with a membership of 51,903 as against 610 functional societies and 46,167 members on 31.03.1991 (OMFED,1992), Ananda pattern dairy co-operatives gone upto 1060 with 72 thousand members in 1995-96 as against 67 thousand members with 968 functional societies with 67 thousand members during 1994-95 (NDDB 1995-96). If we cost our glance back to the year 1985-86 there were only 352 Ananda Pattern Dairy Co-operative Societies (DCS) with former members of 14 thousand only. so, within a span of 10years from 1985-86 to 1995-96 there have been an increased in the numbers of DCS and members recorded 301 and 5.14 times of growth respectively. On an average farmer membership per DCS was 39.8, in 1985-86 as against 67.9 in 1995-96 indicating increase in membership of DCS in Orissa.

Milk Procurement

Annual average milk procurement per day during 1985-86, 1994-95 and 1995-96 were 9,64 and 56 thousand key respectively indicated average annual procurement of milk per day from an average member were 643 grams, 955 grams and 778 gram for respectively periods. Milk procurement has been increasing per members by 67 per cent during 1985–86 mainly due to devastation caused by food and natural clamaties win the area of operation flood. Here power of nature play dominant role of cause diminishing return where as when the effort of men and machinery and technological development override natural hurdles causing diminishing returns. Members are paid prices according to two axis formula of 'fat' and 'solid not fat' of milk content. In 1992-93 each society pours around 68 liters per day to the State Grid (OMFED, 1993). Increase in milk procurement by DCS from its members by paying reasonable price enhance the marginal productivity of members.

Milk Marketing

Marketing plays a dominant role in case of perishable commodities like milk. But co-operation effort through technological advancement like installation of milk chilling centres in various places covering certain geographical areas he length of freshens of milk to reach the consumer with out loss. Annual average of milk marketing per day during 1985-86, 1994-95 and 1995-96 were 8, 80 and 89 thousand cities. The increase in milk marketing through the co-operative organisation increased by more than 11 (eleven) times from 1985-86 to 1995-96 (NDDB, 1996).

Milk Processing

The Federation has three dairies at Bhubaneswar, Rourkela and Sambalpur for processing the milk received from thirteen milk chilling centres within its operation area of five district milk unions an two milk chilling centres of Ganjam Milk Union, under Indo-Swiss project. With the expansion of Bhubaneswar Dairy to handle 75,000 litres per day the federation augmented its capacity to process 1,15000 litres per day. The details of plants commissioned in Orissa depicted in Table 4.3.

Table 4.3 : Dairy Infrastructure in Orissa

Sl. No.	Name of the Project	Managed by	Capacity (TLPD)	Project Cost (Rs./Lakh)	Expendable Capacity (TLPD)	Date of Functioning
1	2	3	4	5	6	7
1.	Bhubaneswar Dairy	OMFED	75.00	323.00	100.00	08.12.85
2.	Rourkela Dairy	OMFED	30.00	145.00	60.00	17.05.88
3.	Sambalpur Dairy	OMFED	10.00	50.00	30.00	16.05.90
4.	Cattle Feed Plant	OMFED	100.00 MT	111.82	0.00	20.09.85
5.	Tirtol Chilling Centre	Cuttack Union	20.00	51.00	30.00	26.06.85
6.	Kendrapara Chilling Centre	Cuttack Union	4.00	6.00	0.00	01.07.85
7.	Athagarh Chilling Centre	Cuttack Union	2.00	10.00	0.00	29.09.84
8.	Banki Chilling Centre	Cuttack Union	1.80	10.00	0.00	26.06.87
9.	Nimapara Chilling Centre	Puri Union	20.00	46.00	0.00	To be commi-ssioned
10.	Nayagarah Chilling Centre	Puri Union	2.00	10.00	4.00	19.08.84
11.	Tangi Chilling Centre	Puri Union	0.50	4.65	4.00	15.08.88
12.	Dhenkanal Chilling Centre	Dhenkanal Union	10.00	38.00	20.00	29.09.84
13.	Anugul Chilling Centre	Dhenkanal Union	2.00		4.00*	12.03.82
14.	Keonjhar Chilling Centre	Keonjhar Union	10.00	38.00	20.00	25.01.85
15.	Anandapur Chilling Centre	Keonjhar Union	2.00		4.00*	05.12.81
16.	Telkoi Chilling Centre	Keonjhar Union	2.00		–0.00	26.01.93
17.	Baragarh Chilling Centre	Sambalpur Union	4.00	8.12	10.00	17.02.87

* Management Basis

Source : OMFED

Non-Operation Flood Project

At present, out of 30 newly formed districts in sixteen (16) non-operation flood districts of the state, there are 12 districts co-operative milk producers co-operative societies, consisting 225 primary milk production co-operative societies. About 18,000 ltrs. of milk is collected daily through 375 co-operative societies in 225 identified milk cluster Areas (Govt. of Orissa, 1997. pp 9-10). The integrated Dairy Development Project (IDDP) Phase-1 has been implemented in the undivided districts of Koraput. Kalahandi and Phulbani with the central assistance from the financial year 1993-94. In the second phase the IDDP has been implemented in the district of Sundergarh and undivided districts of Balasore and Mayurbhanj. The milk producing farmers of the villages on both the sides of identified milk route of the above districts are helped through the primary milk producer's co-operative societies has introducing artificial insemination, collection, processing and chilling for onward marketing of milk. Till 1996-97 a total investment of Rs. 11 crores has been programmed in such dairy development project. (Govt. of Orissa, 1997 p. 10.)

Conclusion

The basic principle of economic development is to raise the standard of living, augmenting production and eliminating poverty, which in turn depend upon distribution of assets. In a democratic setup of society wedding with socialistic pattern requires necessary steps to provide equal opportunity for all to enjoy the share (benefit) of development. Co-operatives can be exemplary institutions to achieve the goals with out conflicting with the dual purpose of reducing ineuqally and increasing production. Multiplying problems due to net increase in population, under nutrition required to increase the food production at least incommensurate with required diet to maintain good health. So that one can work to achieve certain minimum level of living standard. Dairy development through co-operative system provide input (foods) and technique (like Artificial Insemination) at a an affordable price and assured remunerative price to member producers of milk (output) by selling to the urban programme envisages to increase the milk production in rural areas and establishment of dairy plants on co-operative lines by replicating 'Anand Pattern' three-tire Co-operative organisation. In the prevailing situation such co-op. institutions serves to fight against malnutrition, poverty and unemployment in one hand and providing opportunity to share the benefits of development on the other. So, there is a bright future for such co-operatives awaiting ahead at the outset of 21st Century.

Selected References

Dorsten, F. Van (1986). "Operation Flood" The EEC Connection" ISS/IDPAD Working Paper on Dairy Aid and Development"

Eswarn, Mukesh and Kotwal, A. (1994). "Why poverty persists in India: An Analytical Framework for Understanding the Indian Economy, OUP.

Food and Agriculture Organistion of the United nation (1969). Manual on Food and Nutrition Policy, FAO, Rome.

Government of India (1969-79). Fourth Five Year Plan, p.197.

Government of Orissa (1997). State Agriculture Policy, Dept. of Agriculture, Bhubaneswar.

Jain, L.C., Krishnamurthy, B.V. and Tripathy, P.M. (1985). "Gross without Roots: Rural Development under Development Auspices". Sage Publication, New Delhi.

National Commission on Agriculture Report (1976). "Rural Employment" Ch. 58, Ministry of Agriculture and Irrigation, Govt. of India.

National Diary Development Board (1979). "Operation Flood", Govt. of India, Ministry of Agriculture and Irrigation, New Delhi, pp. 3-5.

National Diary Development Board (1996). "30th Annual Report".

Olson, Mancur (1971). "The Logic of Collective Action: Public Goods and The Theory of Groups, Harvard Universsity Press, Cambridge.

The Orissa State Co-operative Milk Producers' Federation (1992). 2nd Annual Report.

The Orissa Co-operative Milk Producers' Federation (1993). Operation Flood in Orissa: Progress at a Gland.

Raju, K.V. (1996). "Diary Cooperatives and Economic Rationality" in Rajagopalan, R. (Ed) Re-Discovering Co-operation, Vol. 1, Bases on Co-operation, pp. 160-176. IRMA.

Rama Krishnayya, M. (1997). "New Economic Policy and Co-operative Movement" in Mishra, Baidyanath (ed.) Co-operative Movement in India, A.P.H. Publication Corporation, New Delhi.

Saha, Deepak (1997). "Cooperative Dairying in Maharashtra: lessons to be Learned" *Economic and Political Weekly*, Vol. XXXII (39), Sept. 27 to Oct. 3.

Saha, T. (1995). "Liberalisation and Indian Agriculture: New Role of Farmers Co-opeatives" *Indian Journal of Agricultural Economic*, Vol. 50(3) p. 491.

Singh, R.K.P. (1995). "Performance of Management of Dairy Cooperative Socities in Bihar - Research Report, Dept. of Agriculture Economic, Rajendra Agriculture University, Pusa, p. 82.

Somjee, Geeta and Somjee, A.H. (1989), Reaching out to the Poor: The Unifinished Rural Revolution, Macmillan, London.

5

Natural Resources and Co-operation

Prof. Raghuraman Narayan*

The beginning of co-operative movement can be traced to middle of the nineteenth century in the philosophy of Robert Own. The first co-operative was started in England in 1844. A group of unemployed workers (weavers) started a co-operative, known as Equitable Pioneers of Rochadadle. It's objective was to provide consumer goods to workers at fair prices. In Germany, co-operatives were chosen as an alternative to exploitative society. Co-operatives can provide an egalitarian and just society.

The principles of co-operation extend beyond the scope of mutually helpful society. It is to promote the welfare and progress of the society. The co-operation aims more than material progress.

Co-operation builds democratic institution of equal partners. It is different from joint-stock companies as one member will have one vote, not one share one vote. That principle of one-vote-for-one person serves the equity principle. All members actively participate in the functioning continuously. Country like India can get the benefit of the co-operative movement. It can provide participatory function for country's development. It will increase the self-confidence of the people.

* Department of Economics, Madura College (Autonomous), Madurai—625 011

In other forms of the organisations, the decisions are taken by the people above and followed by the people below. But, in co-operative sector, the ultimate authority rests with the members of the General Body. Even if there is difference in opinion, the collective decision is binding on others. Co-operatives are not merely economic organisations. They are democratic institutions. Co-operatives provide an alternative to the autocratic functions of capitalistic enterprises.

Co-operatives Beyond Liberalisation

Our liberalisation policy focus more on market policies. There was no reference about the co-operative movement. Once co-operative movement was considered as a key to protect the poor from exploitation. Agricultural service co-operatives were started all over the country to protect the rural poor. Consumers co-operatives aimed at protecting the poor from the middlemen/traders. But, all the efforts have failed for so many reasons.

Many said (experts) that the co-operatives have failed as they are not spontaneous but government included one. Now, very successful water-cooperatives have sprung up.

Co-operatives for Rural Development

Each for all; all for each - is the basis behind co-operative movement. They have a common goal to reach. There is no standard definition for co-operation. It is one which belong to the people who use the services, the control of which rests with all members, and the gains of which is distributed among the members of the population, in proportion to their services.

Calvert says—'as a form of organisation wherein persons voluntarily associate together as human beings on the basis of equality to promote common economic interest of themselves'.

Pochdale principles of co-operation lays emphasis on the following—(a) open membership (b) democratic control (c) distribution of surplus in proportion to purchases (d) limited interest on capital (e) religious and political neutrality (f) cash trading and promotion of education.

Honest, efficient and progressive co-operative society is the slogan for an ideal co-operative movement. Saxena says, the right co-operative should eliminate waste in effort and opportunity, eliminate and also help in the exchange of ideas and experience.

The Food and Agricultural Organisation (FAO) says that co-operatives are useful organisations to assist small farmers to improve food production positions in the market and their earnings.

The co-operatives are playing an important role in rural development. For example, rural credit is still made available to farmers through rural credit co-operatives. Marketing co-operatives have made only a small advancement towards it's goal.

Many co-operative societies in Rural India have failed to take-off due to political interference, exploitation of the officials as members (majority) illiterate. Government-induced co-operatives have mostly failed in India. Only spontaneous co-operatives have made success.

Section—I

Agriculture earns one-third of the domestic product. The performance depends on soil improvement, irrigation, fertiliser consumption, better farm management technique contribute collectively for the farm out-put. The Indian irrigation system started from fourth millennium B.C. Increasing population necessitated improvement in irrigation.

Why Water management ?

Inadequate Rain

The major part of the country receives rains only for four months. It is spread over from June–September. The critical period of crop varies from 105 days for Jowar, 120 days in the case paddy, 150 days in the case of sugarcane.

To boost production; new agricultural strategy, agricultural price stability (it is very important. Due to fall in cotton prices many farmers committed suicide during 1997-98 in Andhra. Only co-operative regulated markets can check fluctuation in prices). intensity of cropping, cropping patten, and yield impact on irrigation.

Sources of Irrigation

The most important source of irrigation is wells. It accounts for 50.4 per cent of the total irrigated area. There are two types of wells. One is open and the other; tube wells. Wells are spread over large areas of Punjab, UP, Haryana, Bihar, Rajasthan and Tamil Nadu.

The second important source of irrigation is canals, accounting for 36.1 per cent of the total area. Large areas of land in Punjab, UP, Bihar, Rajasthan and Tamil Nadu are irrigated by canals. Third comes tanks, lakes and other surface water irrigation sources.

Presently, 85 per cent of the water resources consists of surface water in the form of rivers, and lakes. Only 15 per cent of the water used for irrigation comes from wells of both category.

Section—II

In many less developed countries (India also) the people more prone to poverty are living in dry land belt areas. With no perennial source of irrigation changes in monsoon result in changes in their incomes.

Ridley Nelson in his paper to World Bank has come out with the following suggestions to manage dry lands. Desert does not mean sandy dumes and also lands with uncertain water for drinking and irrigation. Too many people and livestock may be the main cause for desertification. In the process, the vegetable cover is lost.

The only course for rural development is managing dry lands.

Investment on dry land areas should be more than plentiful rainfall regions. People themselves may be aware of adoptive strategies. The need of the hour is suitable technology and participation by the affected people (The concept of co-operation is introduced by the author at this stage).

A dry land may receive less than 800 millimetres of rainfall. High transport cost and other costs make the dry land people to keep off from high technology. Due to different rainfall pattern the same technology may not be susceptible for all years.

People in such areas should produce rain-fed crops in the use of low-cost moisture conservation.

The highest challenge with technology in dry area that plants do not grow without water. Under risk environment, the families are risk averse.

A project of Barkino Faso supported by OXFAM suggests contour bunding, using stone bunds or small retaining walls placed on the contour yielded an economic rate return over 30 percent.

Participation of local people is important for the sustainable development of rural areas (mainly agriculture) and eradication of poverty. It was successful in West Africa, Kenya etc. This approach has been tried by the International Institute for Environment, the Ford Foundation and Agahagan Foundation. MYRADA in India, a NGO, is adopting such methods. It is only a survival strategy.

Water Management

Water is important for human beings for living and agriculture as an input. Our growing population, consequent growing demand for food, water is necessary in increasing quantity. But, water is not available in sufficient quantities at the right time.

In India the supply of water depends on water by rains. It varies from region to region, season to season and year to year. It is low in western Rajasthan (100 mm - annually) and 11000 mm at Cherapunjee in Assam.

Water Management Components

It involves generation, distribution and institutional arrangements, preservation, distribution and harvesting of water.

Forms of Water Management

(a) Groundwater. (b) Surfacewater.

Groundwater management consists of sinking wells, construction of tanks, use of pump sets. Groundwater development form bulk of in minor irrigation programme, which is essentially a people's programme (co-operative effort). It is mainly done by the people co-operatively by raising resources for themselves or institutional help. This programme impose less expenditure for the Government. It is instant and reliable source of irrigation for the people.

Role of Farmers and Government in Water Management

Augmentation of water, conservation and judicious use are the main aims of water management.

The judicious use of water is in the co-operative effort of both government and farmers.

Government's role can be laid down as follows-

a) Assessment of groundwater potential
b) Pointing suitable areas for groundwater development.
c) Monitoring groundwater level and quality.
d) Augmentation of groundwater resources by water spreading, construction of bunds, ponds, pits etc.
e) Mixing groundwater with surface water for saline-fresh water irrigation.
f) Providing extension service.

Farmers' Role

(a) Must know the storage capacity of the wells month-wise and seasonwise.
(b) Addition to climate, rainfall and soil they should choose the cropping pattern.
(c) They may adopt springer, drip irrigation instead of flood irrigation.
(f) Prevent seepage of water.
(g) Selection of well sites on the advice of hydrogeologists.
(h) There should be one pit for one farm.
(i) There should not be any cropping within 50 ft. radius of wells especially rice, sugarcane etc.
(j) Avoid planting Eucalyptus in dry areas.,

(It is for only swamp regions. In Tamil Nadu they grow this crop in Pudukottain district as a consequence the underground water fell from 20 ft. to 500 ft. within twenty years)

(k) Excessive use of groundwater should be avoided.

Involvement of Beneficiaries in the Water Management Process Through Co-operatives

Water management system can be a success only when the beneficiaries take part in it. It is true for any system and all the more for water co-operatives. The participation includes improving field channels, levelling of land and building to avoid the water waste when it is taken from the water body to the fields. The equitable distribution of water is not possible even when there is government set-up to work in the process (So why, the IBRD recommends 'Tradeable water rights' in future. It suggests handing over the water distribution and augmentation to the private investors, who may price water. Only water pricing can result in judicious usage of scarce water. In India, the co-operatives may replace private investors)

Only when there is public participation there will not wastage in construction cost. It may suggest the right way in distribution channels which may lead to fair distribution.

It is from this point of view that organising water users into co-operatives societies does open out a way for their problem. The problem of equitable distribution may well be tackled by the co-operative societies. It is only here the co-operative societies can take over the distribution below the out level by forming 'KULABA CO-OPERATIVES'. It may involve the members (water users) for the mutual benefits. It may expand itself as INTEGRATED AGRICULTURAL SERVICE SOCIETIES. The entire canal system may be taken up under it's control.

Why Co-operatives for Water Distribution ?

The water co-operatives is most suitable for setting up distribution system. It is very good at primary level. The general body meeting should select it's executive members. The general policy that should be adopted for water distribution, rate of water (pricing water ! - is the latest call by the World Bank for judicious distribution of scarce resource) and other important issues are decided in the general body meeting.

The co-operatives are more suitable for farmers, as they can also provide other services, like credit, marketing ware-housing etc. If the farmers of Andhra Pradesh were to get such facilities, there would not have been suicide cases among cotton growers of Andhra. The farmers were deprived of assistance to use the right pesticides and poor prices for their product. The democratic decision making and supportive services make water co-operatives all the more the 'Right Choice' !

Warabhadi co-operatives are for equitable distribution of water. Warabhadi means, fixation of turns. They fix the time, the quantum of water supply according to the area of command. Adequate, timely and assured water supply is the key to rural development.

Rural development depends on water. The available water should be evenly supplied to all the end users. Fixed day, fixed time and fixed period will help the farmers to decide on their cropping pattern.

Water is an essential input in farming. Only farming holds the key for rural development. Using the water for the right crop may help the farmers to boost their income.

Many non-farming activities also provide employment opportunities for the villages only when the farming is in good state.

Economics of Water

Now water has been recognised as an economic good all over the world. The quantity and quality of water decide the rural development. Water resource management has assumed greater importance in the world.

Economics will play an important role in water resource decisions. It is because—

a) Economic efficiency is key to economic development.

b) Opportunity cost is to guide future water allocations.

c) Price and other economic incentives require for conservation of water and efficiency.

d) Investment decisions require economic analysis.

e) Water resource augmentation will decide the future of rural areas, as they bank on agricultural produce, where in water is an input.

The only way to increase water supply is to go in for watershed management, conservation of forest as pre-requisite for water conservation.

Watershed Management

In ancient India, the kings maintained the watersheds by digging up lakes (fresh water), ponds and wells. The ponds served as source of water supplies to the people for drinking and domestic purposes and also drainage. Due to mismanagement the tanks in India lost more than 50 per cent of their storage capacity.

Though the Government spent several crores to maintain the watershed through many rural employment schemes, not even 5 per cent of the target reached. In that respect India is one. The money was siphoned off to the pockets of officials and politicians.

Urbanisation has taken away many watershed in Madurai. Madurai, the second biggest city in Tamil Nadu was having numerous lakes, ponds wells etc. In mid-sixties water table around Meenakshi Amman temple was at 12 ft. Now it is more than 400 ft. It is due to unsustainable exploitation of groundwater and all the recharging channels are blocked. Almost all the lakes around Madurai are used to accommodate Government buildings.

Remaining lakes were used to build Tamil Nadu Housing Board colonies. At one stage or other the watershed management must be taken care of.

The conservation of natural resources like forest and water, the twin factors of the rural people, have assumed greater importance. Spontaneous people's movement have come to in many parts of the country. In this paper case studies of forest conservation and water management are given.

Co-operation means, collective decision making and execution. They need not be registered bodies under co-operative acts. In many cases of Government included co-operatives, the movement has failed. In place where it is spontaneous, they have succeeded. Here are few case studies which explain that voluntary co-operation from people alone will keep the environment resources intact. Environmental resources are 'key' to rural development.

Forests are destroyed to make way for industries, which pollute water and the air. Communities, individuals and non-government agencies are now acting to a save the country side. There is a conflict going on between development conservation.

Here is an example of people's co-operation that has conserved a forest being plundered by officials and politicians.

Wood is an easy way of mopping money for politicians and officials. Several crores can be take away unnoticed by them especially teak, dark-wood; sandalwood are some of the types.

Rajasthan

Kaladevi wildlife sanctuary is one of the examples of people's co-operation for maintaining the rural ecology. It spreads over 674 square kilometer, of 1334 squares km of Rathambor Wildlife Sanctuary. It falls in Madhopur district. It is semi-arid region, where bear, leopard, blue bull and hyena are found in large number. There are 20 villages inside the region where people live on subsistence farming. Things were all right till Britishers were in India. After Independence, the government started exploiting the forest for wood, timber and charcoal. The forest contractors are the agents to siphon off the wealth of the villagers to politicians and officials.

The life of the rural people is linked to water for living, agriculture, tree growing for fuel and fodder. Any damage to the fragile eco-systems will affect the life of the farmers. Besides cutting of wood, the grazziers of Mewar region of Western Rajasthan migrate to this region with 1,50,000 sheeps.

To save themselves Rabris formed an association called 'Baragaon ki panchayat '(body of 12 villages under a single panchayat) in 1990. They started a campaign to keep out of the migrant sheep. They also formed Vana Suraksha Committee was formed to protect the forests. They formed an executive with a forest official as a member. The body has informal recognition, but not legal recognition. Each and every village around Kaladevi has FPC (Forest Protection Council) to protect the forest.

They have a body at village level and the representative of village level samitis form an apex level association.

The voluntary co-operative has representative character. The member represent all communities in the village. Every village have representation at apex committee on numerical strength basis.

Even the panch patels are members. However, women have no role to play.

No one is allowed to carry an axe into the sanctuary area. The villagers are allowed to carry only dry and dead wood for fuel, that too for personal consumption. For housing wood can be cut. The quantity is fixed by the committee. These rules are flexible. Old people can carry axe as they may find it difficult to cut the fuel wood. Those who violate the rules are punished. For violators they impose a fine of Rs. 11—Rs. 1100. The money collected forms villages resource fund and is used for common village purposes.

The village do not allow the mining operations, even though it is a lucrative occupation for them.

The forest protection councils impose social and religious sanctions. It has no legal sanction, though it does the work of the forest department.

In 1996 a seminar (workshop) was conducted by forest department to study the participatory management of protected area. Indian Society of Public Administration discussed about the sustainable development of subsistence resources. Their main demand was for water. They said water should be made available inside the sanctuary both for forest animals and human beings. The people (FPC) demanded powers equivalent to the forest rangers.

It is a classic example of spontaneous, co-operative act of the people to protect their own interest.

Economic of Water Management

With shrinking water supply and ever increasing demand resulted in water management studies. There are two factors affecting water resources in irrigation system. They may be classified under the following:

a) Factors affecting demand for water.

b) Factors affecting it's supply.

The factors which affect the demand for water may be listed as the price of the water, population, the stage economic growth and technology.

Higher pricing will limit the water use. Population, agricultural production may push the demand for water to a higher side.

Supply of Water

The supply of water is limited to the water availability site. Construction of dams, irrigation canals, and rolling of the Earth may improve the water supply.

Management of water in agriculture may be done at the following two levels. They are:

(a) On the farm level.

(b) Off the farm level.

Water resource economics studies the following aspects in water management.

(a) Management.

(b) Conservation and administration.

(c) Public formulation.

Maximum production at minimum water use is the ultimate in water management.

Section—III

Theoretical suggestion to conserve water and augment it.

Prof. Posten, water expert of World Resource Institute Washington, suggests the following for water augmentation. It also includes water conservation. Water saved is water augmented.

It includes plugging the water leaks, recycling of water for industrial use (MFL recycles water for it's) more efficient technologies in irrigation (e.g. drip, sprinkler, mist irrigation), and pricing system that gives incentive to use less water.

Water Conservation through Pricing of Water

Manteen Thobani in his paper on Formal water Markets: why, when, and how to introduce tradable water rights!' (Ref. - World Bank Research Observer - Volume -12 No. 2- August 97)

In many countries the government owns water (India also) and the official decides, who gets the water, how it is to be used and how much will be charged for it.

Water users associations may be formed consisting of farmers to bring out economic use of water. Even world wide, only agriculture consumers 80 per cent of the water and the domestic use is only (8 per cent). Low-value, high water intensive crops are grown even in arid areas. Such practices should be stopped. Diverting water from farming to domestic users in urban areas may result it social conflicts.

Government should assure the poor to have access to water. The rich people may be prepared to pay a high price depriving poor of his share. (Free water supply pipes are located in poor habitat and individual connections are given to better-off and making them to pay a higher price).

Even for farming farmer growing high-value commercial crops should be made to pay electricity charges for their pump-set electricity connections.

Many dams do not supply adequate water to the farmers in time.

No government has control over the quality of the water supplied to the domestic users. Many developing economies do not protect the eco-systems. The Municipal wastes entered into water pipelines meant for drinking and lead to water borne-diseases. Industrial wastes, the run-off of agricultural chemicals also spoil the underground water. Mining and forestry have combined together to erode water sources. (For example, artisan wells were common in South Arcto district in 1960s'. Now the tubewells are sunk for several hundred feet to get water supply for irrigation. The reason : Mining at Neyveli. Nobody bothered about the social cost of losing fertiled lands unfit for farming for the years to come.)

The polluted water lead to degeneration of the land. I am happy atleast few years back the Department of Agriculture, Thanjavur gave up pesticide spraying. They say heaven has not fallen by giving up pesticide spraying. (I had a discussion with one of the Officers Rangaraja (1996) and questioned the decision of giving pesticide spraying. He said many chronic pests are due to the pesticide spraying as they are pesticide induced. He may be correct).

Unsustainable pumping of underground water is threatening the livelihood of thousands of farmers. Even non-agricultural users harm the fragile eco-system.

Pricing of water will correct the situation. Water conservation is possible by only when water is priced.

Water Pricing and It's Effect on Poverty Reduction

Water pricing will reduce poverty in several ways. The scarce resource will be redeployed for more productive purposes, thus leading to increased output and employment.

In my opinion water prices should cover the cost of water recharging. People should pay tax according to the depth and the output of water used.

People's Solution to Water Problem

The following case studies give us confidence that the water problem can be solved (to some extent) by the people themselves.

Case Study—I

Saurashtra

Shyamji Antala is revered by the farmers of Saurashtra for good reason. He used cost-effective methods to recharge 2.5 lakh wells in the region.

In Saurashtra region there is no single perennial river. There are countless riverlets with rocky bed. They keep coming during every monsoon and die there-after.

Sri. Antala connected the dry wells with riverlets by a 9" diameter cement pipe. In two days after the rain started the water started perculating. The farmers feel that a good shower will fill the wells and help them to get one additional crop of groundnut. It would fetch them a profit of Rs. 6000 - (June 1997 - India Today-June, 15).

Antala prescribes various methods. If there are no riverlets he has another solution to recharge. In Gundasara village, he proposed the villagers to dig six ft. by six ft. tanks with connected bed near each dry well. Then he studied the area where water naturally collects during rainy season. These were connected to the tanks by loosely made canals. And the upper portion of the tank in turn, connected to the well by pipe. Once the rains trigger off, the flow of water, the tanks get filled up, the mud settles to the bottom, and the clean water trickle down to the depth of well. Now by the technique 217 of the 277 wells are briming with water. Gudasara villages get an additional income of Rs. 18 lakhs. A simple way to drive poverty from arid villages.

Now Shyamji Antala is a Rain God to the people.

Case Study—II

Bihar

Gandhiji's way of water management is followed by the

people of Relegaon Siddhi, a tiny village in Bihar. Once it was a tiny village with no notable agricultural activity.

Anahazare, a noted activist against corruption, started trapping water co-operatively. People's direct participation in trapping water was a success.

In a country with lakh of villages with no access to safe and pottable drinking water, Siddhi's way is a leading light. The community based efforts yielded water. The community effort made the desert bloom.

Ralegaon village is a show-piece to India and foreign people. A villager said "If you trap every drop of water that falls on Earth, the water problem is solved. You need no external help".

In Palamu district, 125 villagers have solved the problem that way. They found that the Government is of no use in solving their problem. They joined together and built 175 small dams with some technical and monetary assistance from the government. Even non-government organisation came to their help. The period of their achievement is 1994-95.

How They Do It ?

The Ralegoan Siddhi model adopts the following techniques.

a) Storage

b) Diversion.

The big dams catch only 8 per cent to 12 per cent of the total rainfall. Rest go a waste. The Sidhi model store the rain water above the surface., submergence storage, and adopt the simple techniques to divert water from the slopes to the catchment areas.

Case Study—III

Tamil Nadu

Ramanthapuram is a dry district in the state. People adjust their life to water scarce conditions as camels do in deserts. Drought is perennial in the district.

In the ancient times, Kilavan Sehtupathi constructed 'Periakamai' where the flood water of Vaigain stored and the surplus is let off to the sea.

No elected government could find a permanent solution to their water problem since 1960's. Now a young collector, B. Anand

(1997), is trying to find a modern way to solve the problem.

According to the Collector, Naripayur will be a role model. They are going to establish 45 desalination plants. The cost of treating 1000 lts. is Rs. 90/- only.

Case Study—IV

Karnataka

A group of farmers in Jamkhandi, Bijapur district believed in the idea of self-help is the best help. They formed an association, named Krishna Teera Snagha. It means the association Krishna river farmers. They constructed barrage across Krishna (three in number) and solved their water problem. That is across Krishna, Malaprabha.

Though they live near to the river water problem created near-drought conditions. Then they joined together to solve their problem of irrigation and drinking water.

Case Study—V

Gujarat

No programme can succeed unless there is people's participation. Here is a role model story of a group of villages managing the watersheds co-operatively. The participation by the beneficiaries make any programme a success.

Bharuch is a district in Gujarat. It is undergoing silent revolution in watershed management. They have an integrated approach to water management. They link up agricultural intensification with soil and moisture conservation and institutional development to turn marginal land to quasi-rent land.

They formed micro-water sheds across riverlets.

Bharuch once enjoyed the conventional irrigation system through a canal. But, in course of time it was not sufficient.

Bharuch received only 900 mm rain enough to raise only one crop. Then they adopted contour bunding to store water, soil, optimising the use of water, changing crops according to water availability.

The Agakhan Rural Support programme has undertaken the work of water resource development, watershed development, water conservation, agricultural extension, biogas plants, and credit schemes. Savings are also promoted.

The Gram Vikas Mandals initiated many projects for the benefit of the villages which helped them to maximise the benefits from the available resources.

They also started tree growers association in 1993 with 190 members.

Pani Panchayath (Maharashtra)

Fifty kilometers from Pune, against the backdrop of Prandur fort, village Mahur is situated. It is a rain-shadow region. It receives 500 mm of rains every year. The rainwater runs of because it is a hilly region. Only very little water is left for the farmers for their farming activities. Fifteen years ago the farmers depended upon rain-fed agriculture and their income was supplemented by labour. The rate of migration was very high. Atleast one member of a family migrated to Bombay.

All that is changing now. Now you can see flowers, greeny stretches of vegetables etc.

In 1971 Government built a small check dam to store rain water in the village. For ten years the villagers did not know anything about the use of it. They heard that the water can be drawn through pumps only by 1980.

The villagers formed 'Gram Gurav Prishthan mobilised Rs. 2.5 lakhs, the Government provided 50 per cent subsidy. Thirty hrs. power pumps were installed. It served 35 members, who owned 50 acres of land.

The allocation of water was not in a random manner. The largest holder of the land did not get more water. Each land owner was allowed to irrigate only two acres of land. (It is a fine principle of pure co-operation. It is like, each member one vote). Water was distributed equally after ascertaining how much of water needed to irrigate one acre of land. Their incomes rose by 15 times, because of 'Pani Pachayath' (water co-operatives'). Floriculture made them net more income. It is the case of small farmers with one-and-half acres of land. Their monthly income from floriculture was between Rs. 2000 - 2500 a month. There was change in cropping pattern. From traditional rice or bajra, they switched over to flowers and fruits.

Now the principles of Pani Panchayath (water co-operatives) is in force in many other villages like; Naigaon villages of Purandar taluk.

According to Mr. Salunkhe, the first example of micro watershed development programme and land and water management was Naigoan. In Naigoan the average annual rainfall was between 250-500 mm. To prevent run off water they constructed contour bunds around fields and dug up a perculation pond.

Do not say land to the tiller; say water to the tiller. This is the slogan of 'Pani Panchayaths'.

The Pani Panchayath conducted many experiments. They found out half an acre of irrigated land can sustain one person. The Naigoan experiment produced 500 quintals of rice and generated employment for 15 persons. The whole area is covered by hundreds of trees providing fodder for cattle and fuel for humans.

Once the water harvesting is over, the problem of crops and distribution starts. Besides water, the economic needs of the villagers also is to be met. Every villager is to get water regard-less of landholding. On an average every farmer will get water to irrigate one hectare of land. So village was treated as one unit of planning.

Big dams will be connected to small dams. Pani Panchayaths aimed at low water consuming crops. They say 60 per cent of the water is used to irrigate only 3 per cent of land under sugarcane. Short term cash crops are preferred to long term, water consuming sugarcane.

As landless also entitled for his share of water, people who own more than hectare may sell the lands to landless. The pani Panchayaths result in land distribution.

The Naigoan experiment spread to other villages and they also strike a balance between cash-crops and food crops. Community horticulture has become common. (demonstration effect !) Mr. Salunkhe says that is has been proved that village problems can be solved at micro level itself.

Even the Planning Commission has included 'Pani Panchayath' in 20-point programme.

At present (1996) 1600 villagers in 20 villages are benefited by Pani Panchayats. 3000 acres of land sustain 20000 villagers. It is due to availability of water.

The reverse migration is taking place (from cities to villages) Pani Panchayats (water co-operative) made deserts bloom.

Case Study—VI

Afforestation (Rajasthan)

The previous case study deals with conservation of forest. This case study describes people's participation in afforestation, a unique co-operative venture.

This study goes around Aravali region of Rajasthan, bordering Haryana. The width of the Aravali system varies from 10 kms to 100 kms and height varies from 300-900 mts.

The highest peak is Mount Abu, which 1700 mts. The Aravali hill system has always played an important role in maintaining the ecology of the region. It also serves as an important watershed of the region. Rivers like Chambal, Luni and Banas received the run-off from the hill. The literal meaning of Aravali means 'wall of rocks'.

It prevents desertification that lies in the North-West of the hills.

Deforestation

Till the end of the century it was sporting thick fores. It was home for variety of animals and birds. The plant species of rare kind was in abundance. But, in the recent past there was deforestation for wood, timber, charcoal etc. Sudden increase in population in that area and increasng cattle population resulted in rapid phase of deforestation. Extention of agriculture also supplemented the cause of deforestation.

Traditionally women had to toil to get fodder, fuel and water in this region. In eighties the deforestation was rapid in Haryana and Rajasthan region of the Aravali Hills.

To prevent that the Forest Department started participatory development of the region.

The NGOs, Government and people started afforeseting 1.5 lakh hectares of the land. In Haryana the common land was in the hands of the local people, unlike Rajasthan the forest department was owning most of the land.

Case Study—VII

Karnataka

Tapping water Resources (Water Co-operatives)

Even voluntary and non-government organisations look forward to the Government's help. Here is a Karnataka example, which proves that even without the help of Government or NGO's, people can collectively solve their problems.

The place is Jamakhadi, 600 km. away from Bangalore.

Controlled Use of Forest Resources

The Community controlled Regulated Access Management System was adopted to replace open access system. Under open access system, people were allowed to exploit forest resources without any control. Under regulated systems the community itself impost certain restriction for sustainable availability of natural resources. Slowly the villagers accepted these ideas and became participants of the movement. 33000 hectares of land in 293 villages had to be afforested to attain sustainability. Gurgoan, Rawet, Faridabad, Mahendergarh, and Bhiwani districts of Haryana came under this scheme. (CCRMAS)

The programmes costed enormously. The Europeon Union offered 82 per cent of the cost. The rest was borne by the Government of Haryana.

Village Forest committees were formed by the villagers by community participation of five districts of Haryana. The Committees have 13 members with sarpanch as the chairman. Forest department official was a member - secretary.

Role of Women

Atleast three women and members of the SC/ST were made members. They had to report to the General Council. Micro plan for each village was prepared.

The micro plan decided the area that should be under plantation, afforestation and requirement of fuel wood etc. They choose the species of trees according to the nature of the soil.

Nurseries

To provide employment and involve in the planning, the women of the villages are asked to supply nurseries to the department.

Incentives were offered to communities for guarding the tress from human and animal damage. The villages received Rs. 500 per hectare of plantation per year. (This method was followed by former Tamil Nadu Chief Minister Bkathavasthalam. He asked the forest department to plant teak wood trees on Cauvery bunds in 1960's. He allotted the job of maintaining the planted saplings to the village SC/ST landless. Now almost all trees are intact with a growth of five feet. They are valued at several hundred crores. He is an unsung hero of war.

Problem of Grazing

The plantation extension and afforestation reduced the land for open grazing for the villagers. The village/forest committee, so to solve the problem, different types of grasses were tried in plantation area. Open areas available between saplings were utilised for growing grasses. Wide open were left in between sapling. The fodder grown was made available to the villagers as per their requirements. In two years the fodder supply increased enormously and also the cattle population. We know the cattle is the 'mobile form' of villagers wealth.

The grass seeds were purchased from the market. The villagers were encouraged to collect grass seeds from the common land. The villagers were not allowed to cut the grass till it was fully mature. Fodder trees protect the land against erosion, cattle generated biomas for fuel and manure. In five years it produced 30000 tonnes of manure.

The work load of women reduced. Women need not go long distance to collect fodder. The Project Aravali, started in 1990, will continue till 1998.

Objectives Achieved

It has not only reached the targets but also exceeded. That is the outcome of 'co-operation' or 'people's participation'.

For example, the fodder supply increased. In this village it annually increased from 750 quintals to 1400 quintals.

Employment more than one crore labour days have been generated in Aravali project, women labour increased by 38 per cent. (Share of employment generated).

'Van Jothi Chulas' improved the efficiency of wood stoves.

In addition, they enjoy the following benefits:

- Now they can make the new stove with mud and sell it.
- Milk production increased.
- Now the area is much more efficient.

This is the 'magic' of voluntary co-operation or people's participation.

People's Voluntary Co-operation : A case study of Madhya Pradesh

Watershed Management (Water Co-operatives)

Less than few years ago Neemkheda, a village in Madhya Pradesh was under the grip of drinks (alcohol, indebtedness and brawls.). The village is in Dewas district of Madhya Pradesh. Today things are different. Now there are fewer fights and the brewing of illicit liquor has come to stop. The burden of debt also has come down very sharply. Earlier, the youths of Neemkheda were migrating to Indore. Now it has disappeared. One could see a sense of purpose in their faces.

The cause for sea-change in the life style of the village, 50 km away from Indore, is environmental regeneration. Now the young men of the village are engaged in bunding fields, escavating ponds, planting saplings, building underground dykes, are some of the occupations that changed the face of the villages. Now they fight to preserve the environment. It is well-known that poverty and environment are interrelated. Once the environment is protected the poverty is out.

The change was possible because of Samaj Pragati Sahyog, a non-government organisation, which has been working in this area from 1993. It is an example of how a non-government organisation can create assets and employment. (Many of our government sponsored anti-poverty scheme helped only the officials and the politicians. Late Rajiv Gandhi said that out of Re. 1 spend on poor, only 20 paise. reached them, the rest is siphoned off by the others outside the village.) The ongoing environment restoration programme (1997-98) established itself to get the positive results.

How It Is Started ?

The SPS entered when it came to the village to repair the ravages of the Government indifference. They undertook the construction of watershed development work with the help of 110 tribal households with a population of 900. It is largely an agricultural village and little land under irrigation. Within three years 95 per cent of the lands are bunded, to prevent soil erosion. Farm ponds were built to store water for the second crop. And in the nullah that flows through the village, underground dykes have been built to raise the water levels in nearby wells. Experiments have been conducted to limit the use of chemicals, fertilisers and pesticides. (In Thanjavur district of Tamil Nadu in 1996 two Dy. Directors of Agriculture (Mr. Rangarajan and Mr. Venkatesan suddenly decided to give up pesticide spraying in the district. When everybody predicted a holocaust, nothing happened. They say that many of the plant diseases are only pesticide induced !).

The programmes had short term impact on employment and income. Work is available in lean season also. Unlike the Government sponsored activity, the workers received a minimum wage. Women earned as much wage as men for the same job ! (It is one of the long cherished aim of our trade unions)

Now soil erosion is arrested and the water tables have gone up. There is more greenery than two years ago.

The Sign of Troubles

The first sign of trouble shown up in 1996. The dykes that have been built will keep the water in the 'nullah' for a longer time and help families down stream irrigate the lands. It is possible only when the water in 'nullah' is not over exploited by building under water channels that emptied the nullah in no time. Natural resources are only for the community not for individuals.

In 1996, the villagers engaged in afforestation during monsoon. They choose 20 acres of empty land. There was problem of grazing. For that they grew grass on one - third of the area.

Many in the village were after short-term gains more than long term sustainable development.

Pride of the Community

It is a success only for the community and it's co-operation. Mere Government's initiative or non-government organisations cannot perform unless the people's co-operation is there.

The village watershed committee turned the desert into boom. The watershed committee receives funds from the State Government for construction and it's maintenance. Twenty members are in operation for more than one year. The members of the committee have already experienced in construction of contour bunding, escavation of farm ponds, construction of gasbian structures in the riverlets etc.

It is the committee that decides the work to be done and the execution of it. It meets twice a month to discuss the farmer's needs. Any request from farmers is fulfilled only when entire committee accepts the need of it.

Criterion for Job

If the funds are large to carry out the programme, there is not problem. If the work hours are less, they had some criterion to choose people for employment.

- Men and women from landless families are offered employment on the basis of 'first' priority.
- If they need more people for work the second preference was given to those with unirrigated landholding.
- Third preference to those who are in the village as paid employment.
- If the workload is much higher, all those who are willing to work in the village were given employment.

Equity

Equity is prime aspect of co-operation. The principle of equity is satisfied when the people of disadvantages position are given employment.

The principal of co-operation is made the prime force for the development of the village within a short period of 5 years.

References

Dr. Purnima Rao and Mr. Swani ' New Economic Policy problems and alternatives Friedrich (1993)

Guy, L,. Moigine & others - A Guide to Formulation of Water Resources Strategy, World Bank—1994.

Finance & Development - June 1994 (Quarterly by IMF)

Hindu Survey of the Environment - 1992; 93; 94; 95; 96; 97)

6

Marketing Co-operatives in India

Dr. S. N. Tripathy*

In varied agro-climatic conditions, India produces the largest number of various agricultural commodities. While the success in accelerating agricultural production has been made possible because of institutional reforms, technological changes and fixation of remunerative prices, it has been conceived that through adequate marketing support we can ensure and augment continuous agricultural production. This is because a marketing system which protects the interest of the producer and the consumer, is the key to agricultural prosperity. The success of agricultural development and ultimately the welfare of agricultural class depends on the efficiency of marketing system. In view of the perishable nature of agricultural commodities which are susceptible to climatic variation resulting in bumper harvest in one season, leading to seasonal gluts and decrease in prices, while on the contrary, there could be failure of crop resulting in shortages, scarcity and hike in consumer prices.

Problems

The prevailing marketing structure in rural India has been in the grip of serious problems like defective methods of buying and selling, use of under-weights, presence of large army of interme-

* Department of Economics, Aska Science College, Aska (Orissa)—761 111

diaries and middlemen taking a lion's share of the seller's dues. Exploitation by middlemen through secret fixation of prices and thereby grabbing a big portion of the payment due to the cultivators. Lack of grading, standardisation, and transport bottlenecks are the problems associated with the marketing system which results in increasing cost of marketing and adverse affect on marketable surplus.

Co-operative Marketing

Co-operative marketing is an important aspect of the co-operative movement. It has identified itself as the best suited agency for handling the problems of agricultural marketing by virtue of their performance as procurement price support agency for different agricultural produces. The marketing co-operatives are generally owned by the farmers themselves. They are organised to find incentive marketing outlets for their products at reasonable prices. In recent years, marketing co-operative play an important role in agricultural trading of the country pertaining to foodgrains, oilseeds, pulses, jute, cotton, spices, plantation crops like rubber, tea, coffee, coco, fruits, eggs and dairy products etc.

Progress of Marketing Co-operatives

The progress of marketing co-operatives was not upto the mark until the All India Rural Credit Survey Committee (1954) report was brought to light. The Committee brought out the concept of state partnership in co-operation, as a result, the marketing co-operatives gained a new dimension and direction towards its progress.

In 1958 the National Agricultural Co-operative Marketing Federation (NAFED) was established as the apex body of the marketing co-operatives. Its main functions are co-ordination and promotion of marketing activities of its members at the national leave. The NAFED has been playing a commendable role in stabilising market prices of perishable commodities like onions and potatoes in principal producing areas by strategic market interventions at times on its own and sometimes as an agency of the Government.

In 1963, the National Co-operative Development Corporation (NCDC) was set up on the basis of the recommendations of the ALL

India Rural Credit Survey Committee. The NCDC promotes programmes relating to proceeding, storage and marketing of agricultural produce through co-operative societies and other allied activities. It also extends financial assistance to the co-operative marketing societies.

The Dantwala Committee (1966) emphasised the need for co-operation and integration among the various co-operative organisations after assessing the pattern of co-operative marketing distribution of inputs to farmers and supply of consumer products. In 1968 the Reserve Bank of India conducted a survey for marketing co-operatives in order to examine the co-operative friendly factors.

The RBI was of the opinion that effective linking of credit with marketing was crucial for marketing co-operatives.

Structure and Achievement

At the state level, co-operative marketing is of two tier system with Primary marketing societies at the taluk level and the State Co-operative Marketing Federation as the apex body. The net work of marketing co-operative structure comprises over 6,000 primary marketing societies of which 3,500 are special commodity marketing societies, at the district level, there are 160 Central marketing societies, at the state level there are 29 general purpose state level co-operative marketing Federation and 16 Special commodity Marketing Federation. At the All India level, there is the National Agricultural co-operative Marketing Federation (NAFED). Besides, there are 8 state level Trade co-operative Development Corporation/Federations, an Arecanut Co-operative Marketing Federation and a national level Tobacco Co-operative marketing Federation.

The marketing of agricultural produce through co-operatives has recorded a spectacular performance. The co-operative marketing societies marketed agricultural produce valued Rs. 169 crores during 1960-61; this had increased to Rs. 1,950 crores in 1980-81, and subsequently, Rs. 7,500 crores in 1993-94. The striking features of marketing co-operatives in India is that in states like Punjab, Maharashtra, Uttar Pradesh and Gujarat 75 percent of the total value of the agricultural produce have been made through marketing co-operatives.

Organisation of Marketing Co-operatives in Orissa

The marketing co-operative structure in the state of Orissa have been classified as general purpose marketing co-operative societies and specialised community marketing co-operative societies. Under general purpose marketing sector, there is Orissa state co-operative marketing federation at the Apex level and 56 regional marketing co-operative societies (RMCS) at the block or regional level. The RMCS purchases surplus agricultural produce from the growers, process and market the same at remunerative prices. They also distribute chemical fertilizers, seeds, agricultural implements and consumer goods among the rural people at reasonable prices.

Under specialised commodity marketing co-operative societies, two apex co-operative societies, namely, the Orissa State Tribal Development Co-operative Corporation and the Orissa state co-operative oil-seeds grower's Federation are functioning in the State for the eliminating the middlemen in the market operations. The specialised marketing co-operative society collects minor forest produce from the tribals paying supporting prices as well as market the produce.

Progress of Orissa Co-operative Marketing

Trends relating to progress of Orissa State Co-operative Marketing Federation has been analysed in Table 6.I.

It is seen from the Table 6.I that during the period 1980-81 to 1985-86 there has been increase of members from 161 to 616 which

Table 6.1 : Progress of Orissa State Co-operative Marketing Federation (Members, Working Capital, Total Turnover) during 1980–81 to 1995–96

(Rs. in lakhs)

Particulars	*1980–81*	*1985–86*	*1990–91*	*1995–96*
Members	161	616	826	829
Working Capital	3041	6024	8765	7555
Business Turnover	1788	1755	3243	7525

Source : Compiled from "Cooperative Movement in Orissa" various issues. Published by Registrar, Co-operative Societies of Orissa, Bhubaneswar.

further increased to 826 by 1990-91. In percentage terms, the increase has been 282% during 1980-81 to 1985-86; which further registered an increase of 34% by 1990-91. The working capital marked an increase from Rs. 3.041 lakhs to Rs. 6,024 lakhs during 1980-81 to 1985-86. This investment of working capital during 1985-86 to 1990-91 has registered an increase from Rs. 6024 lakhs to Rs. 8765 lakhs. With regard to business turnover the increase in investment has been from Rs. 1755 lakhs to Rs. 3243 lakhs during 1985-86 to 1990-91. The Table clearly shows that although the investment of working capital has declined during 1990-91 to 1995-96 there has been an increase business turnover from Rs. 3243 lakhs to Rs. 7525 lakhs; registering an increase of 132 per cent.

Progress of Regional Co-operative Marketing Societies in Orissa during the period 1980-81 to 1995-96 has been depicted in the Table 6.2.

Table 6.2 : Progress of Regional Co-operative Marketing Societies (Number, Members, Working Capital, Total Turnover) during 1980–81 to 1995–96

(Rs. in lakhs)

Particulars	*1980–81*	*1985–86*	*1990–91*	*1995–96*
Numbers	63	64	64	56
Members	25	32000	33000	26824
Working Capital	4249	4661	3789	3551
Total Turnover	2203	540	671	842

Source : Compiled from "Cooperative Movement in Orissa" various issues. Published by Registrar, Co-operative Societies of Orissa, Bhubaneswar.

Table 6.2 reveals that there has been uneven trend of progress with regard to members of the Regional Societies and investment of working capital during 1980-81 to 1995-96. However, it is heartening to note that business turnover has registered an increasing trend since 1985-86. This increase has been Rs. 540 lakhs to Rs. 671 lakhs during 1985-86. This increase has been Rs. 540 lakhs during 1985-86 to 1990-91, which further enhanced to Rs. 842 lakhs by 1995-96. Thus, there has been an average annual increase of 5.5% total business turn over during 1985-86 to 1995-96.

Strengthening Co-operatives

The marketing co-operatives are, however, suffering from certain impediments. They are organisational, managerial, structural, financial and operational problems. Because of infrastructural bottlenecks these societies fail to operate effectively. It is imperative to bring all farmers, families having marketing surplus, within the co-operative fold.

Marketing co-operatives provide an institutional arrangement to solve the marketing problems and therefore, their success largely depend upon their efficiency, productivity and service.

In the light of above analysis; it is suggested for strengthening and streamlining agricultural marketing facilities. The policy thrust should be intensification of surveys to reviews the marketable surplus and the past-harvest losses and strengthening of different organisations in the states for meeting the mounting requirements of training for market functionaries.

7

Strengthening Co-operatives in Tribal Areas

Dr. Kulwant Pathania*
Yoginder Singh Thakur**
Anita Pathania***

Co-operation means working together. The principle of co-operation is as old as human society. It is the basis of domestic and social life. Montague says that science points out the way to survival and happiness for all mankind through love and co-operation. According to E.R. Bowen "Co-operation is the Universal Instrument of Creation" Dr. R. Philips is of the opinion that the co-operative association is an association of firms or households for business purposes an economic institution through which economic activity is conducted in the pursuit of economic objectives. The co-operative planning committee defined it, co-operation is a form of organisation in which persons voluntarily associate together on the basis of equality for the promotion of their economic interest. The ultimate aim of the co-operation is to develop men-men imbued with the spirit of self help and mutual aid in order that individually they may rise to a full personal life and collectively to a full social life. The genesis of co-operative movement and its applications in the economic field can be traced after the industrial revolution in England. Co-operation as a new Philosophy which is

* Senior Lecturer, Deptt. of Commerce, H.P. University, Shimla
** Ph. D. Scholar, Deptt of Commerce, H.P. University, Shimla
*** M.Ed. Student, Deptt. of Education, H.P. University, Shimla

the true and ultimate goal of the co-operative movement.

Co-operative occupies an important place in the Indian economy. Perhaps, in no other country in the world, has co-operative movement as large and diversified and involves participation of as many people as in India. The co-operative movement has left, almost no sector of the economy untouched. National prosperity of the country depends on the progress of rural-area. Co-operatives provide all necessary commodities at a reasonable prices in rural area. Primary level co-operative societies have been recognised at a very basis for economic development in rural areas. Co-operative helps in increasing production, maximum utilisation of available resources increasing employment opportunity, removing poverty and also improving standard of living. It is very helpful for economic growth, reduction of disparity in income and wealth etc. Agriculture is the backbone of the economy. For the development of the economy, it is necessary that agriculture should be developed in a fast rate. Farmers should be provided credit to meet their needs.

Agricultural credit is very important instrument in facilitating the process of agricultural development, and stabilizing the growth of rural economy. Co-operation plays a major role in supplying of agricultural credit, and agricultural inputs like seeds, fertilizers and pesticides agricultural storage agricultural marketing and processing, dairy, poultry, fishery sericulture and other subsidiary occupations, whole sale and retail trade and consumer distribution, rural and small scale industries including handloom, housing, urban credit etc.

There should be proper involvement of society in the co-operation, so that living of standard may improve. Farmers as well as weaker section should be given proper attention. So it is observed that co-operative plays a significant role in the economic development of the country.

Tribal Scenario

The tribals who constitute about 8 per cent of country's population are concentrated in 21 States and five Union Territories. Half of the total population is confined to Orissa, Bihar, Madhya Pradesh. The tribal areas of Himachal Pradesh constitute 42.49 per cent of the State's geographical area. They have 4.22 per cent of the total population in the State (1991 Census).

The tribal economy is still a primitive one in the main. The tribals are traditionally agriculturist and pack tradesmen. Their subsidiary occupations are weaving, spinning, silver-smithy, wood carving and artistic metalware, manufacturing. They have also adopted cash crops like kuth, potato, apple, peas, hops etc. They have been mercilessly exploited by the middlemen, big traders and contractors. Money lenders have been charging exorbitant rates of interest from them. Traders have been buying their produce at rock bottom prices and selling their wares to the mat very high rates, thus, exploiting them both ways. The contractors, have been paying them very low wages. This made the Dhebar Commission remark in 1962: "The contractor has become a law unto himself. He has a pull with the officers in the department. The tribal who seldom knows the rules is at his mercy."

With the opening up of these areas, increase in literacy and political and social awakening, things have been changing but not at the desirable pace. The main bottleneck in the way of rapid development has been lack of finance to cumulatively meet peoples day to day needs, their social, religious and cultural obligations (which mean a lot of expenditure for every and above all, investment needs).

The tribal populations in India is the most vulnerable and most unfortunate social group, because it is highly unorganised and exploited in the country. The exploitation is social, economic and political as well as cultural. The tribal caste in India may be dived into three major groups.

(i) South Indian Tribals which are still in semi-nomadic stage.

(ii) North-eastern Region tribals, who are relatively more developed and growing politically conscious, and

(iii) The tribals found in large concentration in Central India.

The tribals are exploited on the following grounds.

1. The most important form of tribal exploitation is alienating them from their lands by non-tribals. Though, some or the other ways, land alienation of tribals is being carried on by

individuals, private enterprise and, of course, the Government itself. Thus, since the recent past the landless tribals are growing in number.

2. The tribal's workers as landless labourers work in nearby agricultural field, plantation etc., of their settlements. The landless tribal labour has been cheap source of labour supply for non-tribal agriculturists and plantation owners. The tribal labour is paid less than the non-tribals and they are also not given other benefits as permissible under labour legislations by their employees.
3. The tribals work with forest contractors. The tribal workers are used to collect the forest producers and generally paid lower wages.
4. The tribals exchange their little forest produce for other goods and services with near by town and village businessmen. So it is very easy for the business-men to exploit the tribals by offering throw away prices.
5. The tribal agriculturists are exploited by several ways. An interesting observation has been made by a study team on tribal development programme, appointed by M.P. State Government (1969). If the tribals needed any thing, they have to pay high price.

Therefore, the co-operatives have to shatter a very highly exploitative socio-economic set-up on one hand, and build up a self sustaining growth base by augmenting agricultural and allied resources for moderation of tribal areas. This is really uphill task entrusted to co-operatives in the context of tribal development process.

Problems of Tribal in Himachal Pradesh

The tribal areas in Himachal Pradesh, consist of Kinnaur and Lahaul Spiti districts and Pangi and Bharmour tehsils of Chamba district, are very vast in area, i.e., 42.49 per cent of the total areas as of the states, and scantly populated i.e., 3.13 per cent of Pradesh's population. Snow, glaciers, high altitudes and highly rugged terrain, criss-crossed by fast flowing rivers and their tributaries are the peculiar striking features of the tribal belt.

Although, the different tribals of the different tribal areas have their own problems on the basis of geographical, social, and economically, yet some problems of the tribals are very common, which are listed as under:

a) Tribals are exploited by the landlords, money lenders and other middlemen.
b) There is a problem of communications. Road construction should be started on war footing.
c) Problems of electrification.
d) Literacy percentage is less. There should be an expansion in educational institutions.
e) The percentage of workers employees is less in tribal areas.
f) There is a shortage of medical facilities in tribal areas.
g) Sources of income are very limited of tribal people.

For the sound development of the cooperative movement, it is absolutely essential that cooperatives become self-reliant and self governing in as short time as possible. For this, we have to develop proper management capacity right from the level of village cooperative societies, on which our future success will largely depend. Otherwise, any facility by way of credit, inputs etc., provided to farmers will not help realisation of desired objectives.

Tribal Development in Himachal Pradesh

The centre as well as state governments are paying special attention towards the tribal areas. A variety of measures have been initiated and implemented to ameliorate their socio-economic conditions, for their educational advancement and economic upliftment. In order to cover the 37 per cent of the "dispersed tribals" (i.e. those tribals who live outside the tribal areas and their concentration pockets in non-tribal areas which account for 10% of the tribal population of the state), Modified Area Development Approach (MADA) was devised during the Sixth plan. The entire tribal population of the state was brought under the ambit of the sub-trial plan in 1987-88. The Stage plan flow to the tribal sub-plan has been always above par, starting with 3.65% in 1974-75 and reaching upto 8.78% at the end of Seventh Plan. During 1993-94, it is to be the tune of Rs. 53.05 crores which is 14 per cent higher than the last year. The state is also getting special central assistance (SCA) since 1981. Resultantly, the tribal areas are by and large receiving the fruit of economic development.

The state government has constitued project Advisory Committee, Tribal Advisory Council and even financial powers have been decentralized for the Pangi are to enable the Resident Commissioner, Pangi to ensure effective implementation and monitoring of the sub-plans in that area. The stage government has also formulated sound personnel and transfer policies, keeping in view the remoteness, isolation and inacessibility of these areas. Helicopter travel facility has also been extend to the public and the employees. Strict measures have been adopted to curb the exploitation of the tribals in the fields of agriculture, forest produce and the extension of credit.

Cooperatives : The Instrument of Survival

Co-operatives unlike any other form of organisation are considered to be the best instrument for improving the socio-economic lot of poor tribals and bring them at par with the non-tribals. Prof. D.R. Gadgil had emphatically remarked long back that the co-operative was the best form of organisation for development. The upliftment of the tribals depends to a great extent on the degree of their self-reliance. They can achieve in through the elimination of middlemen, moneylenders, traders and contractors by organising their life and economy on co-operative lines. Bedi (1954) indicates in his study that co-operation was introduced in the country as a remedy for rural indebtedness. Kulkarni (1960) advocates that co-operation seeks to prevent the exploitation of the weaker sections of the community. The scope of co-operative development among the tribals in India has been emphasised repeatedly by economic and developmental experts and thinkers. The Tribal Commission (1962), the Special Working Group on Co-operatives for Backward Classes (1962), Report of the Committee on Tribal Economy in Forest Area (1967), Study Team in Co-operative Structure on Tribal Development Project Area (1970), Study Group on Relief of Indebtedness, land Alienation and Restoration in Tribal Development Area (1973) and various other reports and studies have strongly recommended co-operativisation of the tribal economy.

A comprehensive cooperative has set up in promoting tribal agriculture building up agro-forest based processing and to arrest exploitation of tribals would result in certain conducive effects from the view point of development and welfare.

1. Co-operatives help to build up resource position in tribal areas.
2. Co-operatives help to diversify the activity pattern of tribal regions.
3. They may also help to resolve tribal underemployment.
4. Co-operatives may considerably enhance the incomes in tribal areas by injecting an element of regularity as well as stability in it.
5. Co-operatives are the best organisation for promoting self-help and mobilizing the tribal socio-economic change.
6. Co-operatives can help the authority or authorities to ensure social justice for tribals who are the "poorest among poor" in India.

Significance of Co-operatives in Tribal Areas

The significance of the co-operatives in tribal areas may be adjudged from the findings of the following studies.

Misra (1973) observes that the co-operative is an instrument of economic change in tribal areas. International co-operative alliance (1980) emphasised the need to develop agriculture cooperatives for the benefit of small farmers. Mahalingam (1981) advocates that co-operatives are the only means for the development of tribal communities. Bedback (1982) emphasises that co-operatives play a glorious role in tribal development. A similar study has been conducted by Hegde (1983) on co-operatives for tribal development and his finding is that the co-operatives are better agencies than other available for growth and social change in the context of democratic socialist planning.

Patel (1983) had pinpointed that co-operatives provides all possible facilities in the form of credits to develop agriculture. Khachi (1981) has expressed his opinion about the role of co-operatives in tribal areas and has stressed that the democratic character of the co-operatives should be restored and there should be different types of co-operatives societies in them. Guru (1984) observes that a co-operative plays a significant role in the tribal areas. Similar views have also been expressed by Verma & Pathania (1986). Shash (1986) finds that involvement of the tribals in their on development through co-operativisation of their economy perhaps provides the best strategy. He further says that a co-operatives is the only answer to stop the exploitation of the innocent and poor tribals.

In addition to these studies, a number of rural development programmes have also been undertaken on experimental basis like the Martandam Project (1921). Dr. Rabindra Nath Tagore's Sriniketan Experiment (1922), Rural Reconstruction Project in Baroda (1932), Firka Development Scheme in Madras (1946), Etawah Pilot Project in U.P. (1948), Small Farmers" Development Agency projects (1971) etc. have heavily leaned on people's participation through voluntary organisations. In all these experiments the co-operatives have played a significant role.

It is observed from the foregoing discussion that co-operatives play a dynamic role in the development of tribal areas as well as for overall economic development. Co-operatives help the tribals in achieving the goal of increased production, maximum utilization of available resources, increased employment opportunities, removal of poverty, curtailing exploitation and in improving their standard of living.

Performance of Co-operatives in Tribal Areas

The co-operative movement in tribal areas is performing the important functions of granting credit and marketing as well as distribution of essential commodities. There are different types of co-operative societies functioning in tribal areas of Himachal Pradesh. Some of them are: Tehsil Co-operative Marketing and Supply Union, Agricultural Co-operative Multi-purpose societies, Specialised marketing societies, Agricultural credit societies, Food growing societies and Non-agricultural credit societies etc. The role of these societies can be analysed on different counts.

Membership

In 1991-92 the membership of all types of co-operative societies in tribal areas was 0.324 lakhs and 1995-96 it increased upto

0.382 lakhs during 1991-92 to 1995-96 which shows an increase of 0.058 lakhs in membership during this period.

Capital Mobilisation

In 1992-92 the share capital of all types of co-operative societies was Rs. 221.39 lakhs, in 1995-96 it had gone upto Rs. 352.78 lakhs which shows an increase of Rs. 131.39 lakhs in share capital from 1991-92 to 1995-96. In 1991-92 the total number co-operatives societies were 178 were indicates an increase of 59.34 per cent over 1991-92 to 1995-96.

Deposits

In 1991-92 the deposits of different co-operatives societies was Rs. 20.73 lakhs. In 1995-96 it had gone up to Rs. 42.49 lakhs. There was an increase of Rs. 21.76 lakhs from 1991-92 to 1995-96 or an increase of 104.96 per cent in deposits. Increase in the quantum of deposits indicate that the tribals find co-operatives as a safe custodian of their small savings.

Working Capital

In 1991-92, the working capital of different co-operative societies ws Rs. 1127.28 lakhs. In 1995-96 it had gone up to Rs. 2216 lakhs. There was an increase of Rs. 1088.72 lakhs from 1991.92 to 1995.906 in working capital or an increase of 96.97 per cent. The percentage increase in working capital is very high in tribal areas, if it is compared with the percentage of all co-operative societies in Himachal Pradesh (say 99 per cent).

Credit Business

Short and Medium terms loans are given by the co-operatives societies to the small and poor farmers for the development of agriculture. Some times loans are given for setting small and cottage industries. The main purpose of this loan is to uplift the tribals. In 1991-92, the loan which was given by the co-operative societies were Rs. 13.37 lakhs. It had gone upto Rs. 54.94 lakhs in 1995-96. There was an increase of Rs. 41.57 lakhs in loans, during 1991-92 to 1995-96 or an increase of 310.91 per cent.

In 1991-92 the recovery of different co-operative societies was Rs. 14.9 lakhs. In 1995-96 it had gone up to Rs. 48.84 lakhs. There was an increase of Rs. 33.94 lakhs from 191-92 to 1995-96 which indicates an increase of 227.78 per cent of recovery of loans advanced.

Distribution of Fertilisers

Co-operatives stimulate agricultural productivity by supplying the fertilizers, different agricultural implements, pesticides and insecticides to the farmers. In 1991-92, the total value of fertilizers supplied by the co-operative societies was Rs. 140.92 lakhs, which increased to Rs. 37.81 lakhs in 1995-96 which shows an increase of 153.41 per cent over 1991-92 to 1995-96.

Distribution of Consumer Goods

Consumer goods or necessaries of the life are mainly supplied or distributed through co-operatives societies in the village level i.e., sugar, clothes, atta, pulses, milk, rice, ghee, salt etc., are supplied by co-operatives in tribal areas. In 1991-92, the total value of the consumer goods supplied or distributed by the co-operative societies in tribal areas was of Rs. 1217.95 lakhs, which had gone upto Rs. 996.46 lakhs in 1995-96, which shows a decrease of Rs. 221.49 lakhs. During this period decrease in the value of the distribution of consumer goods in tribal areas was recorded (18.18) per cent.

Population Coverage

People covered by the co-operative societies in tribal areas were 47 per cent in 1981-82 which increased upto 75 per cent in 1984-85, while over all coverage of people in Himachal Pradesh by co-operative societies were 87 per cent in 1984-85, which was higher as compared to tribal areas of Himachal Pradesh.

From the overall analysis, it is observed that co-operative societies are emerging as an important institutions in the tribal areas covering about 3/4th of the population and mobilising the savings of these areas.

Profitability

The total number of fair price shops operating in tribal areas was recorded 125 during 1991-92 and their number has increased to 151 in 1995-96 which indicates an increase of 20.8 per cent. The number of societies which were in profit has increased from 119 to 151 during 1991-92 to 1995-96. Further the societies which are running in loss, their number has also increased from 29 to 42, indicates a hike of 44.82 per cent. Interesting to note that the number of those societies which were neither in loss nor profit remained static i.e., 8 during 1991-92 to 1995-96.

Performance of Cooperatives in Tribal Area of Himachal Pradesh

Sr. No.	*Indicators*	*1991-92*	*1992-93*	*1993-94*	*1994-95*	*1995-96*	*%age over the year 1995-96*
1.	No. of societies	178	182	200	195	201	12.92
2.	Membership (in lakh)	0.324	0.330	0.367	0.375	0.382	17.99
3.	Share Capital (in lakh)	221.39	348.54	318.30	341.63	352.78	59.34
4.	Deposits (in lakhs)	20.73	21.62	31.62	40.91	42.49	104.96
5.	Working Capital („)	1127.28	1370.47	1533.81	1926.76	2216	96.57
6.	Loans advanced (short term and medium term (Rs. in lakshs)	13.37	28.64	68.74	64.39	54.94	310.91
7.	Recovery of loans advanced (in lakhs) (Both S.T. & M.T.)	14.9	14.99	34.86	41.17	48.84	227.78
8.	Value of fertilizers distributed (in lakhs)	14.92	24.53	31.98	58.91	37.81	153.41
9.	Value of consumables goods retailed by co-peratives (Rs. in lakhs)	1217.95	988.04	1115.82	1071.04	996.46	–18.18
10.	No. of Fair Price Shops	125	132	134	148	151	20.8
11.	No. of societies running in profit)	119	124	119	116	151	26.8
12.	No. of societies (in loss)	29	29	67	27	42	44.82
13.	No. of societies (No profit no loss)	8	28	9	30	8	Nil

Source : Annual Administrative Reports of Co-operatives for the years 1991–92 to 1995–96.

Conclusions

It is observed and evident that co-operative movement occupies an important place in the upliftment of the socio-economic structure of the people. The co-operative movement is helping in stepping up agricultural production and helping cultivators to raise their standards of farming. The co-operative movement is widely spread in the country, covering almost every village. The co-operatives provide adequate and timely credit and supplies for agricultural production is of paramount importance. Such credit is made available to needy people. The cooperatives help in the distribution of essential consumer articles.

The co-operative movement is playing a significant role especially in tribal areas of Himachal Pradesh. There are different types of co-operative societies functioning in tribal areas. Standard of living, per capita income, literacy percentage and production is increasing year by year with the help of co-operative societies. Tribal Commission is performing its job well in the development of tribals. Tribal sub-plans are being constituted annually for their development. In order to step up the pace of development of the co-operative movement in tribal areas, assistance by way of share capital contribution, managerial subsidy, financial assistance for construction of godowns, purchase of vehicles etc. are being provided by the co-operative societies functioning in tribal areas. Even the co-operatives societies are facing so many problems in stepping up the pace of development. Inspite of many sincere efforts, non-tribals are exploiting the tribals mercilessly. For the development of co-operative movement and to make this movement mass movement in tribal areas, the following suggestions have been advocated.

Suggestions

1. The primary co-operative in a village should be charged with the preparation of production plans for each of its members so that production can systematically be raised.
2. Identification and setting up of production and processing co-operatives in tribal areas like plantation and horticulture crops, agricultural and forest produces etc.
3. Identification of market for tribal produce in the country and outside.
4. Setting up of appropriate marketing for co-operatives.
5. To promote minimum accepted housing standards, the housing co-operatives shall be set -up.

6. The district co-operative banks should be directed to act as the central force in ensuring success of the plans of the people.
7. Steps should be initiated to encounter the illegal action of forest contractors who have been controlling forest labour co-operatives.
8. The lumpsum state aid (central and State Government financial assistance) should be given to meet capital expenses connected with staff salary, establishment expenses, share capital and margin money requirements, education of tribals for co-operative membership etc.
9. The managerial and operational aspect of tribal co-operatively and TDC's shall be given top priority. The financial frauds and policy lapses committed by the co-operative personnel and management committees should be vigorously dealt with thorough appropriate legal measures. The reasons for growing losses as already pointed out are corrupt practices, inefficiency in recovering overdues, low investment in actual objectives etc. And also the preponderance of the non-tribal officials who often exploit the very organisations in which they work, so the tribal youth may be trained suitably in co-operation and absorbed in the co-operative service sector.
10. No doubt, if the farming community is properly activized and serviced through village co-operatives, can augment agricultural production.
11. The locational aspect of co-operatives in the tribal areas is of paramount importance. To increase the effective participation of tribal men and women in co-operation, the different kinds of co-operatives shall be appropriately located at strategic points within the tribal settlements.
12. The tribals are often exploited by businessmen who exchange tribal marketable surplus for various consumer goods. This barter economy aspect of tribal economic life should be eliminated through the effective monetization process of their exchange. In this regard the LAMPS and unified credit cum marketing societies can play a very important role by dealing in a wide range of consumer articles.

13. Credit should be made available to all producers irrespective of whether they are owners of land or tenants.
14. The production processing marketing aspect of co-operatives have to be appropriately co-ordinated and integrated for realizing better fruits of their functioning. This job could be done by Tribal Development Co-operative Corporations/ Federations existing at the state levels.
15. Distribution of essential consumer commodities through co-operatives in tribal area should be given immediate and full attention.

The co-operatives are better agencies for rapid growth and social change in the context of democratic socialist planning therefore, they can serve as engines of people's participations in development process are efficiently. In the context of area development planning (i.e., tribal sub-plans) the role of co-operatives shall be redefined and appropriatic economic and legal actions have to be taken to improve their operational efficiency. The financial inadequacies as well as managerial inefficiency of tribal cooperatives shall be given top priority in the revitalisation process of these organisations for rapid tribal growth. Therefore, a comprehensive policy for co-operative development in tribal areas is warranted at present. The comprehensive policy for development co-operatives in tribal areas should aim at achieving a self sustaining diversified co-operative structure. Then the cooperative will be able to make a dent on the tribal exploitation.

References

1. Annual Tribal Sub-Plans, 1996-97, Tribal Development, Himachal Pradesh, Shimla.
2. B.B. Goel and P.K. Kamra, Co-operatives Hold the Key to Rural Development, *Kurukshetra*, 1986, pp. 6-13.
3. E.R. Bowen, The Cooperatives Road to abundance (1953) p. 96 (abstract from B.S. Mathur's book co-operation in India).
4. Kulwant Singh Pathania, Co-operatives in Himachal Pradesh - Key to Tribal Development, *Third Concept*, Vol. II, Oct-Nov. 1997, New Delhi, pp. 43-47.
5. Phillips, Economic Nature of co-operative association p. 74, quoted by Yehuda Don: Year Book of agricultural co-operation, 1960.

6. Report of the co-operative planning Committee (1946).
7. S.R. Gupta, Reflections on Tribal Development, *Indian Co-operative Review*, April, 1975.
8. Y.S. Verma and K.S. Pathania, Regional Desparities in the Performance of Co-operatives, *Indian Cooperative Review*, April, 1988.

8

Role and Performance of Dairy Co-operatives in Rural Development

A Micro Level Study of Keonjhar District Co-operative Milk Producers Union

Dr. Surendra Nath Behera*

The establishment and growth of Co-operatives is regarded as one of the important instruments for socio-economic change and for human development. The International Labour Organisation considered "Co-operatives to be established and developed as a means of increasing national income, export revenues and employment by a fuller utilisations of resources aimed at bringing fresh areas in to productive use. In India Co-operation has developed and is being developed as a constructive instrument for economic and social upliftment. As an emerging sector it is not only desired but also desirable. It is no more confined only to credit movement. There has been horizontal and vertical expansion of the Co-operatives. It is embracing wider and wider fields of action and is considered as a diversified movement.

The 'White Revolution' or 'Operation Flood' has emerged as an integral part of rural development. In part the poverty alleviation programmes like IRDP, ERRP etc. making provision of assets for poor, deprived, down-trodden and weaker sections of the

* Reader and Head, Department of Economics, D.D. College, Keonjhar (Orissa)—758 001

society find a meaningful reality in supply of Jercy Cows as a regular source of income.

They Study Area

The study area comprises of Sadar Block of Keonjhar Sadar Sub-Division of Keonjhar District. The Sadar area is situated in between 450.26 square Km. consisting of 227 Villages as per 1991 census. Out of the total population of 11,6,724 S.C. and S.T. Population constitute 58,036. Most of them are agricultural labourers, landless labourers and rural artisans.

Major part of the Sadar area are covered by hilly and forest lands. Seasonal employment causes scanty income for the poor. The operational Flood Programme is an alternative and supplementary source of earning livelihood for the rural poor. The programme is carried on in the District through the District Rural Development Agency. The Keonjhar District Co-operative Milk Procedures Union Ltd. was established in 1978. In 1981, 13 members of Milk Societies in the District Level were constituted by 313 beneficiaries as primary members of the Society.

Out of the total population only 20% people have their sufficient agricultural land. Most of the villagers are agricultural labourers, landless labourers and rural artisans belonging to the weaker sections or lower economic state of the society.

Objectives of the Study

(i) to study the socio-economic status of the Milk Procedures and their attitude to establish Dairy Co-operatives.

(ii) to analyse the strategies adopted by the Government to establish Dairy Co-operatives to enhance Milk Production.

(iii) to assess and evaluate the economic benefits reaped by procurement & marketing of the quantum of milk in terms of Socio-economic change and living standards of the rural poor.

(iv) to examine operational constraints, managerial handicaps and identify the problem areas.

(v) to suggest policy measures to overcome the operational constraints and strengthen the Dairy Co-operatives for their smooth, and effective functioning.

Methodology and Tools of Data Collection

The study has been made by using well structured interview schedules. Data have been collected by purposive sampling. The sampling units are the 120 beneficiaries or Milk Producers of 11 chosen villages. Collected data are being scrutinised and tabulated for analytical purpose. The present study is of survey type, diagnostic as well as remedial in nature. The universe of this study constitutes all the Milk Producers of Sadar Block of Keonjhar District.

The Analytical Frame Work

The Operation Flood Programme which is an integrated diary development programme has made considerable progress in achieving its outlined objectives. The programme was started in 1970 and almost three phases of the programme has been ended so far. The first and the second phase were ended in 1981 and 1985, while the third phase of the operation Flood (OF-3) was officially closed on April, 30 1996. The third phase had sought to set up 70,000 Primary Dairy Co-operative Societies (PDCS) all across the Country covering 6.7 Million families. Compared to this the actual achievement was 71,800, PDCS and 9.2 Million families. The White Revolution seeks to augment the production of Milk. Distribution of Milk is made men and women self-employed. The OF-3 has been operational since 1988. It is functioning with World Bank and IDA financial assistance and also National Dairy Development Board (NDDB). Gujarat has been the biggest beneficiary of OF-3. The operational achievements and handicaps in Orissa with a micro economic analysis of Keonjhar District is shown below.

Most of the Milk Producers of the Sadar block of Keonjhar District are weaker sections. There are 227 villages with 1,16,728 inhabitants of which Scheduled Tribes constitute 58,036 (49.7%), Scheduled Castes, 11,306 (9.6%) and General 47,382 (40.5%). Most of the Milk Producers are the weaker sections of the community remaining below the poverty line.

The Table 8.1 below shows the district profile of Milk Production in Keonjhar District.

A substantial section of the Milk Procedures do not have agricultural land or adequate land holding to earn their livelihood.

Table 8.1 : District Level Production and Yield of Milk

1.	Milk Production (000 MT)	21.6
2.	Share from Indig. cow	10.7
3.	Share from C.B. Cow	7.3
4.	Share from Buffaloes	3.6
5.	Average yield/Animal/Day (in kg.)	
	Ind. Cow	0.452
	C.B. Cow	2.851
	Buffalo	1.510
6.	Per Capital Availability of Milk/Day	41 gm.

Table 8.2 below shows the land holding pattern of Milk producers and total cattle possessions of the surveyed Milk Producers.

Table 8.2 : Land Holding Pattern and Cattle Possessions

Sl. No.	*Land Size*	*No. of house-hold*	*Own Desi Cow*	*Own Cross breed Cow*	*Loan Cross breed Cow*	*Total*
1.	Landless	18 (5)	–	–	5 (19.2)	5 (2.2)
2.	Small (Less than 1 acre)	60 (50)	65 (44.8)	–	10 (38.4)	75 (33.1)
3.	Small (Less than 4 acres)	30 (25)	50 (34.8)	29 (64.4)	08 (30.7)	87 (38.4)
4.	Large (More than 4 acres)	12 (10)	30 (20.6)	16 (35.5)	03 (11.5)	49 (21.6)

Figures in parantheses are percentage.

An analysis of the above table neucals that 5% are landless those are provided with 2.2% of total loan cows. Out of total 120 households, 60 of them (50%) are small landholding producers and out of the total 44.8% are own cows and 38.4% are loan cows. It is evident from the table that relatively largest percentage (38.4%) the cross breed cows are provided on loan basis to the small land owners, those also own largest number of Desi cows to supplement their meagre earnings.

Table8.3 shows the occupational pattern of the Milk Producers.

Table 8.3 : Occupational Pattern

Occupation	*Culti-vation*	*Agri-cultural Labou-rers*	*Busi-ness*	*Service*	*Dairy*	*Total*
Primary	15 (12.5)	55 (45.8)	15 (12.5)	10 (8.3)	25 (20.8)	120 (100)
Secondary	20 (16.6)	20 (16.6)	10 (8.3)	05 (4.1)	65 (54.1)	120 (100)

Figures in parantheses are percentage.

It is revealing from the Table 8.3 that of the 120 Milk Producers 45.8% are agricultural Labourers while 20.8% are the persons depending upon diary as a source of earning livelihood as primary occupational. Compared to this 65 out of 120 (54.1%) consider diary activity as secondary occupation.

In order to strengthen, the dairy co-operatives for socio-economic upliftment of the rural poor several efforts have been made by the Keonjhar Milk Union. It includes a package of strategies of supply of inputs such as cattle feed and fodder, veterinary services etc. Though large number of Desi Cows are available in 27 villages of Keonjhar Sadar area, the productive capacity of these cows is very less due to milk productive capacity of these cows is very less due to mismanagement and lack of proper care. In order to enhance milk production and generate income to the rural poor under different financing schemes, the Keonjhar Milk Union has taken the responsibility to supply high yielding Milk Cows through the District Rural Development Agency (D.R.D.A.) under different anti-poverty Programmes. Accordingly, the beneficiaries ware selected from different villages and provided loan by the Banks with subsidiary to purchase high breed cows.

Table 8.4 shows a comparative picture of cattle induction in the Sadar Block and the District over time.

Table 8.4 : Comparative Picture of Cattle Induction

Year	*District*	*Sadar Block*
1987–88	160	18
1988–89	733	45
1989–90	1218	80
1990–91	2133	110
1991–92	1170	135
1992–93	1342	140

Source : D.R.D.A., Keonjhar, 1997. Though cows in number are increasing both in the District and the Sadar the induction of cattle in the Sadar is insignificant.

Table 8.5 shows the extent of Loan cows provided to the villagers.

Table 8.5 : Loan Cows of Surveyed Villages

Sl. No.	*Name of Villages Surveyed*	*Total Villagers Surveyed*	*Villagers provided with Loan Cows*	
			No	*%age*
1.	Silisuan	8	2	25 %
2.	Raisuan	15	3	20 %
3.	Padmapur	15	3	20 %
4.	Bhatunia	12	3	25 %
5.	Banajodi	10	2	20 %
6.	Gobardhan	12	3	25 %
7.	Mohadeijoda	10	2	20 %
8.	Hatikucha	10	2	20 %
9.	Danua	8	2	20 %
10.	Mukuna	10	2	20 %
11.	Handibhanga	10	2	20 %
	Total	**120**	**26**	**21.7 %**

Thus, out of the total 11 villages in 8 villages only 20% of the villagers are supplied with loan cows which is disappointing. The loan cows of cross breed type are purchased from OMFED and Andhra Pradesh. They are of higher cost for which it very difficult to repay the loan on the part of the rural poor. Those who have taken the first cow are defaulters and are not eligible to get the second. Due to high fodder cost they are unable to maintain the high yielding cows. Lack of proper co-ordination between the villagers and the society is another cause of disappointing picture of loan cows.

The yielding capacity of the cows depend upon regular and proper feeding. The cattle feed should be provided by the Milk Union at a lower price than the market price which is not done properly. It is too difficult for a rural milk producer to purchase cattle feed from the market, particularly during the pregnancy time of the cattle. What ever fodder is supplied is of inferior quality. Poor farmers have not chaffing machine of their own who are facing trouble for better chaffing of the straw which are not being utilised by the cows leading to wastage. The quality of balanced feed produced by the Utkal Gosamiti is not available to the farmers as no such arrangement is being done by Animal Husbandry Department. The study shows that only 33.3% of the Milk Producers use daily 5 kg cattle feed. Insufficient cattle feed obviously reduces the productivity or yield of milk. Green fodder is not scientifically treated and the traditional method of feeding is not adequate for cross breed cattle. Hence, the Union has started fodder cultivation programme.

For the development of the dairy sector and enhance milk production Artificial Insemination (A.I.) is a modern technical method, which is provided by the Keonjhar Milk Union with the financial assistance of N.D.D.B. The Union is providing A.I. facilities through Co-operative Societies by establishing A.I. Centre at Village level. In operation Flood-II, the Union also provided with the help of state Government funds towards purchase of liquid Nitrogen and semen.

Table 8.6 shows the progress of Artificial Insemination in Sadar Block.

The birth rate of cows depend upon A.I. done. The Table shows more of male calfs compared to the female calfs. Despite the progress of Artificial Insemination there are problems of inadequacy of doctors and live-stock Inspector. Treatment of the cows is

Table 8.6 : Progress of Artificial Insemination

Year	*A.I. Centre*	*A.I. Done*	*A.I. Success*		*Calf*			
					Male		*Female*	
			No.	*%age*	*No.*	*% age*	*No.*	*% age*
1982–83	1	35	30	85.0	18	60.0	12	40.0
1983–84	3	60	45	75.0	20	44.4	25	55.5
1984–85	3	82	60	73.1	35	58.3	25	41.6
1985–86	3	110	82	74.5	40	48.7	42	51.2
1986–87	6	95	40	42.1	18	45.2	22	55.0
1987–88	5	70	53	75.7	30	65.6	23	43.3
1988–89	8	62	44	70.16	24	54.6	20	45.4
1989–90	10	55	50	90.9	36	72.0	24	28.0
1990–91	11	80	67	83.75	30	44.8	37	55.2
1991–92	8	50	43	86.0	22	51.1	21	44.8
1992–93	6	52	38	73.0	20	52.6	18	47.3
1993–94	6	45	32	71.1	18	56.2	14	43.7
1994–95	5	49	41	83.7	28	68.2	13	31.7
1995–96	2	30	26	86.7	17	63.3	9	34.6

untimely and irregular. Vaccination is not properly done at regular intervals. The cows remain diseased creating a serious havoc of economic burden for the rural poor because of irregular milk supply.

The main objective of Keonjhar Milk Union is to Procure the Milk, Process it and market it and then pay the bill to the producers through Co-operative Societies. The position of procurement and marketing use also not upto the mark. Milk marketing is a problem for the producers as they were bound to sale the milk to the society i.e. to the Milk Union with much lower price than the local market price. No such visible facility was extended to the poor farmers by the milk Union.

A study of the procurement and marketing shows that poor transportation difficulties in the rainy season, lack of co-operation have accounted for a decline on procurement and marketing. Most of the producers sell their milk to the middleman at a low price and also face the difficulty of irregular payment for which they are unable to repay their loan in time.

The economic benefits derived from the dairy Co-operatives is the real indictor of the impact on their socio-economic standard. That can be well imagined by taking the extent of Milk repeat shown in Table 8.7.

Table 8.7 : Extent of Milk Reaped

	No. of Milk Producers	*Percentage*	*Total Milk Production per day (in lts.)*
	45	37.50	1 – 2
	35	29.16	2 – 3
	18	15.00	3 – 4
	12	10.00	4 – 5
	8	6.66	5 – 6
	6	5.00	6 – 7
	5	4.16	7 – 8
	3	2.05	8 – 10
Total	**120**	**100.00**	

It is revealed from the above table that about 12% of the total Milk producers have high yielding cows giving 6 - 10 lts of Milk per. A substantial portion (37.5%) get only 1-2 lts per day. Insufficient green fodder reduces the yielding capacity.

Table 8.8 below shows the monthly economic benefit of Milk Producers assessed in terms of net return in excess of expenditure on health maintenance and fodder on cows.

It is evident from the above figures that due to lack of adequate Milk Production and Marketing and higher expenditure on cattle feed the not benefit of the Milk Producers is less. However most villages keep desi cow for cowdungs and for production of bio-gas to save expenditure on fuel by the rural Distribution of bonus by the society is irregular and inadequate. The selling price per liter of Milk is fixed on only Rs. 7.15 which is too low to cover the cost and reduce the profit of the producers. The minimum cattle feed of a high breed cow is 5 Kg. per day which raise the cost.

Table 8.8 : Monthly Economic Benefit of Milk Producers

No. of Milk Producers	*% of Milk Producer*	*Total Income (in Rs.)*	*Expenditure on Cow (in Rs.)*	*Net Profit (in Rs.)*
25	20.80	429	300	129
20	16.60	643	450	193
12	10.00	858	600	258
10	8.30	1027	800	227
8	6.60	1287	640	647
6	0.50	1501	770	731
5	4.16	1716	850	866
4	3.30	2145	1300	845
30	3.30	2520	1425	1095

Problem Analysis and Operational Constraints

The study reveals that the rural people are used to live-stock management as a subsidiary Occupation to substantiate their basic needs but due to lack of awareness, education, availability of quality of feed and fodder, infrastructural facilities at the door step and paucity of fund the process of alleviation of poverty is lingering.

Traditional method of feed of sending the cattle for grazing lead to various infections and diseases inadequate irrigation has stood a constraint in fodder cultivation programme.

Non-availability of a suitable cowshed and undercare for their health reduce the longevity of the cows. There is inadequate health coverage at the village level.

Supply of poor quality of cows and lack of artificial insemination facility at the door step is a serious bottle neck in the process.

Lack of organised marketing, interference of the middlemen and irregular payment of the Milk bill use some of the major problems in this respect.

Participation of women member is most substantial due to ignorance and lack of co-operative awareness. It calls for emphasis on co-operative education.

Policy Recommendations

On the basis of the above findings, the following policy measures are considers imperative for the improvement of the living standard of the Milk Produces and efficient functioning of the Milk Societies. Changes should be done in the style, system, approach, concept, belief and values. Greater involvement of Milk Producers at the grass root level, particularly the women members in the decision making process will be positive step forward.

Development of fodder resource should receive priority in the development planning not only for achieving higher production of different live-stock products, but also with a view to increase the employment opportunity and income for a large section of rural people. Adequate resources should be provided a pursue appropriate programme.

Strategy to improve fodder production in terms of quantity and quality should include measures for increasing the area under high yielding varieties with the use of improved package and practices. Input technology must be provided at the farmers door step by adoption of suitable extension mechanism. Arrangement of supply of improved varieties of fodder seeds to be available for ensuring fodder supply during scarcity. It will increase the degree of inclination towards dairy forming.

Effective monitoring and evaluation of the Animal Husbandry programme must be taken up for upliftment of the rural poor. They include specific programmes such as artificial insemination, cross breeding and fodder cultivation.

More of cattle induction is imperative that should be done to suitable beneficiaries. Timely supply of inputs to the villages is needed for massive fodder cultivation.

Mobile veterinary services, emergency veterinary services, first aid services and disease control programme must be conducted by the Milk Unions and Government authorities.

Extensive training seminars, workshops, educational programmes and demonstrations should be conducted on extensive scale to create co-operative awareness and improve practical efficiency.

The state Government should provide all assistance to breeders for improving the genetic potential of breeds through upgrading and provide breeding service through making available semen of superior bulls. Improvement of standard dairy farming by improved programme of feeding and management of breedings, veterinary services, feed stuff supplying and related extension services, thereby will increase the yield of the cows.

The rural people should be aware of the latest Animal Husbandry practices in order to obtain optimum production from their Animal Wealth. There is an urgent need to identify, develop and utilise animal resources and organisations at different levels, modern management practices of personnels, policy with autonomy, accountability, performance appraisal and reward, feasibility and economies of livestock forming, modern technology on animal health, active co-ordination and co-operation between institution must be adopted as imperative to make the programme fruitful. An effective machinery must advice, develop assist, co-ordinate supervise and inspect the Milk Co-operative Societies.

Quality cows must be provided to the beneficiaries of their own choice, rather than imposed on them.

Periodic action plan need to be made taking in to account the constraints faced, 'Co-operation has failed, but co-operation must succeed.'

References

S.N. Singh, "Operation Flood - A Retrospect and Prospect" N.D.D.B., Anand, 1981.

A.H. Somji & Geeta Somji - "Dairy Co-Operatives- A catalyst for economic and social change in rural India", Govt. of India Press, N.D.D.B., Anand, 1981.

Dairy India—1987.

The Amul story of Kaira District Co-operative Milk Producers Union Ltd., N.D.D.B. - 1987-88, Anand.

The Orissa Veternary Journal - "SOVENIR" ISSUE—Jan, 91.

K. Sharma, "Govt. efforts towards co-operative Organisations", *Kurukshetra*, June, 1985.

T.R. Gurumoorty, "Role of Co-operatives in Rural Development—Kurukshetra, Nov., 1995

M. C. Vyasa—"Development of Dairy Co-operatives"—*The Telegraph*, 23 rd June, 1997.

D. Prakash - "Co-operative Democracy, *vis-a-vis* Members Education, N.D.D.B., Anand, 1998.

G.R. Madan - "Co-operative Movement in India - A Critical Analysis Mittal Publications, New Delhi.

Rais Ahmed - "Co-operatives and Integrated Rural Development - Mittal Publications, New Delhi.

9

Fisheries Co-operatives in Orissa

A Case Study of Financing Beach Landing Crafts in Ganjam District (Orissa)

Mr. P. Sahu*
Dr. N.B. Pradhan**

Abstract

This paper seeks to study credit and marketing aspects of fisheries co-operatives in Ganjam district of Orissa. Ganjam records poor performance in marine fish production during 1985-86 to 1996-97 due to lower rate of mechanization. The NCDC financing of BLCs can be considered as significant strategy to improve economic status of the fishermen. The study finds that only one PMFCs at Sano Arjipalli is operating efficiently because of efficient management involving fishermen community. Many PMFCs are defunct due to the mismanagement. Some BLCs are out of order due to lack of mechanical supervision and guidance. Marketing structure is not conductive and is adversely effecting the fishermen's interest due to exploitation of middlemen. A suitable reformulation of credit-marketing linkage is suggested for sustainable development of the fishermen.

* Mr. P. Sahu, Lecturer in Economics, Gopalpur College, Gopalpur-on-Sea, Orissa

** Dr. N.B. Pradhan, Reader in Economics, Berhampur University, Orissa.

This paper was presented in the XXX Orissa Economics Conference, Govt. Women's College, Keonjhar (Orissa)

In the planned strategy of rural development in India, co-operatives have been considered as very important since the turn of this century. The basic idea behind the co-operative movement is to promote thrift, self-help and mutual aid through democratic management. A co-operative is an association of persons with common needs and social purpose. It seeks to bring the best out of a human being for the welfare of the entire community.

The fishermen are economically downtrodden and socially at the lower rungs of the society. The fishermen are engaged in this age-old profession for centuries together. Fishing is mostly taken by the traditional crafts as a subsistence in many parts of the country. The typical Indian fishermen with a small indigenous craft and gear is unable to increase his output. Therefore need for replacement of the traditional methods of fishing in India by modern methods of fishing using trawler and mechanised boats was felt.

The fishermen in spite of the good catches netted by them in some landing centres and better prices prevailing in some fish markets are undoubtedly not getting a good share of the consumer price. The urgent need which calls for a break through in the institutional framework and the structure of fish market where middlemen operate in fishing trade adversely effecting fishermen's interest by offering very low price for the fish catches. Fishermen are completely ignorant of fish market and the prevailing prices in the markets; they generally depend upon these middlemen for fish marketing and financial help. There is a chain of vicious circle of indebtedness fostering exploitation, which in turn make the fishermen depend on money lender and fish traders. The challenging answer to these social and economic problems confronted by fishermen community is to organise various types of co-operatives by themselves and to manage these societies properly and effectively to improve the economic conditions and substantially raising the social standards of the fishermen.

Marine Fisheries in Orissa: A Brief Sketch

Orissa has 480 kms. coastline spread over six coastal districts, Balasore, Bhadrak, Kendrapara, Jagatsinghpur, Puri and Ganjam where marine fishing is done through traditional and mechanised boats. As per the survey report of Department of

Fisheries, Orissa, there are 6.5 lakh fishermen in Orissa of which 1.6 lakh are marine fishermen. The marine fisherman inhabit in 329 fishing villages. The marine fishery segment is highly unorganised and complex, the Nolias are still remained unchanged, in spite of the implementation of many development schemes.

Orissa occupies seventh position in India in marine fish production. Total fish production in 1996-97 was 1,33,462 tones for Orissa and 6,009 tones for Ganjam district. Table 9.1 reveals that the fish production in Ganajam district has declined consistently with slight fluctuation during 1985-86 to 1996-97. Whereas in the state this has increased considerable by 2.5 tones.The share of fish production in the district was 12% of the state's production in 1985-86. This share declined to 4.5% during 1996-97. The reason for poor performance of fish landings in the district of Ganjam in lower rate of mechanisation of crafts.

Out of 1.6 Lakh marine fishermen in the State, only 13,578 were covered under Co-operative showing a coverage of 9 percent in 67 Primary Marine Fishermen Co-operative Societies (PMFCS)

Table 9.1 : Trend of Marine Fish Products in Orissa & Ganjam 1985–86 to 1996–97

(Figures in Tonnes)

Year	*Ganjam*	*Orissa*
1985–86	6570	53581
1986–87	5965	55324
1987–88	8799	59960
1988–89	6424	61120
1989–90	5456	77895
1990–91	6617	78192
1991–92	6036	95026
1992–93	5658	119376
1993–94	6108	103925
1994–95	5937	122892
1995–96	6381	123199
1996–97	6009	133462

Source : Director of Fisheries, Orissa, Cuttack

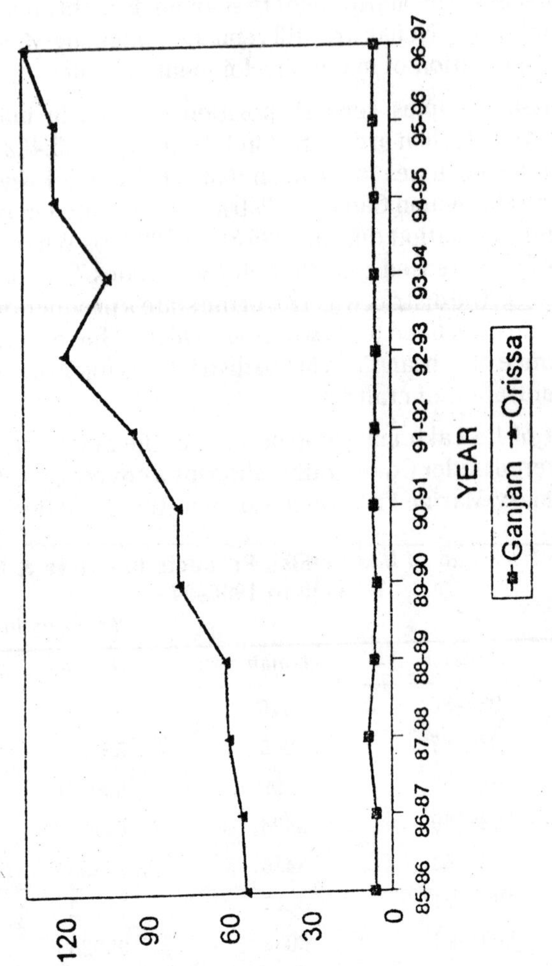

MARINE FISH PRODUCTION IN ORISSA & GANJAM
(1985–86 TO 1996–97)

with an apex society at state level of 5 central district co-operative societies. National Co-operative Development Corporation (NCDC) and banks provide loans to the beneficiaries through the PMFCs (Table 9.2).

Table 9.2 : Credit Flow through Co-operative Societies in Orissa (as on 31st March, 1997)

Particulars	*Inland*	*Marine*	*Chilka*	*Apex*	*Total*
No. of Societies	469	67	80	6	622
Members	38,126	13,578	18,160	481	70,345
Govt. Loan Principal (in Rs.)	1,56,081	88,175	6,84,916	—	9,29,172
Interest (in Rs)	67,308	1,05,549	11,75,801	—	13,48,661
Share Capital Contribution	13,00,400	16,12,600	44,100	52,62,500	82,19,600
Subsidy Released	87,92,781	1,09,55,593	77,64,817	31,50,500	3,06,196

Source : Director of Fisheries, Orissa, Cuttack.

It is also seen that out of the total Fishermen Co-operative Societies, 9 percent were marine, the Marine Fishermen Societies accounted for 20 percent of the membership. About 9 percent of the Government Fishery Loans went to marine fishery sector. The major refinance is provided by NCDC, which finances term loan and working capital to PMFCS and apex Society, which in turn finances the primary societies. NABARD also provides refinance assistance to certain fisheries activities for modernisation of the fishery sector.

PMFCS in Orissa constituted 50 societies in 1984-85 with the member of 9,541 which increased to 67 Societies with the total member strength of 13,578 in 1996-97. Balasore district is having the higher number of 17 societies with 4,199 members followed by the Ganjam district having 14 societies with the highest number of 5,199 members and Jagatsinghpur district is having the lowest number of only 4 societies with 260 members (Table 9.3). Primary Marine Fishermen Co-operative Societies were started before independence in the state. In Ganjam out of 14 PMFCS three societies at Gopalpur, Sonepur and Patisonpur were registered under Societies Act 1860 in 1946. It is found that almost all the Societies were

Table 9.3 : District-wise PMFCS in Orissa upto 31st March, 1997

Name of the District	*No. of Societies*	*Total No. of Members*
Balesore	17	4,199
Bhadrak	14	1,396
Kendrapara	7	845
Jagatsinghpur	4	260
Puri	11	1,699
Ganjam	14	5,199
Total	**67**	**13,578**

Source : Director of Fisheries, Orissa, Cuttack

formed to get Government assistance but it was not functioning effectively with its objections to cater the needs of the members and to develop the fishing activities in the co-operatives. Many of the societies are defunct due to non repayment of loans of the Government and concerned landing banks.

None of the societies in Ganjam is marketing the fish catch by the members of the societies. The members of co-operative societies are compelled to borrow from the money lenders and fish traders during the lean season for their consumption purpose with an agreement to sell fish during the season which leads them to sell their fish at a cheaper rate to the fish traders and to borrow at higher rate of interest to be paid to the money lenders.

NCDC Financing BLC in Ganjam District

The marine fish landings in orissa is still handled by traditional boats operating from open beaches. Among the traditional crafts "Catamaran" are mostly used in south Orissa coast of Cuttack, Puri and Ganjam. Ganjam district is one of the six coastal districts of Orissa with 60 km. of coastline situated in south part of Orissa. It has 26 marine and estuarine fishing villages with total population of 22417. The total number of 3400 non-mechanised boats and 32 BLCs are in operation through 14 PMFCs with total number of 9645 fishing gears used in marine fishing for various types of species engaging 11593 active marine fishermen. The total marine fish production in the district during the year 1996-97 was 6009 tones which landed in 16 fish lending centers viz., Prayagi, Kantiagarah, Gokharakuda, Nolianuagam, Sana Arjipalli, Bada Arjipalli, Reokaturu, Gopalpur, New Boxipalli, Golabandha, Garamapeta, Markandi, Ramayapatnam, Sonapur and Patisonapur. Due to non-availability of infrastructural facilities and sound marketing system, the fishermen are forced to sell their catch to the middlemen at price dictated by the traders. The transportation of fish is done by head loads and cycle loads to the main roads at a distance of 3-4 Kms. from the landing centres.

Objectives of Introduction of Beach Landing Crafts (BLC)

The wooden Catamarans have many disadvantages as it needs to be dried well after each sailing and can be effectively used for only one outing day. Moreover with sinking forests and lacking quality logs being not available the traditional fishermen are facing much difficulties to own a new craft at a reasonable cost.

The development of a new type of user friendly and more efficient fishing craft for operation off open beaches was identified as an improved component of technology development to help the traditional marine fishing communities in the Bay of Bengal region to achieve their ultimate objective to improve the standards of living and quality of life of small scale fisher folk through increase in fish production. The Beach Landing Craft (BLC) was introduced in the east coast of India in 1979 (BOBP Report, 54) with the objective of developing to fishing craft capable of efficient operation from surf beaches. This will enable the traditional fishery folk to exploit the rich marine fishing resources of south Orissa coast in Ganjam District.

The scheme was introduced in 1987-88 in Orissa sponsored by the Central Government for purchase of BLCs through the Primary Marine Fishermen Co-operative Societies on 50 percent subsidy provided by the Government of India. 5 percent of the unit cost is provided by the beneficiary society as margin money. NCDC provides 45 percent of the loan amount at the interest rate of 12.5 percent. It is awarding assistance to the primary marine fishermen cooperatives under this scheme. 32 BLCs (IND-25) have been financed to 7 PMFCs in Ganjam district since 1987 through the Department of Fisheries, Orissa. Total cost of the BLC was

Rs. 1.05lakh with 50 per cent subsidy of Rs. 0.52 lakh. According to the present mode of NCDC assistance 25% as margin money has to be met by the beneficiaries societies, 20% as subsidy by the NCDC and 55% as the loan component.

Repayment of Loan

Seven PMFCs of Ganjam have availed Rs. 14.75 lakhs of NCDC loan as on 31st march 1997. The co-operative societies are found to have paid 33.9 percent of total lob availed Gopalpur PMFCs, the highest recipient of NCDC loan, has repaid the 67.5 percent of the total loan. Though Sana Arjipalli has been financed recently in 1993 it has been paid the highest 75% of the total loans of Rs. 2.36 lakhs. This is no doubt a remarkable achievement of the society.

The two societies have not paid any loan though New Buxipalli PMFCs has been financed in 1989 it has paid the lowest 13.4 percent of the total loan availed. The total outstanding loan comes to Rs. 9.75 lakhs constituting 66 percent (Table 9.4).

The satisfactory performance of Sana Arjipalli may be attributed to successful operation and efficient management of BLCs through the society.

Reasons for Poor Repayment

The poor performance of PMFCs is due to that fact the three BLC financed to New Buxipalli PMFCs belong to the important office bearers of the societies who are not interested for repayment of loan. This does not mean that the BLC are not in operation.

Some beneficiaries are found to be reluctant to repay the loan amount as the crew members of BLCs are no more interested to go for fishing because they prefer more beneficial in fishing through FRP boats. In case of some others engines of BLCs are not in good conditions and are not being repaired because of non-availability of technicians which are to be provided by the Department of Fisheries, Orissa.

Distribution of Catch

There are different types of fishing crafts and gears used for catching different types of fish. Fishing is mainly a team work which involves 3 to 10 members in a group. The sharing of the fish catch goes as follows. If there are four member in a boat of which

Table 9.4 : NCDC Financing Beach Landing Crafts (BLCs) to PMFCS in Ganjam District as on 31st March, 1997

(Rs. in Lakhs)

Name of the MPFCs	*No. of BLCs Financed*	*Date of Finance*	*Amt. of Loan Availed*	*Amt. of Subsidy*	*Total Amt. of loan paid (Principal)*	*Percentage of amount paid*	*Total Amt. Interest paid*	*NCDC Principal*	*Percentage overdue*	*Outstanding Interest*
Gopalpur NAC	6	06.06.87	2.47	2.47	1.66	67.5	1.56	0.81	32.5	0.43
New Buxipalli	3	19.09.89	1.42	1.42	0.19	13.4	1.10	1.23	86.6	0.69
Patisonapur	3	22.12.89	1.42	1.42	0.47	33.1	0.97	0.95	66.9	0.52
Bada Arjipalli	5	20.12.89	2.36	2.36	0.91	38.5	1.90	1.45	61.5	0.98
Sana Arjipalli	5	24.06.93	2.36	2.36	1.77	75.0	0.93	0.59	20.5	0.05
Sana Nolianuagam	5	12.10.93	2.36	2.36	—	0.0	0.18	2.36	100.0	1.18
Bada Nolianuagam	5	09.12.94	2.36	2.36	—	0.0	0.09	2.36	100.0	0.80
Total	**32**		**14.75**	**14.75**	**5.00**	**33.9**	**6.73**	**9.75**	**66.1**	**4.65**

Source : ADF Marine, Ganjam.

boat owner is one, there will be six shares, four for crew members with one share each and the rest two shares for boat and net. If the boat owner has provided the net he will get three shares, one for boat, one for net and one for his own labour. This system is followed in case of the traditional crafts.

In case of the Beach landing crafts (BLCs) 50 percent of the catch is allocated for fuel and maintenance which goes to the owner or society. Balance 50 percent is shared among the crew members.

Marketing of Fish

The fish landings by the BLC boats are not marketed through the societies. The members of the societies sell their share of catch at the landing centres on auction sale basis. In case of prawn they sell to the traders who are pre-determined. Some crew members might have entered into binding agreement to sell the catch to the traders who have advanced loan to them.

Due to lack of marketing facility by the societies the shares of BLC boats are deposited in terms of money value of sale proceeds of catch to the society by the group members for its maintenance and repayment of the loan by the society. It is evident from this study that except in case of Sana Arjipalli the share of the BLC boats are not deposited regularly by the beneficiaries who happen to be the office bearers and leaders of the community in the village.

Need for Credit-Marketing Linkage

Credit is an important component of production and distribution system of the marine fishery sector. In the production process the fishermen (Nolia) community plays the crucial role in the primary production. They belong to low income groups with high mobility and lack of awareness which restricts the availability of institutional finance. The institutional finance is mainly extended for mechanization of traditional crafts, purchase of boats and net. But the politically biased selection process, complex documentation, long waiting time have not made the system successful. The fishermen mostly need consumption loan in the lean period when their income is low and when there are social function such as marriage and death. This demand is well tapped by the money lenders and fish traders. The fishermen play only an insignificant part in the disposal of the catches, the marketing is almost entirely in the hands of middlemen. Then fishermen are turned into bondage labour working for the merchant traders which continues sometime for generations. To make the fishermen free from this bondage a well developed institutional credit marketing linkage is necessary where co-operative societies must come forward to take up marketing of catch by the members.

Conclusion

Study finds that NCDC financing BLCs has helped the fishermen to increase fish production. The problems are associated with inefficient operation of BLCs through co-operative Societies and lack of repairing facilities of BLCs. In some cases the leaders of the community or societies are found to be reasonable for mismanagement of BLCs leading to poor repayment of loans. In case of successful operation of BLCs the repayment position is found to be satisfactory, resulting into economic improvement of the fishermen.

The problem of marketing with the pre-determined traders aggravates the exploitation of the fishermen. For this some kind of institutional arrangement of consumption loan during the lean period is necessary to make the fishermen free from clutches of the fish traders and money lenders. A well directed credit marketing linkage with institution support involving the fishermen communities is needed for the sustainable development of the fishermen.

References

Bal, D.V. and K.V. Rao (1990): Marine Fisheries of India. Tata McGRaw Hill Publishing Company Ltd., New Delhi.

BOBP Report, 174 (1997): 12th Annual State Level Convention, Cuttack.

DFID (BOBP), Post Harvest Fisheries Project, News Letter NO. 12, Oct. 97.

Gupta, S.C. and Ghitkara, S.C. (1993): Future of the Co-operative Enterprises through Managing Local Powers. Indian Journal of Commence, Vol. No. XLVI, N. 174 (Gowalir).

Handbook on Fisheries Statistics (1997): Director of Fisheries, Orissa, Cuttack.

Kurien J. (1979): Co-operatives by Fishermen in kerla. Paper presented in Workshop on Social Feasibility in Small Scale Fisheries development, Madras.

ODA, (BOBP) Informatioin Bulletin-6 (1997), chennai.

Pradhan, N.B. Panda, B.K. and Sahu P. (1998): Optimality in Exploitation of a Common Property Resource: An Evaluation of Marine Fishery in Orissa, Paper presented in the National Seminar oin Development and Environment Controversy in India.

Report on Activities of Marine Sector in Ganjam District (1997): Asst. Director of Fisheries (Marine), Ganjam.

Rowena Lawson, 1984: Economics of Fisheries Development, Prager Publisher, New Delhi.

Srivastava V.K. and M. Sharma Reddy (1983): Fisheries Development in India. Concept Publishing Company, New Delhi.

10

Women Co-operation and Rural Enterprise Development

Dr. M. Soundarapandian*

In India, despite the implementation of five year plans, there has been a growing realisation that rural poverty and unemployment cannot be mitigated with wage employment programme like National Rural Employment Programme (NREP), Rural Landless Employment Guarantee Programme (RLEGFP) and Jawahar Rozgar Yojana (JRY) and the rural development programmes like integrated Rural Development Programme (IRDP) alone.

Lack of adequate attention to small and rural industries has led to large scale migration of population from the rural to Urban areas in search of Jobs. Concentration of industries in cities has, in turn, led to congestion and other problems, including pollution.

The mounting problem of employment has brought into focus the importance of small scale, agro and rural industries as well as development of entrepreneurship in the related fields. Preliminary studies of the planning commission have emphasised that the potentials of this sector should be adequately tapped. Investment per job in this sector would be very low compared to the organised sector. Further, development of this sector would help dispersal of industrial activity reducing inequality and poverty. Development of this sector normally involves acceleration of entrepreneurship movement.

* Reader in Rural Industries and Management, Gandhigram Rural Institute, Deemed University, Gandhigram—624 302

As far as the entrepreneurship development is concerned it may be mentioned that there is no shortage of inherent entrepreneurial talent in the country. What is necessary is to draw out this inherent potential to make the latest talent patent and to galvanise the men, women and the youth to work towards a harmonious blend of personal, corporate and national objective.

Compared to Government Organization like District Industries Centre (DIC) and District Rural Development Agency (DRDA), the role of voluntary organisation in developing entrepreneurial skill is highly appreciable on account of numerous factors which associate with them. To cater to the needs of entrepreneurial development programme, a great amount of co-ordination among various agencies at work is all the more necessary and this alone can steer youth to success in their venture.

The learners of the literacy campaign in Madurai District formed a women organisation and named a "Arivoli Mahalir Iyyakkam" (AMI) for the development of entrepreneurial activities in rural areas. The present study attempts to evaluate the role of the organisation in the rural enterprise development in Madurai District of Tamil Nadu.

Design of the Study

The specific objectives of the study are:

i) To study the growth and performance of Arivoli Mahalir Iyyakkam in Madurai District.

ii) To analyse the role of the Iyyakkam on the rural entrepreneurs development activities.

iii) To evaluate the successful implementation of DWCRA scheme on fair price shops, canteen, cooking powders and washing powders, rearing milch animals etc.,

iv) To suggest various concrete measures for the successful implementation of rural enterprise development in the district.

Based on the above objectives of the study, Primary data as well as secondary data were collected in Madurai District. In order to find out the growth and performance of the "Arivoli Mahalir Iyyakkam" and achievements of the literacy campaign in the district, secondary data were collected from the "Madurai District

Arivoli Iyyakkam Office. Madurai and from the records of the Arivoli Mahalir Iyyakkam Office.

Primary data relating the rural enterprise development activities and impact of DWDRA assistance were collected by the interview method. A total of 30 women groups were interviewed with presented questionnaire. The major activities of the women group such as cooking powder preparation, washing products, fair price shops and canteen were given more importance in the survey period. The findings of the study are presented as the case study in Fair price shops, canteen, cooking powders milk depots, and washing products.

Results and Discussion

The findings of the stud are presented in three sections. They are:

i) Literacy campaign in Madurai District.

ii) Growth and performance of Arivoli Mahalir Iyyakkam in Madurai District.

iii) DWCRA assistance for Arivoli Mahalir Iyyakkam and case studies on rural Enterprise development by Arivoli Mahabir Iyyakkam.

Literacy Campaign in Madurai District

The illiterates under the age group (15-35) in Tamil Nadu accounts for 5.87 millions. Total Literacy campaign projects presently cover 7.45 million illiterates. This includes learners above 35 years also. The campaigns have been implemented in 21 districts. Of the 21 districts, Post literacy campaign was completed in Kanyakumari, Kamarjar Pudukottai and Pasumpon Mathuramalingam Districts. Post Literacy campaign is in the process of having implemented in 10 districts namely, Madurai, North Aroot, Ramanathapuram, Tiruneveli, Dindigul Anna and Coimbatore Districts.

The achievement of Madurai District in the Total Literacy phase is 76.38 percent against the total ranges of 3.28 lakhs. Nearly 3.07 lakhs learners have been enrolled. Among them 2.50 lakhs learners have completed the level III. The target age group for the campaign is (15-35) as per the sanction by the Ministry.

In Madurai, Post Literacy projects was sanctioned in May 1993 to cover 1.80 lakhs neo literates. As much as 1.35 lakh neo-literates are reportedly enrolled. About 1.08 lakh learners attended PLC as on May 1994. The approved cost for post literacy campaign is Rs. 1.46 crores of which Rs. 0.97 Crores was sanctioned from National Literacy mission and Rs. 0.49 Crores from the State Government.

The PLC in Madurai Distract was launched with the main intention of facilitating a continuous approach for after becoming literate, an adult generally becomes motivated to learn more things and shows more interest in reading different types of books and other published materials. He/She wants to use and develop his reading, writing skills. In general, he wants to learn more and continues the process of education. It was felt that if suitable learning opportunities are not provided the neo-literates may lapse back to illiteracy.

The major objective of the Post literacy is to reinforce and consolidate the skills relating to the literacy among the learners, and to equip the learners with better knowledge, perception, skills, attitude, understanding, awareness, functionality etc., of the surrounding society and the nation at large. So, they are equipped to remove the impediments coming in the way of leading a better, happier and more meaningful life that they become active members of the community and participate in the process of social reconstruction and national development.

In Madurai District, each Panchayat Union has one Block Project Co-ordinator (BPC), 2. Assistant Project Co-ordinators (APC) and one office assistant for the implementation of PLC at block level. There is a library in each Panchayat maintained by the Panchayat Co-ordinator. The Panchayat Co-ordinator also co-ordinates and supervises the Centres (Vattam) in the Panchayat area. Generally each Panchayat covers three to four centres which is guided by the Vatta Vazhikatti (Circle Guide). Based on these administrative and organisational background, The Vattam functions twice a week. The reading materials are supplied and circulated among neo-literates among the Vattams. Many self-help groups have been formulated in every Vattam of PLC in Madurai District.

Arivoli Mahalir Iyyakkam in Madurai District

Arivoli Mahalir Iyyakkam (Tamil Name for the organisation of Literacy Campaign women Learners) was formed on 8.3.95 by the neo-literates of Post Literacy campaign in Madurai District. The Officer address for the organisation is : 16, Old Ramanathapuram District Collector's Office, Madurai, - 625020.

The Arivoli Mahalir Iyyakkam (AMI) was Officially registered under the Societies Registration Act of the 1860 (TN Act 27 of 1975) at Madurai on 15.5.95. The office Bears at the time of registration were as follows:

1. V.V.G. Ganeswari — President, Mellur
2. N. Vijayalakshmi — Vice President, Ellis Nagar
3. S. Navanitham — Secretary,E. Kottaipatti.
4. S.Vijayalakshimi — Assistant Secretary, Kallikudi
5. T. Thavamani Devi — Treasurer, Mellakkal
6. G. Mallika — Executive Member, Alli Nagaram
7. A. Pusham — Executive Member, Achampatti

The Neo-literates of the Post-literacy campaign are enrolled as members of the Organisation. The above 18 years girls are eligible to become the member of the Society and they have to pay Rs. 2 as annual subscription. The specific aims of the Society are:-

i) To organise various groups in all villages of the Madurai District in order to implement various women development programmes;

ii) To help the members in maintaining the libraries, developing small savings, insurance and Government assistance for the women groups in Madurai District;

iii) To implement the various schemes like Educational For all, Health For All, mother child care, women Development, Waste land development, water resource Management, environmental protection etc.;

iv) To provide training and assistance to develop the entrepreneurial skills of the women groups in villages to start the small scale industries;

v) To identify the marketing potentialities for the women entrepreneurs.

vi) To generate employment opportunities for the members with non-Profit enterprises; and

vii) To develop the agro-based industries and to popularise and agricultural development schemes in the rural areas.

Under this AMI, at the initial stage, one women team was formed in each Panchayat. During the period of months (May 1995 to December 1995), nearly 240 women teams were organised in Madurai District. The 'Self-help' groups, at the beginning, start to save their excess income by opening an account in the nearby bank (Joint A/c of President and Treasurer of the women group). At the maximum of Rs. 10 to 20 per month, every member provide their savings. Each group consists of 10 top 15 Neo-literates of PLC in a village. After a few months, the saved money was invested in productive activities at a small scale level. The main productive activities are : Preparation of cooking powders, Flouring of Rice and Wheat, cleaning powders, soap powders, Blue drops, Jam, Juice, Bathi, Chips etc.

Before getting the financial assistance from the Government, the AMI also involved in the productive activities with non-profit basis. The women neo-literates are participating during their leisure period. Some groups got training for tailoring, typewriting through the District Arivoli Iyyakkam. The performance of AMI in Madurai District, before getting the Government assistance is given in Table 10.1.

Table 10.1 reveals that during the period of 8 months, the AMI in Madurai district had mobilised the capital resource at an average, of Rs. 281 per women group and they were involved mainly in producing the cooking powders, wheat and Rice flours. Preparation of Phenil, Soap powders, blue-liquid etc., The study revealed the following main features:

i) Before getting the DWCRA assistance, the production was in a small scale level and they earn a meagre profit.

ii) With the limited finance, there was no continuous production and irregular employment opportunities.

iii) The members of the group had equally distributed their produced commodities at the time of marketing problems.

iv) The women neo-literates were involved only during the leisure period in production activities.

Table 10.1 : Performance of Arivoli Mahaliriyyakkam before Getting Government Finance as on December—1995

S. No.	*Divisions*	*Number of Women Groups*	*Average Amt. of Capital Invested per Group*	*Activities involved*
1.	Madurai Corporation	79	4060	Sambar Powder Phenyl, Soap Powders
2.	Madurai Division	76	3055	Wheat, Rice Flour, Samber Powder, Phenyl
3.	Uslampatti Division	55	2637	Liquid blue, cooking powders, Soap Powders, Blue Metal
4.	Periyakulam Division	30	2984	Wire Basket, Phenyl, Ink
	Total	**240**	**3281**	

Source : Computed from the Office Records of Arivoli MahalirIyyakkam, Madurai.

Note : All women groups are involved in smal savings activity and the same capital was invested for the productive activities.

In order to rectify the above difficulties and problem, the AMI had approached the District Collector for the development of the Arivoli women groups in Madurai District.

DWCRA

A mid term review of the implementation of Integrated Rural Development Programme (IRDP) revealed the flow of assistance to women members of target group households or even women headed households had been very marginal. To sub-serve the overall objective of improving the quality of life of rural families living below the poverty line, a sharper focus on providing assistance to women as part of the IRDP strategy was considered essential. Development of women and children. In Rural areas

DWCRA was formulated as a Sub scheme of the IRDP within this frame work.

DWCRA seeks to provide income generating activities to women and also provides an organisational support in terms of a receiving system for the assisted women so that they can become effective recipients of goods and services available in that area. Women's income is known to have positive correlation with the nutritional and educational status of the family and in the building up of a positive attitude towards the status of women. Hence, the necessity of ensuring more income earning avenues for women.

While the target group of DWCRA is the same as IRDP i.e., families having an annual income of less than Rs. 6,400/- (below poverty line) The methodology is through a group. The financial provisions under DWCRA are available only for the group. Individuals are financed on IRDP pattern from IRDP budget. The scheme envisages formation of a group of 15-20 women. The women are expected to come together for an activity of mutual interest to all. The entry point for the group may not be income generating activities but it must be an essential ingredient of the total gamut of activities in which the group is involved. The assistance available to a group are:

a) Rs. 15,000 as one time grant contributed in equal measure by Government of India, state Government and UNICEF, which can be used as:

   i) revolving fund for purchase of raw material and marketing:

   ii) honorarium to group organiser not exceeding Rs. 50/- per month for a period of one year;

   iii) infrastructure support (seed money) for income generating activities; and

   iv) One time expenditure on child care facilities.

b) Travelling allowance at Rs. 200/- for one year for the group organiser.

If the group is registered under the Registered of Societies Act, it can take loan from the bank as a group for economic activities. Individual women members will be entitled to subsidy as per IRDP norms and each member will be equally liable for repayment of the loan. In case the group is informal, it not be able to draw loan from the bank as a group and there the composite loan may be disaggregated into individual loans and subsidies, with the group guaranteeing the total amount of loan.

Training of Rural youth for self Employment (TRYSEM) is expected to cater to fulfilling the skill requirements for beneficiaries of DWCRA also. The curricula, duration of training and rate of payment to trainers and trainees requiring the same should be in accordance with the norms of TRYSEM.

In Madurai District, the Arivoli Mahalir Iyyakkam are registered under the Registration of Societies Act are eligible to get loan from the bank under DWCRA ASSISTANCE.

Arivoli Mahalir Iyyakkam After DWCRA Assistance

As on Ist June 1996, the total members of AMI are 10,840 and number of women groups are 770 in all villages' of Madurai District. The details of members enrolment in AMI in given in Tabel 10.2. The table reveals that the 770 women groups were formed under AMI in Madurai District. Of the total women groups, a large number of groups (28.96 percent) were formed in Madurai Division and lower number of groups (21.56 per cent) were formed in Usilampatti division.

Table 10.2 : Arivoli Women Groups as on 1st June, 1996

S.No.	*Divisions*	*Number of Groups*	*Total No. of Members*
1.	Madurai Corporation	192 (24.94)	2812
2.	Madurai Division	223 (28.96)	3290
3.	Usilampatti	166 (24.56)	2298
4.	Periyakulam	189 (24.54)	2440
		770	**10,840**

Source : Computed from Office records of AMI, Madurai.

For the administrative convenience, the Madurai District was divided into 4 divisions under total literacy and Post literacy campaign. AMI got the DWCRA assistance in two stages. At the first stage, January 1996, 103 women groups got the assistance at the rate of Rs. 15,000 per group in Madurai District. During the Period June 1996, another 113 women groups got the assistance under DWCRA at the rate of Rs. 25,000 per group. A total of 226 women groups got the assistance of Rs. 43.70 Crores under DWCRA scheme. The activities of AMI under DWCRA scheme are given in Table 10.3. It is clear from the table that the 216 self-help groups, in addition with their savings and by using DWCRA assistance, have involved in the rural enterprise development. Such as preparation of cooking powders (18.06 percent) rearing milch animals (12.5 percent), running fair price shops (12.5 percent), providing domestic credit/household credit needs (10.19 percent), Production of ink, shampoo, cleaning powders, Jam, pickle, bakery etc., (9.72 percent) in Madurai District. The above said activities were predominantly

Table 10.3 : Rural Enterprise Activities of AMI with DWCRA Assistance

S.No.	*Activities*	*Number of Women Groups*	*Percentage*
1.	Cooking Powders	39	18.06
2.	Tailoring, Typewriting	19	8.79
3.	Milch Animals	27	12.50
4.	Cooking vessels, Canteens	14	6.48
5.	Weaving	4	1.85
6.	Fair Price Shops	27	12.50
7.	Blue Liquid, Phenyl	21	9.72
8.	Quarry and Blue Metal Work	6	2.78
9.	Wire Basket and Bags	9	4.17
10.	Ink, Shampoo, Cleaning Powder	14	6.48
11.	Wheat, Rice Flour	14	6.48
12.	Domestic Credit/Household Credit Needs	22	10.19
		216	**100.00**

Source : Office records, AMI, Madurai.

done by the groups. A lower percent of groups had involved in tailoring (8.79 percent) renting cooking vessels and ornaments for marriage purpose and running canteen in BDO office, (6.48 percent), weaving (1.85 percent), blue liquid, phenyl production (9.72 percent) quarry and blue metal work (9.72 percent), wire basket and bags designing (4.17 percent), and preparation of wheat and Rice flour (6.48 percent). It is inferred that most of the women groups had concentrated mainly on fair price shops, rearing milch animals and domestic credit activities.

Rural Enterprise Development By AMI, Few Case Studies

The performance and achievement of the Arivoli mahalir Iyyakkam in Madurai District in employment and income generating activities through the rural enterprise development are discussed in this section. The research team had visited many villages (nearly 20 villages) and investigated the 30 women groups about the functioning of the women groups with the DWCRA assistance. The findings of the field visit are summarised below with a few case study analysis.

Fair Price Shops

The AMI in Madurai District had involved in running the 27 fair price shops in various villages. In addition to the DWCRA assistance, the Madurai District Co-operative Bank had provided the loan assistance to the women groups for running the ration shops. Nearly 200 card holders got the benefits in each fair price shop of the women teams. The women groups are supplying the very essential commodities through the ration shops. The supplied commodities are rice, kerosene, sugar and wheat at reasonable rate with the correct weight measurement.

In Vachampatti, Keelavazhvu Panchayat Union of Madurai District, one AMI group under the president of Mrs. M. Thavamani is running the ration shop service to the public from September 1995 with the assistance of DWCRA and Madurai District Co-operative bank. The experience gained form the fair price shops in Vachampatti are reviewed below:-

i) The fair price shops run by the AMI charged a lower price for all essential commodities than the shops run by the CMS marketing society. Both the AMI and CMS marketing society purchased the commodities from the Pandian Super Market,

Madurai. But they charged the different prices. These findings are presented in Table 10.4

Table 10.4 : Rates Charged by the AMI and CMS Marketing Society in Fair Price Shops in Vachampatti

S.No.	*Commodities*	*Rates Charged by* CMC Marketing Society	AMI	*Quantity* supplied per Month per Card
1.	Rice–I Quality (1 kg.)	4.00	3.75	20 kgs.
2.	Sugar (1 kg.)	9.25	9.05	½ kg. per Unit
3.	Wheat (1 kg.)	4.75	4.50	3 to 5 kgs.
4.	Kerosene (1 lt.)	3.25	3.00	3 litres

Source : Field visit at Vechampatti Village.

ii) The AMI Groups had charged the profit of 13 percent for rice, 14 percent for wheat and 70 paise per Kg., of sugar at the selling price, as per the Government norms. In addition to this profit, the used Gunny bags are calculated as an additional income.

iii) The gross profit includes the transport cost and salary to one sales girl and one assistant. Two women got the employment regularly in each ration shops. One Sales girls got the salary for Rs. 250 per month and one assistant got Rs. 150 per month.

Mrs. Thavamani, President of the AMI in Vachampatti Village revealed some difficulties and suggestions for the successful functioning of Fair Price shops by the AMI group in all villages. They are:-

i) Lack of accommodation for shops - Now in Vachampatti, the ration shop is conducted by the AMI in the community hall of the village. It lacks storage facilities, lighting facilities etc.,

ii) The AMI group are purchasing the commodities from the Pandian super Market at Government rate. But the Pandian Super Market is supplying the under weight bags of sugar and rice to the maximum of 2 to 3 kgs per quintal.

iii) At an average, each ration shop in the Village allotted for 20 family cards. But the monthly quota supply was insufficient level for the distribution of the essential goods.

These are the main problems faced by AMI Group in running the ration shops in Vachampatti. The president is very happy to say that the beneficiaries of the ration shop are satisfied with the ration shop run by the AMI, because, they are receiving the essential commodities at lower price and with the correct weight measurement. The problems could be solved by providing the buildings, supply of goods at correct weight and in the sufficient level to the ration shops.

Production of Soap Powder Phenyl etc.

A team consisting 15 members under the Presidentship of Mrs. Panchavarnam (30 years Old) is producing soap powder in large quantities before and after getting DWCRA assistance, in Achampattu. In the initial stage, each member invest Rs. 400/- for the production of soap powder (Surf Powder). During their leisure period, they are preparing the powders for two hours per day. The team got the training for the preparation of soap powders from the Arivoli Mahalir Iyyakkam at the central level.

A book "China China Ettu Eduthu" published by Bharat Gyan Vigyan Samiti (BGVS) Resource centre, Madurai is also useful for the production of soap powder and all other products. The required raw materials for producing the soap powder are washing soda (1 kg.,) R. P. Soda (3/4 kg.,) Sillary (250 ml.,) D. Blue (10 gm). Dinopal (10 gm), Tri-Sodium- Phosphate (TSP) (30 gm), STPP (20 gm), and Scent (10 ml.) By using these materials, the team produces 2 kg., of soap powder every time. At an average, the team has produced 20 Kg. of soap powder per month before getting DWCRA assistance.

After getting the DWCRA assistance, the team continues the production of soap powder and also involved in providing the domestic credit needs in the Achampattu village of Madurai District.

The Group sells the powder at the rate of Rs. 3.50 per 100 grams and earns the total sales revenue of Rs. 35 for 1 kg., production. The actual cost of production is only Rs. 21 and earns a profit of Rs. 14 per Kg.

Mrs. Panchavarnam revealed some of the difficulties which have been listed below:-

i) Without publicity and advertisement, it is difficult to market the product in the open market, even though, the products of AMI group is sold in the market at lower price than the established company product, for example, "SURF" - Rs. 28 for 1/2 Kg., and the AMI group products - Rs. 35 for Rs. 1 Kg.,

ii) The produced soap powders are equally distributed among the members for avoiding the difficulties in marketing and the group also losses the profits from the production.

iii) The group have to face the dangerous effects without using the hand gloves at the time of preparation.

iv) There is no building facilities for the bulk production.

If the AMI got the marketing facilities in the centre of the Madurai city by establishing a shop and make some advertisement for such products, the above said problems could be solved and the women entrepreneurs development in an unexpected level.

The research team had visited the Phenyl production centre at A. Vellalapatti, Mellur Block. The group consisting of 12 members is headed by S. Indira. They are producing the phenyl as per the suggestion of the Book "China, China Etta Eduthu" and training by the AMI of Madurai District.

The requirements for producing the phenyl are : Pine Oil (500 ml) soft soap (250g), Rosanam (125 gm), Jasmine Scent (10 ml), By using these materials, the group has produced 15 bottles of phenyl. The cost of production was Rs. 4/- per bottle. But the phenyl was sold at the rate of Rs. 9 per bottle.

In order to solve the marketing problem, the group approached the private clinics and Government Hospital in Mellur and sell the Phenyl regularly to the hospitals. The Group earns a regular income through the production the Phenyl. The group also sell the product at the lower rate than the market rate of the established products.

Canteen by Women Group at BDO Office

The Arivoli Mahalir Iyyakkam in Madurai District is running the 7 canteens in Panchayat Union Offices, namely, Usilampatti,

Chellampatti, Sedapatti, T. Kallupatti, Thirparankundram, Madurai, West and Vadipatti. The Canteen is functioned in the DWCRA Building in every Panchayat Union Office. The women group is paying a rent of Rs. 150/- per month. The experiences gained from the Thirupparkankundram canteen run by the women group are discussed in this section.

A women group consisting of 10 members under the presidentship of Mrs. Santha, Palaniammal (Secretary) and S. Padma (Treasurer) was formed on 30.10.1995. At the initial stage, the group involved in preparing the cooking powders and turmeric powders. Before getting the DWCRA assistance, the group earns Rs. 100 per members from the production of cooking powder etc., After getting the DWCRA assistance, the team involved in running the DWCRA canteen at Thirupparankundram Panchayat Union Office. The team got the DWCRA assistance of Rs. 15,000/- on January 26, 1996 and the Canteen was started on the same date.

Of the total 10 members, 7 women are actually involved in the canteen work. Everyday, the canteen is functioning from 9 A.M. to 7 P.M., and the items supplied in the canteen are : Tea, Coffee, Milk, Vadai and the Variety rice, meals etc., The total sales at an average, per day is Rs. 800/- They earn the 25 to 30 percent of profit from the total sales. The seven women members working in the canteen got the salary of Rs. 25 per day. They got the employment for 5 days a week except Saturday and Sunday. In the mean time, the excess or unsold items are also used by the members. The group is also supplying the food items for bulk orders like marriage and other ceremonies. During the period of 8 months period, the group repaying the DWCRA loan was Rs. 2,250. The only problem revealed by the women group (Mrs. Santha) is that the rent charged by the Panchayat Union Office for the Canteen building. The research team find the speciality of the group, at the time of field visit, that the all women members equally shared their work in the canteen and they got the equal salary of Rs. 25 per day per head.

Milk Depot

In Achampatti Panchayat, a women team was formed under AMI in the year 1995 with 16 scheduled caste members including 14 neo-literates and 1 volunteer Instructor of Post Literacy campaign. The group started the savings as Rs. 10/- per month. Before getting the DWCRA assistance, the members were involved in producing cooking powders, phenyl and blue drops. Most of the members are having one milch animals in their houses. The neglected scheduled caste people did not get the benefit of IRDP, so far, in this village. Only after forming the women group, the members get the DWCRA assistance through the AMI of Madurai District.

Mrs. Meenakshi is the Secretary for the group. She made some important observations about the running of milk depot with the assistance of Rs. 15,000 under DWCRA scheme. They are as follows:-

i) If the total DWCRA assistance, Rs. 10,000 was distributed to the women member having a milch animals, as advance, for the regular supply for the milk to the women group.

ii) The remaining Rs. 5,000 were used to purchase 3 milch animals for the women group and handed over to 3 women members for rearing.

iii) There are 3 women members involved in this activities as full time for account maintenance, procurement of milk and clearing the vessels and supply of milk to the hotels in towns.

iv) At present the milk turnover is 38 liters in the morning and 21 liters in the evening.

v) The milk purchased at the rate of Rs. 6 per litre from the members and sold to the hotels and to the public at the rate of Rs.8 per litre. But the actual market rate for the milk is Rs. 9 per litre.

vi) After deducting the salary for the 3 women members (a total of Rs. 2,000 per month), the remaining profit was utilised for repayment of loan. The women group, so far, repaid the amount of Rs. 1,000/- to the Bank.

The women group pointed out some difficulties and problems in rearing milch animals under DWCRA scheme. They are :

i) There is no separate building for running the milk depot and for improving the enterprise.

ii) The financial assistance of Rs. 15,000/- is not enough to purchase the High breed variety of Milch animals.

iii) The members have to purchase the fodder for their milch animals from the town on credit due to the financial problem.

These problem could be solved by providing separate buildings, enhancing the DWCRA assistance to Rs. 30,000 per group and setting up of a store for milch animal fodder by the women group of AMI of Madurai District.

The AMI has also developed the such type of milch animals programme in Ayyappanayakkanpatti, Vadipatti Block and in Alanganallur Panchayat Union.

In Conclusion, empowering women through the employment and income generating activities under Arivoli Mahalir Iyyakkam of Madurai District is successful in reducing the gender gap and development of women after getting education through the Mass Literacy campaign. Such type of voluntary organisations could be encouraged by the Government and the Public for the Women's Movement.

11

Problems and Prospects of Primary Handloom Weavers' Co-operative Societies in Orissa

Radha Krishna Panda*

The handloom industry in India is the largest unorganised sector and constitutes an integral part of the socio-economic trait of rural India. Traditionally, this industry has shown a remarkable performance even in the international market. This sector with three million handlooms is able to produce about 4,000 million meters of cloth and provides employment to about 10 million population (Khadi Gramdoyog, March 1989, pp 286). Again this sector contributes 30 percent of the total textile production of the Country in the year 1991 (Report of the Village and small scale industries committee, 1991).

Though this industry is the symbol of the self sufficiency in the Gandhian terminology and has been moulding the socio-economic destiny of rural India, But in this days of modernisation and advanced sophisticated technology, the active role of handlooms is hardly felt. Their problems are manifested in the sphere of procurement of raw-materials, installation of equipments, finance, marketing and so on. Lack of competitiveness is the fundamental criterion associated with this industry. In order to overcome these multifaceted problems the formation of weavers Co-operatives is a possible institutional ultimatum.

* Deptt. of Economics, Somnath Science College, Ganjam (Orissa).

Handloom industry thrives due to the active participation of weavers who are economically backward. They are one of the vulnerable and weakers sections of the community. If they remain backward, the rural economy will suffer from some serious handicaps. In the backdrop of all these things, the weavers had been brought to the realm of Co-operation during the post independence era. Unlike any other Co-operatives, "Weavers Co-operatives Society is a voluntary business association of weavers devoted for the all round development of the industry in the collective benefits of all the member weavers". "This Society also runs with a democratic principle that it is for the weavers by the weavers and of the weavers. " W.C.S. is an institutional attempt to bring about the socio-economic transformation of masses of weavers. Historically, the performance of handloom industry in Orissa finds even the international acceptance. The weavers of Sambalpur, Bargarh and even Berhampur have shown spectacular performance in the art of the weaving. As per the report made by Directorate of Textiles, Orissa, "By the end of May' 1997, the total weavers population 4,15,261 of the state are having with 1,19,005 looms." Out of 1,19,005 looms, 1,10,124 have remained in the fold of Co-operatives. Further, it clarifies that by the end of 1997 there are 841 active PHWCS.

Like Industry, Fishery, Poultry Co-operatives, the Weavers Co-operatives are the functional co-operatives which remains under the statutory control of the Director of the Textiles, declared as Additional Registrar. However, the statutory responsibility of Audit, supervision and inspection ultimately rests with the Registrar of Co-operative Societies. WCS includes three types of societies such as handloom societies, powerloom societies and sericulture societies. By the end of 1997, there were about 841 primary handloom societies, 5 powerloom societies and 63 sericulture societies. Thus in any discussion of WCS, the proportionate share of handloom is maximum and it remains at 92.51 percent. So to say about the problems of WCS are the problems associated with handloom industry. In the fitness of all these things, this paper is an exhaustive attempt to evaluate the performance of handloom WCS.

Objectives of WCS

WCSs have been functioning in different states with the mission of the following objectives.

(i) To supply raw-materials to members and for the purpose of making purchase thereof in bulk.

(ii) To create funds to be lent to members for initial and running expenses of the Industry.

(iii) To provide technical assistance to the members in producing goods of new and improving patterns and to provide common services as dying, printing and bleaching.

(iv) To arrange collective sale of cloth produced by members.

(v) Generally, to promote the industry acts in such a way that its benefits percolates to the workers.

If the above objectives are rightly pursued, a WCS can become the friend, Philosopher and guide to the weavers, who are economically less fortunate.

Working of PHWCSs

Generally the operation of WCS is associated with the concept of either/or. Either the societies help the members to carry on the work individually or the members work collectively in the society and share the profit. In Orissa the first type is in vague. Again, all the primary WCSs which operate it the micro level are federated into an apex society which operate at the state level. In the year 1956," "The Orissa State Apex Weavers' Co-operative Society" was formed with the sacrosanct objective of providing regular work to all the weavers through Co-operatives. Therefore, it can be correctly stated that Co-operative is a true path from poverty to plenty.

Certainly, the weavers' Community are the fragmented and disintegrated array of the socio-economic structure of rural India. Many a times they are in the vicious trap of poverty. They are frustrated in the superior echelon of the society. They deserve adequate smile through the efforts of Co-operation. Thus, co-operative is a small and simple measure for the benefits of small and simple people within a small and simple area requiring small and simple needs.

Role of WCSs

WCSs performs a plethora of functions for the all round development of its members.

(i) To protect the weavers from exploitation by the village money lenders and business intermediaries is an important role of WCS. In the absence of WCS, the weavers go on borrowing money capital as well as raw-materials from the village money lenders or business intermediaries. Due to the evil intention of the later, either they pay exorbitant rate of interest or are compelled to sale their produce even at below equilibrium price. Thus co-operative is a way of emancipating the masses of weavers.

(ii) WCSs are aimed at working regular employment to weavers as well as their invested physical capital.

(iii) WCSs rightly arrange right quality yarn and right dyes to the weavers at right prices. In order to ensure timely supply of different varieties of yarn, there are six co-operative spinning mills in Orissa. These six spinning mills are located at Nuapatna (Cuttack), Tirtol (Jagatsinghpur), Khurda, Gobindapur (Dhenkanal), Bargarh and Kiroi (Sundargarh).

(iv) The Directorate of Textiles & the apex WCS through PHWCSs impart training to weavers for modernisation and diversification.

(v) A part of the total profit earned by the PHWCSs is declared as bonus payment to the weavers.

(vi) In order to gear-up marketing of handloom clothes, the Govt. of Orissa was guaranteeing 20 percent price subsidy to the weavers. But this system has been alternated in the year 1988-89, by introducing Market Development Scheme. As per this programme, was PHWCS receives 15% of its working capital as matter of special aid, which can be used for maintaining price subsidy. PHWCSs have been more successful due to this effort.

(vii) In order to introduce weavers to Market, the PHWCS have been instigating weavers to participate in different state level and national level Cloth exhibitions and workshops.

(viii) In the year 1985 a constitutional reservation plan have been introduced to protect the interests of the weaves of handloom Industry. Accordingly 22 varieties of cloths have been reserved for handloom sector, where the entrance of powerloom sector is strictly prohibited. As a matter of fact the role of PHWCSs have expanded progressively.

In the light of the above facts, and an attempt has been made to focus the different statistical evidences pertaining to the growth and performances of PHWCSs in Orissa.

Growth & Performance of PHWCSs in Orissa

Table 11.1 explains the growth pattern of PHWCSs in Orissa. In the year 1980-81 there were 492 PHWCSs with 64 thousand individual members. With the period of in a half decade the number of PHWCSs and the number of individual members had increased to 755 and 90 thousands respectively. Thus, the percentage growth rates were 53.45 and 40.62 respectively. But the number of PHWCSs steadily declined accompanied with a negative growth rate during 1990s which is evident from Table 11.1. Thus, the PHWCSs in the light of growth rate is not satisfactory.

Table 11.1 : Growth Pattern of PHWCSs in Orissa

Years	*Number of PHWCSs in Orissa*	*% growth Rate*	*Total Individual members (000)*	*% growth Rate*
1980–81	492	—	64	—
1985–86	755	53.45	90	40.62
1990–91	866	14.70	98	8.88
1993–94	863	-0.35	103.85	5.96
1996–97	841	-2.55	110.124	6.04

Source : Directorate of Textiles, Orissa.

Table 11.2 highlights the total working capital, share capital, No. of Looms, Employments, production, sales, value of cloth produced respectively.

Working capital wise the year 1991-92 witnesses a falling tendency from 5793.09 lakhs to 4316.41 lakhs. The amount of share capitals has shown increasing frend over years during the period under study. In the year 1991-92, the number of looms were 1,04,290 and in the year 1993-94 it remains at 1,05,662. The employment opportunities of the indutry have steadily increased from 209 thousand in the year 1990-91 to 211 thousands in the year 1993-

Table 11.2

Years	Working Capital (in lakhs)	Share Capital (in lakhs)	No. of looms	Emp. (000)	Prod. (Lakh sqm.)	Sales (in lakhs)	VCP (in lakhs)	Value of Clothes remain unsold (in lakhs)
1990–91	5793.09	192.7	104290	209	516	2933.7	4587.2	1653.8
1991–92	4316.41	391.3	103513	207	461	3552.3	5099.22	1547.6
1992–93	N.A.	N.A.	104951	210	418	N.A.	N.A.	N.A.
1993–94	8365.80	326.9	105662	211	382	4645.4	5326.03	680.03

Source : Annual Audit Reports from the Office of the Registrar of Co-operatives, Orissa.

94. But one vital item, i.e. total production of the industry in Lakh sqm, has fallen steadily over years. So to say, there has been a secular deterioration in total production. Total sales of clothes have shown an increasing trend during the four years periods and the value of clothes produced has also shown an increasing trend. Similarly, the value of clothes remain unsold, through points out a diminishing but certainly there has been a cumulative stock of the industry which is a bad sight. Therefore, falling production and the cumulative stock of final goods in the inventory are the negative symptoms in the annals of progress of this industry.

The Progress of PHWCSs in Ganjam District

After a thorough study about the progress of PHWCSs in Orissa, it is imperative to study the progress of PHWCSs in Ganjam District. Table 11.3 indicates the performance of PHWCSs in terms of the Nos. of PHWCSs and the total individual members. In the year 1990-91, the total Nos. of PHWCSs were 68, which has decreased to 65, making a negative growth rate of 4.42 percent. After 1992-93, it has remained standstill at 65 over all the years. The number of individuals members have increased from 5,882 to 7,365 over all the years. Thus, the performance of PHWCSs in the light of individual members remains satisfactory.

Table 11.3 : Performance of PHWCSs in Ganjam District

Years	*Number of PHWCSs*	*% growth Rate of PHWCSs*	*Individual members*	*%age growth of Individual membership*
1990–91	68	–	5882	–
1991–92	68	0	5919	0.62
1992–93	65	–4.42	5984	1.09
1993–94	65	0	6222	3.97
1994–95	65	0	6522	4.82
1995–96	65	0	6771	3.81
1996–97	65	0	7065	8.77

Source : Office of the Asstt. Directorate of Textiles, Berhampur.

Table 11.4 explains the total working capital and share capital of the PHWCS in Ganjam district. The working capital of all the years from 1992-93 to 1995-96 remaining lower in comparison to the year 1991-92. But it has been increased in the year 1996-97. Simiarly, the amount of share-capital goes higher over the years from 1990-91 to 1996-97.

Table 11.4 : Total Working Capital and Share Capital of all the PHWCSs in Ganjam

Years	*Working Capital (in Lakhs)*	*Share Capital (in Lakhs)*
1990–91	N.A.	19.88
1991–92	734.15	20.42
1992–93	611.00	20.47
1993–94	687.20	24.17
1994–95	675.63	29.80
1995–96	676.21	N.A.
1996–97	842.73	N.A.

Source : Office of the Asstt. Directorate of Textiles, Berhampur.

Table 11.5 explains the performance of PHWCSs in the light of profit and loss. In the year 1990-91, the number of profit making untis were 64 and the number of loss making units were only 4 and

Table 11.5 : Performance of PHWCSs in the light of Profit and Loss

Years	*No. of Profit making* PHWCSs	*No. of Loss making* PHWCSs	*No. of No Profit/* No Loss making Units	*Total PHHWCSs*
1990–91	64	04	–	68
1991–92	64	04	–	68
1992–93	53	15	–	68
1993–94	52	12	01	65
1994–95	55	10	–	65
1995–96	57	08	–	65
1996–97	51	09	05	65

Source : Asstt. Directorate of Textiles, Berhampur.

the no. of no-profit, no-loss making units were nil. But in the 1996-97 out of 65 PHWCs the number profit making units, loss making units and no-profit/no-loss making units remains at 51,9 and 5 respectively. As 21.5 percent of PHWCSs out 65 PHWCSs are suffering from loss and no-profit/no-loss, therefore, the performance of PHWCSs are not absolutely satisfactory.

From the above, it is ample clear that the performance of PHWCSs in the light of growth rate, accumulated stock of final goods, the rising trend of loss etc. is not satisfactory. Two possible reasons may be surfaced for the overwhelming deadlock of PHWCSs. On one side, it may be market failure, i.e. the lack of sufficient demand for the products produced by PHWCSs. On the reverse side it may be the marketing failure, i.e., due to improper marketing strategies adopted by the co-operatives. The negative consequences of market failure as well as maarketing failure unfortunately reside with the Weavers who constitute the architects of handlooms industry.

Obectives

In view of the aforesaid analyssis, an attempt has been made in this study to evaluate the different bottlenecks associated with the market as well as marketing. At the same time, the socio-economy or Weavers has been studied to assess the negative impacts of market failure as well as marketing failure.

Scope of the Study

This paper has relied on primary data as well as secondary sources data. Primary data have been collected from the scattered Weavers of five different villages Dengaosta (Patapur Block), Pitala (Sheragada Block), Mundamarai (Dharakote Block), Gada demodarpalli (Dharakote Block) and Suramani (Sorada Block) and the PHWCS of Gada Damodarpalli. These villages has been purpositively selected on the basis of their easy accessibility and as the author has been closely associated with the villagers because of his place of work. The second any data have been collected from the official files and publications of Directors of Textiles, Orissa; the Registrar of Co-operatives, Orissa and the Assistant Directorate of Textiles, Berhampur.

Methodology

Technique of Multi-stage sampling has been adopted in order to get an unbiased estimate of the socio-economy of Weavers. For MSS, data have been collected at different stages like state level, district level and micro level. Thus, it is hoped that the findings of the study may easily be considered to assess the due picture of PHWCS in Orissa in totality.

Further, simple arithmetic mean, simple Average of Price Relatives method for the calculation of sales price index number, ratio analysis, percentage calculation etc. have been introduced to obtain the findings of the study.

PHWCS - A Case Study of G. Damodarapalli

Table 11.6 highlights the progress and performance of G. Damodarapalli PHWCS. This society was founded in the year 1978. Since 1990-91, this society has been witnessing an increasing trend in the membership. The total membership of this society remains at 71 during the year 1990-91, which increases to 76 in the year 1993-94, and further increases to 104. The absolute growth of membership during the year 1996-97. compared to the year 1990-91 happens at 46.47 percent.

Working capital wise there cyclical fluctuations. In the year 1993-94, this amount falls to 792.679 from the previous peak 1001.929 in the year 1992-93.

The performance of this society in terms of share-capital proceeds with secularly-increasing trends. If one compares the share capital in the year 1990-91 to 1996-97, he will find that there has 25.1 percent increase in this figure. Here, it is noteworthy that the share-capital of the society consists of the membership fees and undistributed annual profits of the society.

Total production of cloths in money terms undergoes falling trends in the year s 1994-95 and 1996-97. Further there happens a spectacular fall in the production of clothes in the year 1996-97 in comparision to the year 1995-96, which is clearly reflected in Table 11.6.

Table 11.6, further suggests that the sales of clothes have increased continuously over the years from 1990-91 to 1995-96 with the exception of the year 1996-97. The year 1996-97 suffers

Table 11.6 : Progress of PHWCS—Gada Damodarapplli

Years	*Individual members*	*Total Working Capital (in 000)*	*Total Share Capital (in 000)*	*Total Production (in 000)*	*Total Sales (in 000)*	*Total Unsold items* (in 000)
1990–91	71	829.572	52.125	N.A.	451.3	319.1
1991–92	72	1008.028	57.885	480.134	414.3	384.7
1992–93	75	1001.929	58.515	579.519	593.4	433.6
1993–94	76	792.679	61.015	1380.0151	1197.5	292.8
1995–96	81	N.A.	66.875	1106.686	1234.4	294.9
1996–97	104	N.A.	116.875	1408.002	1240.8	467.3
1997–98	104	N.A.	156.875	786.803	788.2	426.0

from a negative sales growth to the tune of 26.48 percent. It is due to the impropoer, marketing strategy and lack of sufficient market.

The total unsold items in money terms, reflected in Table 11.6 represents non-marketability of different items which is a cummulative expansion of the past years. The discussion with the executives of the society reveals that in order to exhaust the old stock, the total production had been reduced by 55.88 percent in the year 1996-97.

But it is not desirable on the ground that the fall in production will adversely affect the employment position of the weavers. Therefore, in order to ensure adequate strength and vigour to the PHWCS, the marketing strategy should be rectified and modified in an effective manner.

Table 11.7 illustrates the calculation of price index number. For the said purpose, the years 1991-92 and 1996-97 have been selected as the base year and current year respectively. Further, six representative commodities have been choiced for this pur-

Table 11.7 : Preparation of Sales Price Index taking 1992–92 as the Base Year

Range of Commodities	Prices in 1991–92 (P_0)	Prices in 1996–97 (P_1)	Price Relatives $\left[\frac{P_1}{P_0} \times 100\right]$
Saree-White (Y–40)	45	65	144.44
Saree-Check (Y–60)	70	110	157.14
Lungi (Cotton)	45	72	160.00
Towel-White (Y–40)	09	16	177.77
Towel-Check (Y–40)	18	26	144.44
Dhoti (Y–60)	40	65	162.5
			Σ I = 964.29

Sales Price Index Number for the year 1996–97

$$= \frac{\Sigma I}{N} = \frac{946.29}{6} = 157.715$$

pose. The price level of the stated commodities have been collected from the official files of the PHWCS, G. Damodarpalli.

Accordingly,

The sales price Index Number for the year 1996-97 = $\frac{\Sigma I}{N}$

[Where ΣI = Summation of Price Relatives for the years 1990–91 to 1996–97.

N = Number of commodities selected]

$$SPI = \frac{946.29}{6} = 157.715$$

Therefore, the rise in the price level for the commodities produced by PHWCS happens to the extent of 57.71 percent.

If we compare the rise in total sales in the year 1996-97 to the year 1991-92, We will find that there has been a sales growth of 90.02 percent (Table 11.6). Since the percentage growth of sales is greater than the percentage growth of the price level (51.71), therefore, the current price level for different commodities is satisfactory. Thus, in order to get profit there shouldn't be price-rise rathe PHWCSs should be engaged in sales-promotion activities.

Socio-economy of Weavers under PHWCSs

In order to assess the socio-economy of weavers, 60 weavers households under different PHWCSs have been sampled. Table 11.8 focusses the distribution of total labour force in the industry. From this table, it is evident that the propertionate share of female

Table 11.8 : Distribution of Total Labour Force

Different Types of Workers	*Part-time Labourers*	*Full-time Labourers*	*Total*	*% Share of each category of labour force in the total labour force*
Male Workers	68	50	118	33.55
Female Workers	68	72	140	42.17
Child Labourers	50	24	74	22.28
Total	**186**	**146**	**332**	**100.00**

workers remain maximum at 42.17 percent and the proportionate share of child workers remain minimum at 22.28 percent.

Table 11.9 suggests the product-range of this Industry. Weavers manufacture different clothes like towels, sarees,lungis, dhotis, napkins etc. Maximum number of Weavers produce cheque-sarees and towels and the proportionate share of these two items remain at 32.79 percent. On the other hand the products like bandha sarees and stripe sarees for which the market is more awaited,

Table 11.9 : Product-range of Different Sample-households

Product Range	No. of Weaver Households Produce	% Share of each in the total Product Range
Towel – 26	40	32.79
Towel – 40	08	6.59
Stripe-Saree	48	3.27
Cheque – Saree	40	32.79
Bandha - Saree	06	4.92
White – Saree	08	6.56
White – Dhoti	16	13.11
Total	**122**	**100.00**

N.B. : Though in this paper only 60 households have been sampled, but the total households in this Table 11.9 remains at 122 because few house-holds produce more than a single product.

they are produced minimum and their share in the total production remains at 4.92 and 3.27 respectively.

Though the Weavers are in the fold of Co-operatives, many-a-times the farmer procure yarn, dye and other requirements frrom the market due to the improper supply of raw materials by the later. Table 11.10 suggests the souce of raw-materials for the weavers. Though co-operatives meet a sizeable needs, still the share of local retail market in bridging the production gap of the industry is quite eye-catching and the proportionate share of the local retail market happens at 33.33 percent.

Table 11.11 declares the quality of services of PHWCS, our of a large number of services offered by the PHWCSs, the maximum

Table 11.10 : Source of Raw-materials

Major Source of raw-materials	*No. of Weaver-household*	*% Share of each item*
Local-market (Relailers)	20	33.33
Whole-salers	06	10.00
Govt. & Semi Govt. Agencies	Nil	–
Co-operatives	34	56.67
Total	**60**	**100.00**

Table 11.11 : Quality of Service of the PHWCSs

Different Services	*Number of Weavers*		*Total*
	Satisfied	Not Satisfied	
Supply of Yarn	40	20	60
Supply of appliances	33	27	60
Loans to member weavers	12	48	60
Payment of Wage to members	22	38	60
Welfare package to members	2	58	60

number of members are unsatisfied for the tasks like supply of loans, payment of wage and welfare package to members.

For a variety of purposes like modernisation of looms, diversification of business, to meet the unforseen cosumption expenditures; Many-a-times, the Weavers are in need of finance. In addition to, for the purpose of restructuring and revitalising the unit, they are in need of all types of term loans. The PHWCS hardly meets these requirements, Tabel 11.12 amply demonstrates the fact that the percentage share of non-institutional sources and commercial banks remain at 51.61 percent of the total financial requirements, of the total financial requirements of the weavers.

Income Pattern of Weavers

From the study, it has been calculated, if an average labour

Table 11.12 : Source of Finance

Different Sources	*No. of House-holds*	*% Share of each Agency*
Govt. Schemes	02	3.33
Commercial Banks	25	41.66
Rural Banks	Nil	–
Co-operatives other than W.C.S.	02	3.33
Non-Institutional Sources	31	51.66
Total	**60**	**100.00**

devotes full time work for a month he will be able to produce 90 Towels and 25 Sarees. The wage rate for towels varies from Rs. 5 to Rs. 7. Thus in terms of towels the happens between Rs. 450 to Rs. 630.

Again, in terms of saree the wage rate ranges between Rs. 12 to Rs. 17. If a weaver household concentrates in the weaving of sarees he will be able to receive an income from Rs. 300 to Rs. 450 per month. Further, it has been reported that due to the improper supply of suitable yearn, the weavers remain unaffiliated, with their work. Thus, due to extremely lower income generating potential of this industry, it is to considered as a profession, rather it is a way of life. Table 11.8 makes it clear that majority of the weavers in this industry are part time workers and the percentage share of part time workers remains at 56.02 percent. Further in the total labour force of this industry the percentage share of ladies remains maximum at 42.17 percent.

Due to improper remuneration in this industry the traditional weavers have entered into other sectors of the economy in the form of agricultural labourers, construction workers, vegetables venders, Hawkers and like that. Thus lower income generating potential of this industry have disintegrated the social division of thę labour in this industry.

Due to the rigidity of the income at the lower level, coupled with high income-inelastic demand of the members makes a mismatch between the income and expenditure pattern. As a matter of fact, the weavers become forced to be indebted.

Table 11.13 highlights the average per capita monthly consumption expenditure of sample households. Maximum number of weaving households about 43.33 percent are found with lower consumption expenditure ranging Rs. 0 to 500. The per capita consumption expenditure of Rs. 2,000 and above are found minimum.

Table 11.13 : Average Monthly Per-capital Consumption Expenditure of Sample Households

Ranges of Monthly Expenditure (in Rs.)	*No. of Households*	*% Share of Each Range*
0 – 500	26	43.33
501 – 1000	20	33.33
1001 – 2000	11	18.33
2001 & above	03	5.00
Total	**60**	**100.00**

Table 11.14 highlights the different items in the basket of consumption. The percentage share of food items remains maximum at 74.0 percent. The expenditure incurred for house rent and other intoxicated items remains minimum. Thus Table 11.14 infers that as a major fraction of the current income is diverted towards food items, therefore the weavers are confronted with subsistence income.

Table 11.14 : Items of Consumption

Items of Consumption	*% Share of Each-item in the total expenditure of all the households*
Food	74.00
Clothing	5.00
House Rent	0.50
Tea and Coffee	3.00
Pan/Cigarette/Snuff	0.50
Alcoholic Drinks	1.00
Medicine	5.00
Miscellaneous	11.00
Total	**100.00**

Table 11.15 clarifies about the work environment of the weaves. The work environment has been judged on the basis of three parameters like adequate floor area, good roof electrification of the unit. As it is evident from Table 11.15 that 70 percent of total weavers are not available with electricity, therefore, the work environment is not certainly congenial.

Table 11.15 : Work Environment

Different Situations	*Yes*	*No*
Adequate Floor Area (More than 100 sq. ft.)	45 (75 %)	15 (25 %)
Good Roof (in tin, Asbestoes or Concrete)	18 (30 %)	42 (70 %)
Electrification of the Unit	22 (36.66 %)	38 (63.33 %)

Table 11.16 exhibits the number and percentage of weavers opting for modernisation and diversification. About 88.33 percent of weavers opt for modernisation and 58.33 percent of the weavers opt for diversification. The personal interview with the weavers reveal that the lack of proper encouragement from the PHWCSs and non-availability of adequate finance stand as the stumbling blocks on the path of modernisation and diversification of the industry.

Table 11.16 : Modernisation & Diversification

Options	*No. and Percentage of Weavers Opt*	*No. and Percentage of Weavers Don't Opt*
Modernisation	53 (88.33 %)	07 (11.66 %)
Diversification	35 (58.33 %)	25 (41.66 %)

N.B. : Data collected through primary survey and official papers have been analysed in the tables from 6 to 16.

Findings

On the basis of the different parameters studied in this paper, the following findings home emerged:

(i) The number of PHWCSs under the SHWCS, Orissa witnesses a declining trend and consequently a negative growth rate of

PHWCSs. (Table 11.1)

(ii) During 1990s the percentage growth of individual members under PHWCSs is not satisfactory in comparison to 1980s. (Table 11.1)

(iii) The amount of clothes remain unsold stands at 680.03 lakhs in the year 1993-94. (Table 11.2)

(iv) The growth rate of the number of PHWCS encounters zero rate of growth and number of individual members witnesses an ever increasing trend. (Table 11.3)

(v) On the basis of working capital and share capital the PHWCSs are sound. (Table 11.4)

(vi) No of loss making and no-profit/no-loss making PHWCSs are on rise (Table 11.5)

(viii) The glaring problem of PHWCSs relates wit unsold accumulated clothes of past years. (Table 11.6)

(viii) The sales price index in the year 1996-97 in comparison to 1992-93 happens at 57.71 percent rise in the price level of clothes produced by PHWCS. It is a better price situation. Thus in order to earn better profit, PHWCSs should be indulged in sales promotion activities. (Table 11.7)

(iv) The percentage share of female workers remains maximum at 42.17 percent and the percentage share of the child workers remains minimum at 22.28 percent. Table 11.9

(x) In order to ensure contineous production, many-a-time weavers collect raw-materials from the local-retail market and the whole-salers also. (Table 11.10).

(xi) Weavers mainly rely on non-institutional sources and commercial Banks to engulf the gap of finance. (Table 11.12)

(xii) Majority of the weavers about 95 percent are confronted with lower income expenditure due to their lower income. (Table 11.13).

(xiii) Substantial part of the total expenditure of the weavers is reflected in food only. (Table 11.14).

(xiv) At the onslaught of economic liberalisation and globalisation programmes of the economy during 1990s, all the marketing co-operatives in general and Handloom weavers Co-operatives in particular are no longer in safety-net. The subsidies in the yarn prices and price-subsidy in the products produced by PHWCSs have been stopped as a part and parcel of the economic liberalisation package. Thus PHWCSs have been compelled to accept the free-play of market mechanism and competition wit the MNCs, big business houses and big industrialists associated with different textile mills. So to say the last vestieges of Co-operatives handloom industry are expected to be cut-off by the liberalisation programme.

It is high time for the PHWCSs to be adaptable to a new business and commercial environment so created during 1990s. At present, the cumulative unsold stocks of final goods in the inventory of PHWCSs are supposed to be the major problems encountered by the PHWCSs. The anti-date for the said problems remains in perfect adaptability of PHWCSs to suit the changed market environment and introduction of a perfectly effective marketing strategy. A suitable protectionist policy can guarantee success. If the problems of PHWCSs are rectified, the member weavers can re-assume the built-in destiny on the path of their progress. In the back-drop of the plethora of problems, following suggestions may be forwarded.

(xv) In order to avert the problems of market, the PHWCSs should concentrate on sufficient product lining and product mix strategy for different segments in the market. They have to abandon the production of old, ill-fashioned and absolute items. As per the study, in order to earn profits, co-operatives can't raise the price-structure rather they must alter the pattern of production and supply of different items in conformity with latest fashion and design of the consumers. This requires a contineous periodical marketing research and better inventory management. The executives of PHWCSs, should be well trained by the Directorate of Textiles.

The PHWCs are the entrepreneurs and sellers. Total Revenue maximisation and profit-maximisation should be their ultimate goals. In the wake of these, the Co-operatives must find out the solutions for the four basic equations of production. They are :

What to produce ?

How to produce ?

Where to produce ?

Whom to produce ?

Better salesmanship demands a quantitative shift in the total products produced by the PHWCSs. Thus the equations of productions, should be transformed into the equations of better selling strategy. Therefore the ultimate aim of the seller is to be:-

What to sell ?

How to sell ?

Where to sell ?

Whom to sell ?

In the changed economic environment of 1990s, the above equations should be rightly solved, so that the PHWCSs as the sellers will come out with best success.

The merchandise of final goods so produced by PHWCSs must not be confined to the selling counters of the society. The products must be well advertised in a sufficient manner wit the help of different mass media, banners & posters in the crowded public places & campaigning.

As per the observation of the author, the PHWCSs don't levelling. A slip containing the name of the weavers, the name of PHWCS, the pattern of the product should be affixed on the respective item. So that a weaver & PHWCS can obtain the complain and suggestion as to the alteration and modification of the product. By this process, consumer's sovereignty is highly rewarded.

The PHWCS don't resort packaging. But the consumer's psychology is a complex phenomenon and he simply not only consumes the service of the product, rather he consumes the package of the product. Therefore the PHWCSs should lay great stress on packaging.

The colour, design and quality should be blended in such a manner that it will be easily recognised by the customers.

Mira Seth Commission Report submitted to the Ministry of Textiles on January 1997 should be implemented thoroughly due to its important recommendations as regards to subsidy, loan waiver scheme, loss guarantee scheme etc. Sufficient modernisation and diversification programme should be introduced. If Govt., different officials and workers affiliated with Directorate of Textiles and Asst. Directorate of Textiles, the executives of PHWCs and the Weavers themselves adapt a positive, sincere and honest attitudes, the PHWCSs can be successful in accomplishing its objectives. To conclude, " The Weavers Co-operatives have been in gruesome conditions, but they must no be allowed to die."

Notes and References

1) R.D. Bedi "Theory, History and Practise of Co-operation", International Publishing House, Merrut, 1997 edition.

2) S. Sundar and N. Mani Mekalai, "Problems of Women Workers in Handloom Industry at Vengamedu", Khadi Gramodyog, March, 1989, pp. 286.

3) Report of the village and Small Scale Industries Committee, 1991.

4) Orissa Handloom Basic Facts, published by Directorate of Textiles, Orissa, Bhubaneswar, 1993.

5) Orissa Handloom Basic Facts, Published by Directorare of Textiles, Orissa, Bhubaneswar, 1997.

6) Staistical Outline of Orissa, Published by Directorare of Economics and Statistics, Orissa, Bhubaneswar, 1995.

7) District Statistical Hand Book, Ganjam, 1993.

8) S. K. Panda, "Guide to Weavers" (Oriya) published by Directorate of Textiles, 1994.

12

Issues and Problems of Co-operatives in India

Dr. Sudhakar Patra*

I

As a voluntary movement co-operatives have become an integral part of India's democracy. Co-operatives have failed in India but it must succeed. This statement shows the need and importance of co-operatives in a country like India with diverse activities. This paper is an attempt to analyse the strength, management and problems of co-operatives in India.

There is a general feeling in the country that co-operatives have not done well. Our records are not so impressive as compared to other countries of the world. Yet, nobody can deny that the co-operative movement in India is the largest co-operative movement in the world. There are more than 3.5 lakhs of Co-operative Societies with 16 crores membership and Rs. 62,500 crores working capital. During Last 90 years of existence since emergence in 1904 in an enactment of Credit Co-operative societies Act. It has diversified and emerged as a very powerful sector of the Indian economy alongwith the private and public sector. This sector is leading in production of sugar, fertiliser, dairy, housing and marketing of agricultural produce. Credit and marketing societies have played a significant role in the development of rural door extricating them from the clutches of money lenders and private traders. During 32 years of it's existence, NAFED'S turnover reached Rs. 400 crores, including Rs. 150 crores of export

* Deptt. of Economics, N.C. College, Jajpur (Orissa)

business. Some of the state-level marketing co-operative federations have emerged equally strong and lead in procurement, input supply, processing and export promotion.

IFFCO & KRIBHCO have set records in fertiliser production. They are contributing to 33 per cent of national production of fertiliser. Licences of setting up 283 Co-operative sugar mills were issued, out of them 222 has already been set up till 1992. Sugar production in co-operative sector is 60 per cent of the annual production of sugar in the country. The value of goods marketed by our co-operative milk societies have reached more than Rs. 6,000 crores. As many as 2442 processing units have been set up in co-operative sector, out of them 113 are soil processing units. Thanks to the initiative of the National Co-operatives Development Corporation for creation of 19447 lakhs tonnes of the storage capacity. As many as 230 cold storage plants are functioning. There are more than 60 dairy co-operatives with nearly 75 Lakh members. These societies in 1992 were daily collecting 97.1 lakhs kgs. of milk, and supplying 80 lakhs litres of milk through 524 milk supply centres.

Despite these achievement there are many weakness in Co-operatives:-

1. Competition from other sector is increasing and Co-operatives are losing their share in the market.
2. Average membership continues to be low.
3. Deposits going down.

India is a country composed of villages, primarily engaged in agriculture and allied activities. Due to uneven distribution of land the landless poor are unable to participate effectively and contribute to agricultural production. As agriculture still alters in the monsoon the worst sufferers are the landless, women and rural artisans. In the event of natural calamities such as floods, drought, pest attack, crop failure etc., the Scheduled Castes and Tribes are most affected as they are landless. Rural artisans such as carpenters, blacksmiths, cobblers, well diggers, masons, barbers, dhobis, who once served as support structure to agriculture under the Zamindari system are also affected either due to culmination of Zamindari or technological transformation in agriculture. The system of social stratification has affected these segments further and subjected them to the practice of social inequality in the form of casteism, untouchability, exploitation, social segregation and social distance. Moreover, the peopie belonging to the lower echelons in the social hierarchy had to lead a life of subordination owing to socio-economic domination of upper caste and class people. The people who are affected in one way or other or experience socio-economic alienation, deprivation, inequality, humiliation etc. are termed as weaker segments for whom programmes of social justice have been felt needed.

Co-Operative Movement in India

The Co-operative movement strives to provide opportunity to these weaker segments by pooling their resources leading to collective and co-operative social action and thereby mitigates their problems and promotes development. The concept of co-operation covered and took concrete shape in India way back in 1904 since introduction of Co-operative Credit Societies Act—a measure designed to eradicate rural indebtedness and provide institutional credit to the weaker segments. Since then the co-operative movement has progressed and penetrated all walks of rural social life, especially in fields of credit transaction, supply of farm inputs, processing, marketing and employment generation. Later organisation of industrial co-operatives specifically meant for women and rural artisans accelerated the process of rural industrialisation. As a voluntary movement, cooperation has now become an integral part of India's roots in democracy, formed part of India' development strategy and paved the way for the socio-economic upliftment of the weaker segments.

The co-operative movement is based primarily on the "spirit of working together" and thereby eliminates monopoly of individuals. It is based on the principle of open and voluntary membership, democratic participation and control, equality and fair distribution of benefits. The co-operative organisation is marked by mutual help and social welfare of individual members.

The definition of co-operative itself highlights social justice and the need to organise co-operatives to bring the weaker segments under its fold for elimination of their socio-economic problems. Co-operation is a form of organisation in which persons voluntarily assist one another on the basis of equality for the promotion of their economic interest. Those who come together have a common economic aim which they cannot achieve by individual isolated action, because of the economic position of large majority of them. The element of individual weakness is overcome by self-help pooling of their resources and by strengthening the bond of moral solidarity between them.

Canons of Co-operatives

(a) Generation of Awareness

Enrolment into co-operatives exposes the rural poor to the avenues of development, their rights, duties, provisions in co-operatives and to the benefits of co-operative action. Co-operative education undertaken accelerates the process of awareness generation and co-operative action leading to development of unity, integrity, co-existence, mutual aid, participation in co-operative business etc.

b) Elimination of Inequality

One of the principles of co-operation is equality and practice of democracy in co-operative endeavor. The rural poor and affected segments are brought under the fold of co-operation for the promotion of economic betterment irrespective of their personal background of caste, class and creed. The co-operative action demands that members should remove their personal prejudices and engage in gainful activity on the basis of equality. This tendency ultimately results in elimination of inequality.

c) Eradication of Untouchability

As there is no chance for social identify of individual members in co-operative business transactions, the social evil of untouchability is gradually eliminated from the minds of members.

d) Promotions of Co-existence

Collective and co-operative action stimulates co-existence resulting in recognition of problems of individuals and assistance for the amelioration. This sense of togetherness and recognition of common problems leads the participating members to interdependence and peaceful co-existence.

e) Practice of Democracy

One of the principles of co-operation relates to democratic control being exercised by the owners of co-operative i.e. the members. This provides an opportunity to all members to participate equally in the affairs of co-operative management and exercise their right of control in such a way that it results in equitable distribution of benefits to all members. Equality is practised in the administration of co-operatives by offering one vote to each member irrespective of their personal background, which is the principle of democracy.

f) Decentralisation of Leadership

The organisation of co-operatives in village has not only facilitated the practice of the values of democracy at the micro level but also ensured the decentralisation of leadership amongst the members regardless of their socio-economic status. To be specific the people belonging to lower castes, women and rural artisans who were once neglected, are now offered the opportunity to become office-bearers either through contest or through nomination and thereby share power in co-operative management. Further more, the organisation of co-operatives exclusively meant for women, Scheduled Castes and Tribes and rural artisans had further accelerated the process of development of leadership amongst these segments.

g) Development of Women

Indian women, due to the practice of sex bias inequality and other socio-economic restrictions are subjected to exploitation, domination, harassment etc. The organisation of co-operatives particularly industrial co-operatives have provided them with opportunities for permanent employment and continuous income flow. Women are also very conscious now of their potential and independently establish rural industrial enterprises through co-operation which has led to the development of women's entrepreneurship.

h) Rural Industrialisation

Besides, women, rural artisans are now-a-days brought under the fold of co-operative action through the establishment of guilds for rural artisans which act as a forum for their development. The establishment of guilds for artisans ensured tapping of fiscal assistance with subsidy from government for generation of employment. This has helped to a great extent in poverty alleviation, checking migration and indebtedness in their midst.

i) Social Solidarity

In view of the collective action under the fold of co-operation there emerges social solidarity amongst the participating members and leads to the development of certain socio-psychological characters such as 'we' feeling, homogeneity of interest, unity in the promotion of interest, integrity and morality and in business transaction leading to togetherness, peaceful coexistence and communal harmony which in turn, promote social solidarity.

Management of Co-operatives

Within the power structure of every society, certain vital integral individuals operate within groups to promote, stimulate, guide, or otherwise influence members to action. Such activity has been called leadership and the individuals have been referred to as leaders, power-holders, men of power, power centres, and power elite. According to Stogdill, "Leadership may be considered as the process of influencing the activities of an organised group in its efforts towards goal setting and goal achievement". According to this definition, the minimum social conditions which permit the existence of leadership are as follows:-

— a group

— common task

— differentiated responsibility

Bernard states that, "Leader is any person who is more than ordinarily efficient in carrying psycho-social stimuli to others and is thus effective in conditioning collective responses". This being the case, the leaders are those who are able to identify themselves socially and psychologically with the group and work in a manner that results in the fulfillment of the goals of the organised group. There must be both special influence and a number of persons involved. This establishes the influence potentiality of the ledgers who get things done willingly by followers, which promotes their socio-economic conditions.

A leader is a person who by virtue of the magnetism of his personality, social status or economic affluence is able to command respect from or dominate the wills of groups of persons so as to be able to mould and direct their energies into channels of his choice. He is the one who is respected and obeyed by his followers. Unless respect and obedience are simultaneously present there can be no effective leadership.

There is also hierarchy among leaders. The superior leaders may be called primary leaders. Junior to these primary leaders there are other leaders who may be called secondary leaders. The secondary leaders are younger than primary leaders and they are also inferior in status. In actual practical all practice and field work are entrusted to the secondary leaders and the primary leaders function as advisors.

Leadership on Co-operatives

Leadership in co-operatives broadly falls into the following categories:

1. Membership leaders.
2. Management leaders.
3. Official leaders.

Membership leaders are the initiators, promoters of co-operatives and directors elected by members. Management leaders are the professional men employed for the day-to-day management of the affairs of the co-operatives. The official leaders include the extension workers and the government officials who are engaged in the administration of co-operatives societies act and in the organisation, administration and supervision of co-operatives. The efficient functioning of co-operative democracy depends on the relative roles of these three categories and their characteristics.

The leadership studies conducted on co-operatives reveals that high caste and class middle to old aged people were selected to leadership position who on account of obvious reasons were unable to manifest dynamism in their functions. In rural co-operatives the poor villagers are unable to feel free in the midst of rich land owners and hence they are unable to participate effectively and have their say in co-operative administration.

The characteristics of management leaders are very much influenced by socio-economic background of our country. To be specific, Indian social structure is marked by inequality, caste, and class bound hierarchy. The economic system in India is also equally known for imbalanced and uneven distribution of means of production and heavy concentration on upper strata. Therefore our socio-economic systems are not effective for functioning and practice of co-operative democracy.

In addition to socio-economic inequality other aspects such as illiteracy, ignorance, unawareness-syndrome, subordination, inferiority complex, lack of initiative on the part of the members, affect emergence and development of democratic leadership in co-operatives. However, of late, spread of formal and non-formal education in rural areas has minimised this problem.

In order to improve its efficiency, the question of proper management of co-operative arises. Management is sine-qua-non for better results and service to the members. This involves proper combination and co-ordination between membership leaders and the staff, appointed by co-operatives to run the day-to-day affairs. It is expected that under the guidance of the directors, the members must draw policy decisions, and the staff must implement the same. This function presupposes complementary roles between these two types of leaders. But many a time these leaders fail to develop complementary discharge of functions to the utmost satisfaction of members. Hence they find themselves at loggerheads, resulting ultimately in indifference, insubordination and exploitation.

The third, typology of leaders i.e. official leaders are meant for the elimination of mismanagement in co-operative societies affairs through implementation of co-operative societies Act. But in actual practice this group seems to overshadow both membership and management leaders as the co-operative movement in India is most spontaneous but State sponsored. In view of this, the Government invariably increase control over co-operatives and thereby paves the way for bureaucratic and political interference in the affairs of co-operatives. Consequently there seem to develop a nexus amongst management, official and political leaders by overthrowing the power of member leaders. As long as this type of tendency prevails in the co-operatives, the movement will hardly succeed in its attempts to work for the socio-economic emancipation of weaker, downtrodden and poverty stricken segments in our society. It is high time now that these three categories of leaders namely membership, management and official leaders show their differences and act collectively with co-operatives spirit, in the interest of their respective co-operative societies community and society at large.

Agricultural Co-operatives

In India crop fails either due to excessive rain or lack of it. Thanks to advanced pest control and improved cultivation systems. The non-monsoon related causes of crop failure have been successfully controlled. However, fragmentation of holdings, increase in input costs, etc. make agricultural production less economical. The marketing side is also no good. The terms of trade have been adverse to agricultural sector. Over 200 million are toiling in the fields to contribute 32 per cent of our GNP while 36 million in the industrial sector account for 28 per cent and 60 million in the tertiary sector 40 per cent poor marketing facilities, intervention of middlemen. etc cut the earnings of farmers. On the marketing side, earnest efforts to protect the poor farmers are therefore called for. "The prosperity of agriculturists and success of any policy of general agricultural improvement depend to a very large degree on the facilities which the agricultural community has at its disposal for marketing to the best advantage as much of its produce as of its surplus". This view of the Royal Commission on Agriculture made 62 years ago holds good even now. An improved system of marketing is the need of the hour. In this article, the need for strengthening co-operative marketing is highlighted.

Marketing Co-operatives

Marketing co-operatives for agricultural produce can well serve farmers interests. The main objective of marketing co-operatives is to do away with middlemen and thereby ensure a relatively higher price for the producers and at the same time a relatively lower price for the consumers.

The first co-operative society was formed in Hubli in 1905. It was designed to encourage cultivation of improved cotton introduced by the Agricultural Department and to sell it collectively. In 1918, the South Canara Planters Co-operative Sale Society was formed in the then composite Madras Province. The Objective was joint-sale of product. In the later years a few more societies were formed. They advanced loans to members to enable them to avoid distress sale of their produce. The Royal Commission stressed the need for group marketing instead of individual marketing. The Central Banking Enquiry Committee (1931) also underlined need for organised marketing. The XI Conference of Registrars of Co-operative Societies (1934) emphasised the importance of co-operative marketing. The co-operative planning Committee (1945) took up an ambitious plan for achieving co-operative marketing covering at least 25 per cent of marketable surplus in a span of 10 years by forming society for a group of 200 villages. All these efforts were only partly successful.

The All-India Rural Credit Survey Committee (1954) brought to light the dismal performance of the existing marketing co-operatives. In a sample of 75 districts surveyed, 63 districts did not have any co-operative marketing society. The committee suggested among other things reorganisation and linking of credit with marketing. The credit and marketing societies were to function in unison so that production and marketing are streamlined helping the farmers and at the same time improving viability of the societies. In 1958 the National Agricultural Co-operative Marketing Federation (NAFED) was established as the apex body of marketing co-operatives. Its main functions are co-ordination and promotion of marketing activities of its members. It also provides marketing intelligence.

In 1963, the National Co-operative Development Corporation (NCDC) was set up on the basis of the recommendations of the All India Rural Credit Survey Committee. The NCDC promotes programmes relating to processing, storage and marketing of agricultural produce through co-operative societies and other allied activities. It also extends financial assistance to the co-operative marketing societies.

The Dantwala Committee (1966) stressed the need for co-operation and integration among the various co-operative organisations after reviewing the pattern of co-operative marketing distribution of inputs to farmers and supply of consumer products. In 1968 the RBI conducted a survey of the co-operative marketing scenario to examine the factors that facilitated the growth of co-operatives. The RBI was on the view that effective linking of credit with marketing was necessary.

Structure and Services

At the State Level, Co-operative marketing is of two tier system with primary marketing societies at the taluk level and State Co-operative Marketing Federation as apex body. The expert Committee on co-operative marketing recommended the two-tier system.

In certain states there is three-tier system with district marketing society in the middle. At the national level NAFED serves as the apex institution. The State Marketing Federation are members of NAFED. The district marketing societies are also federated with it in some cases.

There are 29 states level marketing federations, 173 district/ regional marketing co-operative societies, 2633 general purpose primary marketing societies and 3290 special commodities societies. Their functionaries are operating as a network.

The main functions of the marketing societies are:-

i) arranging the sale of produce,
ii) outright purchase of produce, especially from small farmers,
iii) advancing loans to members on the security of their produce,
iv) renting or hiring godowns and processing yards to facilitate storage and processing of produce belonging to members,
v) transporting produce from members' residence or farms to the market place,
vi) supply of agricultural inputs such as seeds, fertilisers, and pesticides to members,
vii) distributing essential commodities to the public through DPS,
viii) undertaking the processing of produce and
ix) grading and extension works.

Achievement

The value of agricultural produce marketed through the co-operatives was of the order or Rs. 53 crores in 1955-56. It went up to Rs. 3902 crores in 1987-88. By 1990 it was planned to raise the figure to Rs. 5000/- crores. In recent years there has been a downward trend. In all, about 8-10 per cent of marketed surplus is routed through co-operatives.

Among the states, Maharashtra, Uttar Pradesh, Gujarat, Punjab, Karnataka, Tamil Nadu, and Haryana come in the order of their importance. Of the Rs. 3,092 crores worth of produce marketed through the co-oepratives in 1987-88, the seven states along accounted for Rs. 3374 crores or about 85 per cent. The next best performance area of co-operative marketing societies is in respect of supply of agricultural inputs, such as fertilizers, improved seeds, pesticides, agricultural machinery and implements. From. Rs. 392 crores, the value of these supplies rose to Rs. 1675 crores in 1984-85. Over 70,000 retail depots all over the country are engaged in the distribution of these inputs.

Strengthening Co-operatives

Co-operative marketing efforts need strengthening. Improvement in organisational, operation, financial, personnel and marketing areas are required.

Marketing societies need to be linked with credit societies and consumer co-operatives. Every unit should have a strong co-operative base. Size of membership is a factor of significance. Individual producers have to be enrolled as members. Majority of producers are outside the ambit of co-operative marketing system and many members are only partially using the system. These are the basic weaknesses. Member enrolment must be made mandatory for anyone seeking service from the co-operatives 50 per cent of PCSM are making profits, 37 per cent incur losses. Broad-based operations alone can ensure viability.

Supply of inputs to agriculturists is another operation where marketing skill is necessary. Co-operatives are no more monopoly suppliers as they were till 1969. Private traders will outdo the co-operatives, unless PCSMs adopt sound marketing practices. This is a potential area of business. Procurement operations of the State, Governments and the Food corporation of India should be streamlined so that NAFED and State Co-operative. Marketing Federation do not compete with each other. Outright purchase of the surplus from small and marginal farmers should be stepped up so that farmers do not fall prey to the evil designs of private traders. It is necessary to evolve a command area for making necessary operations viable.

Finances of co-operatives are not always that good. Membership subscription is very small. Hence Government participation becomes necessary. Financing of co-operatives by NABARD is to be stepped up. The higher allocation for priority sector proposed in the VIII Plan is a welcome sign.

Staffing of co-operative marketing is another neglected area. Marketing is a competitive field. To be successful in that line a unit has to be professionally managed.

Role of Women in Co-operatives

One great failure is the insignificant role assigned to women participation in co-operatives. It is very disturbing to point out that while we have done well in other sectors, in case of the women co-operative sector, we have gone down rather than going up. The position of women co-operative during last four decades in inputs has gone from bad to worse. Their number was 4809 in June 1998. In 1992 Punjab had the highest number of 2,195 societies followed by 772 in Andhra Pradesh, 500 in Maharashtra, 243 in Gujarat, 228 in Karnataka, 197 in West Bengal, 127 in Uttar Pradesh and about 1001 societies in the rest of the states. Against 16 crores of membership, the number of women co-operatives is only 3.43 lakhs, paid-up capital Rs. 534 lakhs and working capital only Rs. 1,600 Lakhs.

In rural co-operative, which are the largest in the country, there may be involvement of members. In some states, bye-laws provide that women cannot become members. Wherever such provisions are not there, women connected with the dominant interest in the society, are enrolled as members as there is a provisions to co-opt one to two PCSMs in the board of directors. Such directors have no independent voice. Co-operation of few members is not sufficient when we think of the role of women who account for 50 per cent of the target group. What is needed is active involvement and participation of rural women which will act as an agent of change in the rural scenario.

The involvement of women will result in:

1. Increased membership
2. Increased paid-up share capital and increased deposits
3. Increased turnover and business viability.
4. Devoted and loyal membership.

In urban areas, some societies in handicrafts cottage industries, thrift and credit have been organised, but involvement in consumer activities is insignificant. There may be some PCSMs co-operative stores in the country. There may be a few Mahila Nagrik Co-operative Bank. But in general the women have been deprived of the benefit of co-operatives. In a few consumers co-operatives, where membership is larger, it has been proved that those societies have done better. In Orissa with the support of Mahila Vikash Maha Mandal Ltd., Co-operative electronics Units dealing with radios, cassette recorders, voltage stabilisers, electronic clocks and lamps have been set up. These goods are manufactured by the women co-operatives. Encouraged by this experiment Govt. of India proposes to set up 400 such Co-ops. Another back-up to women coops. was provided by Indian Telephone Industries, which has set up five women Industrial Coop. ancillary units. KVI commission has also helped women Co-ops. in processing of cereals, masala grinding etc. Handicraft Corporations have also helped in development of some societies.

One the whole, women continued to play as insignificant role in the development of the co-operative sector. The greater participation of women can ensure the following benefits.

1. Creating social awareness
2. Creating entrepreneurship
    a) Capital needed is small
    b) Know-how of the trade is available.
3. Development of skill
4. Sources of income
5. Reducing unemployment
6. Effective participation in management.

Besides organisation of women in exclusive co-ops, we can have better involvement of women in ordinary co-operatives in following ways :

i) By not debarring the women membership as per the provision of by-laws in some states.

ii) Joint membership also denies legitimate right of the women to become independent member of the society.

II

In the light of the aforesaid analysis in the macro-frame, we can undertake a micro-level study regarding the problem of over-dues in co-operative banks in a tribal concentrated district Boudh in Orissa. The study provides future guidelines to mitigate the problem of over-dues in the co-operative sector. The analysis of data highlights some interesting finding to formulate policy measures for the successful target-oriented banking activities in tribal India.

Objectives of the Study

The specific objectives of this study are as follows :

i) To study the performance and development of agricultural credit through Boudh Central Co-operative Bank.

ii) To analyse the reasons for non-repayment of loans and problems of overdues.

iii) To find out the extent of borrowing and its relation with operational holdings of the borrowers.

iv) To highlight weakness and problems of co-operative bank and to provide suggestions for efficient management of the co-operative banks.

Data Base and Framework

Boudh Central Co-operative bank is situated at the heart of district headquarter of Phulbani. The data are collected in printed questionnaire from the borrowers of agricultural loan belonging to the villages of Teraduda, Gudari, Rajangi, and Kaladi. The borrowers are selected randomly from the list provided by the Boudh Central Co-operative Bank. Purposefully the borrowers are selected from nearby villages within the 6 (six) kilometers of the bank and data are collected on personal inquiry basis. The collected data are classified and tabulated to facilitate analysis.

Terms of Loans

Central Co-operative bank advances loans to (a) Primary agricultural Co-operative societies (PACS) (b) Firm loan to farmers, (c) Non-firm loan for consumer durable. Firm loans are sanctioned to farmers within the area of operation on land mortgage basis and the amount of loan depends on the operational land (irrigated and un-irrigated) owned by the borrower. For example a farmer with one acre of land can avail maximum amount of crop. loan Rs. 3,300/- for khariff crop in case of irrigated and Rs. 1,900/- in case of un-irrigated land. For sugarcane cultivation maximum limit of loan is Rs. 8,000/-. The maximum limit for crop loan is Rs. 10,000/- and for purchase of pumpset it is Rs. 20,000.

The interest rate on loans depends on purpose and amount of loan. The interest rate varies from 13 per cent to 18 per cent. Central Co-operative bank advances loans to PACS at 14 per cent interest and PACS advance loans to members at 16.5 per cent. The interest rates changes as per the Reserve Bank of India guidelines. Crop loans are advanced on short term basis for a period of one year. Consumer durable loans are advanced for a period of three years and maximum period of repayment is usually seven years.

Analysis and Results

The borrowers of firm loan for agriculture and allied activities are classified by the purpose of loan which is presented in Table 12.1. Out of 50 borrowers, crop loans are advanced to 23 which constitute 46 per cent of total borrowers. Due to dry land and rain-fed area of Phulbani 12 borrowers (24 per cent) are given loans for digging well and tubewells. Only three persons are advanced loan for purchase of pump sets and seven persons for plantation.

Table 12.1 : Classification of Borrowers by Purpose

Sl. No.	*Purpose*	*No. of Borrowers*	*Percentage*
1.	Agriculture/Crop	23	46.00
2.	Digging Well/Tube-well	12	24.00
3.	Plantation	7	14.00
4.	Development of old well/pond	5	10.00
5.	Purchase of Diesel Engine/Pump	3	6.00
	Total	50	100.00

The crop loan to 23 borrowers are sanctioned for a period of one year where as other loans are medium loans for three years.

The borrowers are classified according to the amount loans taken and it is found that 18 respondents (36 per cent) belong to Rs. 4,000—Rs. 5,999 class. In this class 13 borrowers are defaulters in repayment of loans. Only four persons have taken loan above Rs. 10,000 and six persons below Rs. 2,000.

Table 12.2 : Amount of Loan Borrowed

Sl. No.	*Loan (Rs.)*	*No. of Borro-wers*	*%age*	*No. of defau-lters*	*%age of defaul-ters to total borro-wers*
1.	Below 2,000	6	12.0	3	6.0
2.	2000–3,999	11	22.0	5	10.0
3.	4,000–5,999	18	36.0	13	26.0
4.	6,000–7,999	6	12.0	5	10.0
5.	8,000–9,999	5	10.0	2	4.0
6.	10,000 and above	4	8.0	4	8.0
	Total	**50**	**100.0**	**32**	**64.0**

The amount of loan sanctioned depends on purpose and operational land holding of the person. Sixty four percent borrowers are defaulters who do not repay the loan in proper installments fixed by the co-operative bank. Thirty percent of borrowers have taken loan above Rs. 6,000 where as 70 per cent have taken less than Rs. 5,999 which indicates that more loans are given to farmers with less operational land holdings, Central Co-operative Bank sanctions loans as per government directions under IRDP, ERRP schemes.

The causes for non-repayment of loans in the time are given Table 12.3. Out of total 32 defaulters, 11 borrowers do not repay due to drought conditions during 1997-98. Thirteen borrowers state that agriculture income is not sufficient to repay the loans. Due to higher consumption and low market price, there is no agricultural surplus income. Three respondents could not repay the loan due to unforeseen medical expenditures and family burden.

Table 12.3 : Causes for Non-Repayment of Loans

Sl. No.	Causes	No. of Defaulters	Percentage
1.	Less Agricultural Income	13	40.6
2.	Draught conditions	11	34.4
3.	Family burden and medical causes	3	9.4
4.	Miscellaneous	5	15.6
	Total	**32**	**100.0**

Thirty eight per cent of the borrowers are small farmers having 1.0 acre to 2.5 acre land holdings. There are nine marginal farmers and eleven farmers having more than five acres of land are among the fifty borrowers. It is clear from Table 12.4 that small farmers can easily mortgage their land holding to avail agricultural loans from co-operative banks.

Table 12.4 : Borrowers by their Operational Holdings

Sl. No.	Land (Acres)	No. of Borrowers	Percentage
1.	Less than 1.0 acre	9	18.0
2.	1–0–2.5	19	38.0
3.	2.5–5.0	11	22.0
4.	5.0–7.5	8	16.0
5.	7.5 and above	3	6.0
	Total	**50**	**100.0**

Observations

Co-operative banks are the most important source of institutional rural credit. The small and marginal farmers mostly depend on these co-operative banks for short term kharif and rabi crop loans. The Boudha Central Co-operative bank under study has not been successful in making profits due to non-repayment of loans in time. The bank is not effectively managed due to lack of proper identification of beneficiaries and political pressures to sanction loans.

On the other hand agriculture is not a lucrative occupation in Phulbani district as the land is rain-fed dry land. The agriculture in Phulbani is a gamble of monsoon and a good crop year is always followed by a drought year in this area. So the borrowers and farmers are not able to repay the loans in time. Further, an increase in output due to good crop results in sharp fall in price of the commodities in the local markets.

The co-operative bank is forced to sanction loans to the people under IRDP, ERRP and other schemes without the credit worthiness of the borrowers which result in non-repayment of loans. The present study of Boudh Central Co-operative Bank provide similar results as other Central, Co-operative Banks of the state faces the problems of overdue to loans.

Conclusion and Suggestions

The working of the Co-Operative movement is not quite satisfaction even though there is a tremendous increase in the number of Co-Operative banks and societies. Their total membership and amount of loans given may sound spectacular when we compare the figures over a period. The amount of overdues is also increasing with the growth of the movement. The funds of co-operative banks and societies and after misused and mismanaged.

The following conclusions can be made out of the present study.

i) Maximum number of borrowers of Central Co-operative Bank avail short term crop loan.

ii) Borrowers within loan range Rs. 4,000–6,000 are largely defaulters.

iii) Draught conditions and less agricultural surplus income are the main causes of non-repayment of loans.

iv) Small farmers are the maximum beneficiaries of co-operative loans.

It is futile hope to eradicate the poverty of rural masses with co-operation alone when movement is not functioning properly. There is an urgent need to rethink and revitalise co-operative banks and societies. Some of the curative suggestions are as follows:

i) Weaker segments of the society should be given priority in sanction of loans according to the credit worthiness of borrowers.

ii) Sanction of loans should be made strictly as per the principles and provisions and it should be away from pressures of management and politics.

iii) Properly trained and bank management degree holders should be given appointment in higher posts of the co-operative banks.

iv) Periodical review and training be conducted for all co-operative banks.

v) Women should be given equal opportunity with men in co-operative sector.

vi) Loan recovery procedures should be strictly followed and defaulting should be checked.

References

Attwood D.W. and B.S. Baviskar (ed) (1988): Who Shares? Co-operatives and Rural Development, Oxford University Press, New Delhi.

Gurusamy S. (1994); Strength in Co-operation, Social Welfare, Vol. 41, May, 1994, Page 14-15.

IGNOV (1990): Rural Development Administration, RD.D1, Block-3, Ch.1.

Yesudian P.J. (1971): Rural Credit and Nationalisation of Commercial Banks in India, Economical Christian Centre Publication, Bangalore, pp.10-19.

13

Agricultural Financing and Problems of Overdues

Dr. R. N. Mishra*

Agriculture occupies a significant place and has been regarded as the 'back bone' of Indian economy. India is a country of villages. About 80 per cent of its population reside in the villages and agriculture constitutes the primary occupation of about 70 per cent of population of our country. It provides employment to about three-fourth of the working population and accounts for about 50 percent of the national income. Even to-day agriculture in India is taken as a 'way of life' than a mode of business.

The importance of agriculture cannot be ignored despite rapid industrialisation in the country. To realise the goal of a modern welfare state it has become necessary not only to achieve self-sufficiency in matters of food and agricultural raw-material, but to highly mechanised agriculture so as to throw up surpluses to be made available for investment in other sectors of economy as well. In India, prior to the year 1950, agriculture was neglected sector and no deliberate effort was made by the government to uplift the living standard of cultivators. For development of the agriculture, the government is making all out effort since 1950's. But, still the growth rate of agricultural output is not impressive.

Agriculture is no doubt an important industry and like other industries it also requires capital. From among the various factors

* Dr. Mishra belongs to the faculty of commerce, Science College, Hinjlicut (Orissa)

for the growth of agriculture, non-availability of adequate and timely agricultural credit is one of the reasons for low productivity. Agriculture cannot develop unless credit facilities are available to the peasantry. The supply of credit will be highly effective in rehabilitating the agriculturists. The need for such credit has become all the more important in the context of new strategy and the introduction of high yielding varieties of crops.

For rapid agricultural growth, adequate agricultural credit facility is highly essential. It is also axiomatic that credit requirements in agriculture cannot be met by private individual resources alone. Profit, being the sole guiding principle of the private money-lenders, they cannot meet the desirable requirement of the farmers. Their financing principles will not help the needy farmers. The farmer is not only to be helped with a loan, but also be given the necessary guidance to make the most effective use of it, so that he may maximise his earnings from the land resources. Agricultural credit extended to farmers is of three types: short terms to purchase seeds, manure, fodder etc.; medium term to purchase cattle and agricultural implements, and long term finance for making permanent improvement in land for reclamation and for constructing well or dug well etc.

Because of vast gap in the supply and need of credit in the vital sector of the economy, the multi agency approach is initiated. The agricultural credit agencies include co-operatives, commercial banks and regional rural banks, government and private agencies.

Prior to the co-operative movement, a vast number of peasants were caught in the clutches of unscrupulous private money lenders. "The private village money-lenders, because of their monopolistic position in the sphere of agricultural finance then had held a large number of indebted peasants in a state of bondage which almost amounted to a sort of semi-slavery"[1]. To save the peasants from the clutches of money-lenders, co-operatives played a very important role, but it is felt that the co-operatives alone cannot meet the different credit requirements of Indian farmers. So a number of Commercial Banks nationalised and Regional Rural Banks (RRBs) have been established in the rural areas of the country to meet the credit requirements of the farmers.

1. Desai, S.S.M., Rural Banking in India, Himalaya Publishing House, Delhi, 1986, p. 200.

With the increasing institutionalisation of agricultural credit, the problem of farmers indebtedness has achieved a new dimension. The farmer is able to get more finance due to multi-agency approach and the burden of debt is also increasing day by day. So far the farmers it made them difficult to repay the advances in time. This non-repayment of agricultural dues has caused serious concern to the agricultural credit system as a whole. When a loanee fails to repay his instalment amount within the stipulate time, the amount is considered as overdue. To-day the mounting overdues of financial institutions; Co-operatives, commercial banks and RRBs has almost paralyzed the country's agricultural credit structure designed for increasing agricultural productivity. The accumulation of overdues has threatened to rob the rural credit institutions and their financing ability. If this scenario is allowed to continue there is very fear that in due course of time the credit institutions would stop financing to agricultural sector. Ultimately the strategy of agricultural development may prove to be a failure.

Objective and Scope of the Study

The problem of recovery of agricultural credit has became a constant source of anxiety for the financing institutions and a lion's share of the banks' funds remain locked. It is observed that on an average banks have to bear the burden of more than 50 per cent of overdues in the state of Orissa on agricultural loans. This results in curtailing the recycling of funds and depriving several new deserving cases.

The present study being affect finding research, aims at finding out the magnitude of the problem, the repayment behaviour of the loanees and different causes of mounting overdues in the agricultural credit sector.

Since it is empirical in nature, the study is confined to only the undivided districts of Southern Orissa viz., Ganjam, Koraput and Phulbani. The scope of the study is made limited only the agricultural finance provided by rural lending institutions; co-operative banks, commercial banks and RRBs non-institutional agencies in the region. Out of the various problems in the agricultural credit sector, because of its acuteness, only the problem of the overdues is selected for the study.

Mounting Overdues in Agricultural Credit

Overdue in agricultural credit is a very serious problem. It undermines the soundness of credit structure of banking institutions. The ever mounting overdues have created an alarming situation during last several years.

This chapter deals with the defaults of various kinds, at borrowers level and institutional level. The survey method has been adopted to study 300 sample borrowers of three districts viz., Ganjam, Korapur and Phulbani of Southern Orissa for the purpose. The finance given by the non-institutional agencies in the field of agriculture can not be ignored in this context. Therefore, an analysis of the agricultural finance provided by the non-institutional agencies to the sample borrowers also has been undertaken and their repayment style has been x-rayed in this chapter.

Analysis has been made in this Chapter from different angles in case of recovery of different categories which will depict a clear picture of overdues in agricultural finance in the three study districts from 1985-86 to 1995-96.

Default at Borrowers Level

Three hundred sample borrowers have been selected from three Southern districts of Orissa. From among the borrowers, 231 (77 per cent) are found defaulters. The district wise types of defaulters is illustrated in the Table 13.1.

Table 13.1 : Types of Defaulters

Name of Districts	*No. of borrowers*	*No. of defaulters*		*Total defaulters*	*%age of defaulters*
		Chronic	*Casual*		
Ganjam	140	52 (44.8)	64 (55.2)	116	82.8
Koraput	130	37 (37.7)	61 (62.3)	98	75.3
Phulbani	30	5 (29.4)	12 (70.6)	17	56.6
Total	**300**	**94 (40.6)**	**137 (59.4)**	**231**	**77.0**

Figures in brackets indicate percentage to total number defaulters.
Source : Compiled from questionnaire

The number of defaulters is the highest 116 (82.8 percent) in Ganjam, followed by 98 (75.3 percent) in Koraput and 17 (5.6 percent) in Phulbani districts. From among the total defaulters, chronic defaulters are 94 (40.6 percent) and casual 137 (59.3 percent) during the period of study. The chronic defaulters are the highest 52 (44.8 percent) in Ganjam, followed by 37 (37.7 percent) in Karaput and 5 (29.4 percent) in Phulbani districts.

To study the behavioural attitude of the sample beneficiaries in repayment of institutional credit the chi-square test has been used both at 5 percent and at 1 per cent level of significance. Since calculated value is greater than the table value the borrowers of these districts do not show any similar tendency regarding repayment of institutional loans. Since the sample borrowers are different in their socio-economic status, their attitude in repayment of institutional loans differ. But when the districts are separated and two districts are selected at a time a study the behavioral attitude, different results emerge. The borrowers of Ganjam and Koraput districts have similar attitudes towards the repayment of institutional credit at 5 per cent and at 1 per cent level of significance. But the borrowers of Koraput and Phulbani districts possess different attitudes at 5 per cent level of significance. But at 1 per cent level, the borrowers of Karaput and Phulbani districts have shown similar attitude in repayment of bank credit. But on considering the behavioural attitude of the borrowers of Ganjam and Phulbani districts it is found that no similar attitude exists between them as regards to the repayment style of institutional credit (at both level of significance).

Default of the Basis of Literacy/Illiteracy

The beneficiaries of the sample districts have been divided into two categories; literates and illiterates. The number of defaulters of both the categories of loanees of study districts are shown in the Table 13.2.

According to the Table 13.2 the percentage of defaulters in literate borrowers category is 81.5 percent which is higher than the percentage of illiterate borrowers. The default among illiterate borrowers is 67.9 per cent in the sample districts. In all these three districts the percentage of defaulters in literate category is higher than the illiterates. In Ganjam the percentage of defaulters in

Table 13.2 : Defaulters according to Literacy/Illiteracy

Items	Districts							
	Ganjam		*Koraput*		*Phulbani*		*Total*	
	B	*D*	*B*	*D*	*B*	*D*	*B*	*D*
1	2	3	4	5	6	7	8	9
Literate	91	79 (86.8)	82	67 (81.7)	21	13 (61.9)	194	159 (81.5)
Illiterate	49	37 (75.5)	48	31 (64.5)	9	4 (44.4)	106	72 (67.9)
Total	**140**	**116 (82.8)**	**130**	**98 (75.3)**	**30**	**17 (56.6)**	**300**	**231 (77.0)**

B = Borrower D = Defaulter

Figure in brackets indicate percentage

Source : Compiled from the questionnaire

literate borrowers category is 86.5 per cent which is higher than other two districts.

From the total credit of Rs. 625.0 thousand, Rs. 454.7 thousand has been given to literate borrowers numbering 194 and remaining Rs. 170.3 thousand has been advanced to illiterate borrowers numbering 106. In case of literate borrowers the loan recovered is Rs. 214.4 thousand or 47.1 per cent, similarly in case of illiterate borrowers the loan recovered is Rs. 85.5 thousand or 50.2 per cent leaving 49.8 per cent unrecovered. From the figures it is observed that the percentage of overdues is high in case of literate borrowers (Appendix I to this Chapter).

Out of the literate borrowers the percentage of urban borrowers is higher than the rural literate. The urban literate borrowers know well that in case of any legal action taken by the bank, it may take years together to get a decree. Thereby the default amount accumulates every year with compound interest. On the other hand the illiterate borrowers are afraid of the legal action taken by the institutional agencies. According to chi-square test, at 5 per cent and 1 per cent level of significant the literate and illiterate borrowers have dissimilar attitude regarding the repayment of institutional loans.

Area-Wise Default

The borrowers have been chosen from different areas of Southern Orissa for the purpose of the study. The area is divided into urban, semi-urban and rural. The area-wise default is illustrated in the Table 13.3.

Table 13.3 : Defaulters according to Area

Items	Districts							
	Ganjam		*Koraput*		*Phulbani*		*Total*	
	B	*D*	*B*	*D*	*B*	*D*	*B*	*D*
1	2	3	4	5	6	7	8	9
Urban	11	10 (90.9)	8	6 (75.0)	3	3 (100)	22	19 (86.3)
Semi-Urban	21	19 (90.4)	9	7 (77.7)	4	3 (75.0)	34	29 (82.3)
Rural	108	87 (80.5)	113	85 (75.2)	23	11 (47.8)	244	183 (75.0)
Total	**140**	**116 (82.8)**	**130**	**98 (75.3)**	**30**	**17 (56.6)**	**300**	**231 (77.0)**

B = Borrower D = Defaulter

Figure in brackets indicate percentage

Source : Compiled from the questionnaire

The Table 13.3 reveals that the percentage of defaults is the highest in urban areas followed by semi-urban and rural areas respectively. The percentage of defaulters in rural is 75.4 per cent, where as it is 82.3 per cent in semi-urban and 86.3 per cent in urban areas of the study districts during the period of the study. In Phulbani the number of defaulters is cent per cent in urban areas. But the percentage of defaulters in rural areas is only 47.8 per cent which is least among all the three districts.

According to the Appendix I, the urban borrowers of the study districts have been financed Rs. 72.2 thousand during the period of study. Similarly, Rs. 90.7 thousand and Rs. 462.1 thousand has been advanced to the semi-urban and rural borrowers respectively. From the amount advanced, Rs. 21.5 thousand, Rs. 40.2 thousand and Rs. 238.2 thousand has been recovered from urban, semi-urban and rural borrowers respectively. The percentage of recovery is 29.7 in urban, 44.3 in semi-urban and 51.5 in rural areas.

The urban borrowers are relatively more clever and know the rules and regulations of the banks regarding repayment of loans. Again most of the literate borrowers are from the urban areas. For all practical purposes the expenditure is definitely higher in urban areas than the other two areas in standard of living. This factor is also a point in making them defaulters knowingly or unknowingly. They avoid and hesitate to repay the loan in time because of the emerging write off concept and other dilly dallying factors. The rural borrowers are not very much influenced by the 'write-off' concept of the Government. Again most of the rural borrowers are illiterates and they fear legal action of financing institutions. As per the Chi-square test of significance, the calculated value is greater than the table value. The test reveals that the borrowers of three areas have no similar attitude in repayment of institutional loans. The behavioural attitude of the borrowers of all the three areas differs to a varying degree depending on their socio-economic factors geographical position, caste, religion etc.

Default According to Caste

The sample loanees of study districts are dived into three categories: General, Scheduled Caste and Scheduled Tribe. Out, of 300 borrowers, 84 borrowers are ST, 56 borrowers are SC and 160 borrowers are from general castes. The share of above borrowers to the total number is 28 percent, 18.6 per cent and 53.4 per cent respectively. Of the total number of defaulters, 55, 42 and 134 are defaulters in ST, SC and general castes categories respectively. The distribution of defaulters on the basis of caste is illustrated in the Table 13.4.

According to the analysis of the Table 13.4 the number of defaulters are the highest among general caste borrowers i.e. 83.7 per cent. But it is 75 per cent in case of scheduled caste borrowers followed by 65.4 per cent among scheduled tribes.

The institutional agencies of the study districts have financed Rs. 114.9, Rs. 100.2 and Rs. 409.9 thousand to ST, SC and general caste borrowers respectively during the period 1985-86 to 1995-96. The Appendix-I, reveals that out of the above advanced amount Rs. 82.5 or 71.8 per cent, Rs. 48.2 or 58 per cent and Rs. 159.2 or 38.8

Table 13.4 : Defaulter as per Caste

Items	Districts							
	Ganjam		*Koraput*		*Phulbani*		*Total*	
	B	*D*	*B*	*D*	*B*	*D*	*B*	*D*
1	2	3	4	5	6	7	8	9
ST	4	2 (50.0)	64	45 (70.3)	16	8 (50.0)	84	55 (65.4)
SC	25	18 (72.0)	26	21 (80.7)	5	3 (60.0)	56	42 (75.0)
General	111	96 (86.5)	40	32 (80.0)	9	6 (66.6)	160	134 (83.7)
Total	**140**	**116 (82.8)**	**130**	**98 (75.3)**	**30**	**17 (56.6)**	**300**	**231 (77.0)**

B = Borrower D = Defaulter

Figure in brackets indicate percentage

Source : Compiled from the questionnaire

per cent have been recovered from ST, SC and general caste borrowers respectively.

Chi-square value reveals that SC, ST that general caste beneficiaries are having no similar attitude in the repayment of institutional loans. As the expected or calculated value is more than the table value at 5 per cent and 1 per cent level of significance, the behaviour of ST, SC and general caste borrowers show no similar attitude in the repayment of institutional loan.

Institution-wise Defaulters

The financing institutions situated in the rural areas of the sample districts are mostly providing credit for the growth and development of agriculture. The co-operative banks, regional rural banks and commercial banks located in the rural areas are the rural financing institutions catering to the needs of agriculturists in Southern Orissa. The institution wise borrowers and the number of defaulters are illusterated in Table 13.5.

Among the three kinds of banks, the co-operatives have the maximum number of borrowers followed by commercial banks and RRBs respectively in the sample districts during the period of

Table 13.5 : Types of Defaulters at the Level of Institutions During the Period of Study

Name of Institutions	*No. of borro-wers*	*No. of defaulters*		*Total defaul-ters*	*%age of defa-ulters*
		Chronic	*Casual*		
Commercial Banks	94	20 (31.7)	43 (68.3)	53	67.0
Co-operative Banks	147	49 (42.2)	67 (57.8)	116	78.9
RRBs	59	25 (48.0)	27 (52.0)	52	88.1
Total	**300**	**94 (40.6)**	**137 (59.4)**	**231**	**77.0**

Figures in brackets indicate percentage to total number defaulters.
Source : Compiled from questionnaire

study. But the percentage of defaulters is the highest in RRBs, followed by Co-operatives and commercial banks. Out of 231 defaulters, the percentage of chronic defaulters are highest i.e. 48.0 in RRBs followed by co-operatives 42.2. and commercial banks 31.7 during the period of study.

The co-operatives, commercial banks and RRBs of study districts have been financed Rs. 309.0, Rs. 183.0 and Rs. 133.0 thousand respectively to the sample borrowers during the period of the study. From the advanced amount Rs. 149.1 (48.2 per cent) Rs.100.1 (54.6 per cent) and Rs. 50.7 thousand (45.6 per cent) has been recovered from the sample borrowers of co-operatives, commercial banks and RRBs respectively. Recovery of loan is lowest in case of the borrowers who have taken loan from the RRBs in comparison to other institutional agencies (Appendix-II to this Chapter).

RRBS is relatively a new concept in rural lending. The state government gives more emphasis in rural lending through RRBs to fulfil the target. Further RRBs are comparatively less experienced in formulating effective methods for recovering agricultural dues. The bank personnel are hesitant to take any definite legal action due to excessive government and political interference. The other two financing institutions are some how active in this regard and their recovery position is bit better, though all of them are in the same boat.

To know the behavioral style of repayment of agricultural credit in case of all the three financing institutions of the study districts, chi-square test has been adopted. On the basis of this test it is found that the borrowers of three financial institutions indicate no similar behaviour in repayment of agricultural credit at 5 per cent and at 1 per cent level of significance. But when the banks are separated and two banks like co-operatives and RRBs are taken together for study, the beneficiaries of both the banks show similar attitude towards repayment of institutional credit 5 per cent and 1 percent levels of significance. But the loanees of RRBs and commercial banks show dissimilar attitude in the repayment of credit at both the levels of significance.

But on considering the level of significance with the borrowers of co-operatives and commercial banks, they are of dissimilar attitude at 5 per cent level of significance at it is similar at 1 per cent level of significance.

Term-Wise Default

The financing institutions advance three types of loans: short term loans to meet the short term needs of the agriculturists, medium term loans meant for semi urgent requirement like purchase of agricultural implements, and long term loans for the capital expenditure of agriculturists. The term-wise defaulters among the sample borrowers are illustrated in the Table 13.6.

The percentage of defaulters is high among the borrowers so far as the short and medium term loans are concerned. But it is very high in case of long term loans. The distribution of defaulters is 75.4 per cent in short term, 76.5 per cent in medium term and 82.0 per cent in long term loans respectively. The percentage of defaulters is high in case of long term loans. This may be due to long interval given to the borrowers for repayment of such loans. Long term loans take more time to generate agricultural income. Further there is every possibility that a long term loans is used for diversified purpose and becomes unproductive. The Appendix-II reveals that out of the total credit of Rs. 625.0 thousand, Rs. 339.0 thousand, Rs. 126.0 thousand and Rs. 160.0 thousand has been financed under short, medium and long term credit respectively.

Table 13.6 : Default : Term-wise

Items	Banks							
	Co-operative Banks		*Commercial Banks*		*RRBs*		*Total*	
	B	*D*	*B*	*D*	*B*	*D*	*B*	*D*
1	2	3	4	5	6	7	8	9
Short-term loan	83	64 (77.1)	49	32 (65.3)	39	33 (84.6)	171	129 (75.4)
Medium-term loan	13	10 (76.9)	38	26 (68.4)	17	16 (94.1)	689	52 (76.5)
Loang-term loan	51	42 (82.3)	7	5 (71.4)	3	3 (100)	61	50 (82.0)
Total	**147**	**116 (78.9)**	**94**	**63 (67.0)**	**59**	**52 (88.1)**	**300**	**231 (77.0)**

B = Borrower D = Defaulter

Figure in brackets indicate percentage

Source : Compiled from the questionnaire

But Rs. 182.9 thousand (53.9 per cent), Rs. 55.0 thousand (43.6 per cent) and Rs. 62.0 thousand (38.7 per cent) has been recovered from the short term, medium and long term finance respectively. The recovery is high in case of the sample borrowers to whom short term finance has been made.

According to the chi-square test, the defaulters of short, medium and long term loans have similar tendency at 5 per cent and 1 per cent level of significance with regard to their repayment of agricultural dues.

Default according to the Forms of Loan

The financial institutions generally give credit to the borrowers in cash, kind or both cash and kind. The list of borrowers and the defaulters regarding the form of credit is explained in the Table 13.7.

The Table 13.7 reveals that out of 300 sample borrowers, 112 borrowers have availed credit in cash only, 43 borrowers availed credit in kind and 145 borrowers availed credit both in cash and kind. The number of defaulters is highest among the loanees who

Table 13.7 : Default according to the Forms of Credit

Name of banks	Mode of Credit							
	Cash		*Kind*		*Both Cash and Kind*		*Total*	
	B	*D*	*B*	*D*	*B*	*D*	*B*	*D*
1	2	3	4	5	6	7	8	9
Co-operative banks	46	31 (67.4)	14	12 (85.7)	87	73 (83.9)	147	116 (78.9)
Commercial banks	52	33 (63.4)	22	15 (68.1)	20	15 (75.0)	94	63 (67.0)
RRBs	14	8 (57.1)	7	6 (85.7)	38	38 (100)	59	52 (88.1)
Total	**112**	**72 (64.2)**	**43**	**33 (76.7)**	**145**	**126 (86.8)**	**300**	**231 (77.0)**

B = Borrower D = Defaulter

Figure in brackets indicate percentage

Source : Compiled from the questionnaire

have received their loan in cash and kind both. It is as high as 86.6 per cent. The percentage of defaulters is 76.7 among the borrowers who have availed credit in kind only. The borrowers who have availed credit only in cash, comparatively a few of them turned to be defaulters. It is 64.2 per cent. The financial institutions advanced credit amounting to Rs. 172.0 thousand in cash Rs. 127.0 thousand in Kind, and Rs. 326.0 thousand on both cash and kind. Out of the advanced amount Rs. 101.0 thousand or 58.7 per cent, Rs. 62.0 thousand or 48.8 per cent and Rs. 136.9 thousand or 41.9 per cent has been recovered from the borrowers mentioned above. The recovery is high in case of the sample borrowers to whom only cash has been financed. (Appendix-II).

For better and proper utilisation of loan, crop loans are given in cash and kind components like fertiliser, seeds etc. expecting that credit supplied in shape of kind or both cash and kind will be utilised for production purposes. This type of loan cannot be diversified for other purpose thereby enabling the borrowers to generate income and could repay the loan in time. But surprisingly it is found here that probably the reverse is true. It is observed that the kind component is very often sold away in the market by the borrowers at a lower rate to get an immediate gain. Those are not of desired quality and are not being supplied in appropriate time, as attributed by the borrowers.

Default and 'Write Off' Concept

The 'write off' concept of the government (both centre and state) has influenced the borrowers not to repay the agricultural credit borrowed from different institutional agencies. The write off scenario has tempted most of the sample borrowers not to repay the institutional credit intentionally. The default caused due to present write off concept is explained in Table 13.8.

The Table 13.8 reveals that out of 300 borrowers, 206 or 68.7 per cent are aware of the write off concept and among them as high as 199 or 96.6 per cent borrowers are defaulters. It is cent per cent in Ganjam District. Ninety four borrowers are unaware of this write off concept. However, It is found that 32 (34 per cent) borrowers are defaulters in this category. In Ganjam district it is 31.4 per cent, which is the lowest in comparison to other two districts. It leads

Table 13.8 : Default due to Write-off Concept

Name of the District	Knowledge of write off concept		No knowledge of write off concept		Total	
	B	*D*	*B*	*D*	*B*	*D*
1	2	3	4	5	6	7
Ganjam	105	105 (100)	35	11 (31.4)	140	116 (82.8)
Koraput	89	85 (95.5)	41	13 (31.7)	130	98 (75.3)
Phulbamni	12	9 (75.0)	18	8 (44.4)	30	17 (56.6)
Total	**206**	**199** **(96.6)**	**94**	**32** **(34.0)**	**300**	**231** **(77.0)**

B = Borrower D = Defaulter

Figure in brackets indicate percentage

Source : Compiled from the questionnaire

to believe that the write off syndrome has affected the psyche of borrowers in an adverse way and they are not prepared to repay institutional loans.

Testing of Hypotheses

In the light of the above findings the hypotheses formulated are tested here.

1. **Borrowers having large land holdings possess better repaying capacity and default among them is less compared to the borrowers with small holdings.**

From the analysis it is observed that borrowers having large land holding are chronic defaulters. It is revealed from the analysis that among borrowers with small (less than 5 acres) land holdings, the percentage of defaulters id 74.0. Where as the percentage of defaulters has increased to 82.1 per cent when the land holding increased to 5-10 acres. The percentage of defaulters has further increased to 87.5 when the land holding is in the range of the 15-20 acres. It is also observed that there is 100 per cent default among big land holders having 20-25 acres and above. This may due to big land holders avail larger chunk of loans. These is every possibility of misuse of the loan by these borrowers. The big farmers default wilfully and they hardly care for the bank authorities or of any legal action. Very often the legal action and the casual behaviour of the bank authorities make them default. Therefore, the hypothesis is proved negative and is not accepted.

2. **Overdues at the level of co-operatives is less compared to other institutional agencies.**

The analysis revealed that among three financing institutions i.e. co-operatives, commercial banks and RRBs, the percentage of defaulters is 67 in commercial banks, 78.9 in co-operatives and 88.1 in RRBs. It is also observed from the analysis that the percentage of recovery is 54.6 in case of the borrowers who have taken loan from commercial banks, where as it is 48.2 and 45.6 among the borrowers of co-operatives and RRBs. The percentage of defaulters, and non-recovery of loan is the highest in RRBs followed by co-operatives and commercial banks.

This is due to, RRB is relatively a new concept in rural lending compared to co-operatives and commercial banks. The state

Government gives more emphasis in rural lending through RRBs to fulfil to target. The bank personnel are hesitant to take any definite legal action due to government and political legal action due to government and political interference. On the other hand, though co-operatives are age old organisations having a wide network and varied experience, inadequate supervision and lack of persuasion by bank officials has resulted in poor recovery. And in this regard the commercial banks have fared well comparatively. The chi-square test reveals that the sample borrowers of three financial institutions indicate no similar behaviour in repayment of institutional credit. Hence, the hypothesis is partially accepted.

3. It is a general belief that supply of credit in kind other than cash and constant post-lending supervision by the lending agencies lead to quick recovery.

For proper utilisation of institutional loan the kind component was initiated apart from cash in rural lending. From the analysis it is revealed that out of the total finance, the percentage of recovery of loan supplied in cash, kind and both cash and kind is 58.7 48.8 and 41.9 respectively. The kind component supplied by the financing institution are not of desired quality and quantity are not supplied at appropriate time. Further, very often the borrowers use to sell the kind component in the market for ready cash. Therefore, the objective of supplying kind component is being defeated and the percentage of recovery is being less among the borrowers to whom credit in kind and both cash and kind have been supplied. Since the percentage of recovery is higher among the borrowers who have availed only cash component, the first part of the hypothesis is found no basis.

The analysis also revealed that the percentage of defaulters is less (48.2) among the borrowers who are being constantly supervised by bank officials. But the percentage of defaulters is 88.0 among the borrowers who are not being supervised. According to chi-square value the borrowers supervised by bank officials and not supervised by bank officials reveals dissimilar tendency in repayment of institutional credit. Hence, the second part of hypothesis is accepted.

4. Awareness of the lending and repayment rules and regulations of institutional agencies is one of the factors

which influence the borrowers to postpone/avoid the repayment of credit.

The Urban, general caste and literate borrowers are mostly aware of the lending and repayment rules and regulations of the financing institutions. From the analysis it is found that the percentage of defaulters is 86.3, 83.7 and 81.5 among urban, general caste and literate borrowers. Similarly, the percentage of recovery is only 29.7, 38.8 and 47.1 per cent among urban, general caste and literate borrowers respectively. The chi-square test also reveals that urban, general caste and literate borrowers show similar attitude in repayment of institutional loans.

The rural, SC, ST and illiterate borrowers are hardly aware of the banking rules and regulations. It is observed from the analysis that the percentage of defaulters is 75,75,65.4 and 67.9 in respect of rural, ST, SC and illiterate borrowers. Further, analysis revealed that the percentage of recovery is 51.5, 58.0, 71.7, and 67.9 in respect of rural, ST, SC and illiterate borrowers. Further, analysis revealed that the percentage of recovery is 51.5, 58.0, 71.8 and 50.2 among rural, SC, ST and illiterate borrowers respectively. The chi-square value indicate that rural, ST, SC and illiterate borrowers have similar attitude in repayment of institutional loans.

This tendency of avoidance or postponement might have developed among the urban, general caste and literate borrowers due to their awareness of lending and repayment rules and regulations of financial institutions. They know that in case of any legal action initiated by the institutions may take years together to get a decree. Therefore, they feel encouraged to postpone or avoid the repayment of credit. Thus, the hypothesis is found to be valid.

Suggestions

The financing institutions and government need take some definite corrective measures to improve the scenario of mounting overdues. It is true that there is no easy solution to check this old malady. But adequate steps should be taken to tackle borrowers efficiently and effectively depending on the circumstances of the case. A few humble suggestions are put forth here under to contain the situation.

1. Pre-lending appraisal like evaluation of agricultural product, assessment of external forces; availability of inputs, local

market structure etc. are to be taken into consideration. Credit may be sanctioned according to the approved schemes of the lending institutions alone. Repaying capacity of the borrower is to be judged carefully before such a decision. Similarly, post-lending supervision and approaching the borrower in right time for repayment may prove effective in early recovery of overdues.

2. It is observed that recovery through legal action is a time consuming process. It takes years together to settle a case. So a method of mediation/compromise with borrowers may help in minimising overdues. It may be in the shape of waiving penal interest or waiving of accrued interest or permitting easy term of repayment. Compromise with borrowers for repayment of dues seems to be a pragmatic approach in the field of recovery.
3. The employees of lending institutions should develop a positive attitude in creating friendly relation with borrowers. They have to create a good climate of personal touch with the borrowers by meeting their express demands instantly. They have to gain fairly adequate knowledge about the behaviour; creditworthiness, personal need and character of the borrower. Such an attitudinal change amongst bank officials may bring both borrowers and lenders close and this relationship ultimately motivate the borrowers to repay the dues in time.
4. Rural lending institutions are providing only production credit to the farmers. But most of the rural borrowers are poor, small farmers, and live below the subsistence level. They very often feel tempted to use production credit supplied by lending institutions for consumption and other non-productive purposes and ultimately turn defaulters. Therefore, total credit need of the farmers should be taken care of. Either these rural lending agencies should also provide consumption credit along with production credit or some other agency/agencies should look after the consumption credit need of rural farmers.
5. The non-institutional agencies usually provide the day to day requirements both production and consumption credit, of the borrowers and the farmers avail such as and when they need. Overdues at this level is minimum because of coercive

action taken against the borrowers. Moreover, because the non-institutional agencies charge exorbitant rate of interest, borrowers very often repay such loans after availing institutional credit a lower rate. Such practices may not be possible on the part of institutional agencies but repeated approach for repayment and quick disposal of legal proceedings may help minimise overdues.

6. In case of co-operatives a list of defaulters with name and address could be prepared at the society level and a copy of the same may be pasted on the notice board of the society and another copy at a central place of the village, So that the sensitive and prestige conscious defaulters may come forward to repay the dues immediately.
7. To reduce overdues in banking institutions a sizeable number of field staff are to be engaged for collection of dues. The staff should approach the borrowers frequently for collection of loans. Apart from their salary, as an incentive, a small percentage of commission on the basis of their collection performance may be introduced. The responsibility should be fixed on the respective field staff for timely recovery of credit.

APPENDIX—I

Recovery of Loan at Borrowers Level

(Rs. in thousands)

Different categores of borrowers	*No. of borrowers*	*Amount financed*	*Amount recovered*	*Amount unrecovered*	*%age of recovery*
1	2	3	4	5	6
Literate	194	454.7	214.4	240.3	47.1
Illiterate	106	170.3	85.5	84.8	50.2
Total	**300**	**625.0**	**299.9**	**325.1**	**47.9**
Urban	22	72.2	21.5	50.7	29.7
Semi-Urban	34	90.7	40.2	50.5	44.3
Rural	244	462.1	238.2	223.9	51.5
Total	**300**	**625.0**	**299.9**	**325.1**	**47.9**
ST	84	114.9	82.5	32.4	71.8
SC	56	100.2	58.2	42.0	58.0
General	160	409.9	159.2	250.7	38.8
Total	**300**	**625.0**	**299.9**	**325.1**	**47.9**
Irrigated	115	274.7	162.5	112.2	59.1
Non-Irrigated	185	350.3	137.4	212.9	39.2
Total	**300**	**625.0**	**299.9**	**325.1**	**47.9**
Cash crop	70	223.0	120.2	102.8	53.9
Traditional crop	230	402.0	179.7	222.3	44.7
Total	**300**	**625.0**	**299.9**	**325.1**	**47.9**

Source : Compiled from questionnaire

APPENDIX—II

Recovery of Loan at Institutional Level

(Rs. in thousands)

Particulars	*No. of borrowers*	*Amount financed*	*Amount recovered*	*Amount unrecovered*	*%age of recovery*
1	2	3	4	5	6
Co-operative Banks	147	309.0	149.1	159.9	48.2
Commercial banks	94	183.0	100.1	82.9	54.6
RRBs	59	133.0	50.7	82.3	45.6
Total	**300**	**625.0**	**299.9**	**325.1**	**47.9**
Short term	171	339.0	182.9	156.1	53.9
Medium term	68	126.0	55.0	71.0	43.6
Long term	61	160.0	62.0	98.0	38.7
Total	**300**	**625.0**	**299.9**	**325.1**	**47.9**
Cash	112	172.0	101.0	71.0	58.7
Kind	43	127.0	62.0	65.0	48.8
Cash and kind	145	326.0	136.9	189.1	41.9
Total	**300**	**625.0**	**299.9**	**325.1**	**47.9**

Source : Compiled from questionnaire

14

Co-operative Movements in India

With special reference to the Ganjam district of Orissa

Dr. (Major) Gouri Prasad Mohapatro*

Before independence, there was an undeveloped and uncoordinated credit structure which was prevailing in our country. The unscrupulous village money-lenders and landlords were playing a pivotal role in the flow of finance to agriculture and the rural sector of the economy. The wealthy people in the villages were exploiting the poor farmers and artisans by extracting high interest rates. In this manner, the wealth got concentrated in the hands of the few people while the majority of rural poor lived a precarious life.

Eradication of poverty from the grass-root level of villages and to get economic upliftment by providing institutional financial help to the needy farmers was one of the basic requirement of the Indian economic every-since from the pre-independence period. Efforts to build up institutional financing for rural sector and specifically to agricultural sector started with the passage of the co-operative credit societies Act in 1904, which aimed at freeing agriculturists from the grips of the money-lenders and enabling them to secure production credit to the extent required by them at relatively cheap rates of interest.

* Dr. Mahapatra, Reader in Economics, Science College, Hinjilicut (Orissa)

The co-operative movement in India started with the objective of giving short-term loans to the small farmers and other economically weaker sections of the society. But later on the co-operative movement got spread into the other fields also. As stated earlier, the need for uplift of the poor masses of India, is being more and more realised ever since the dawn of freedom. Thus co-operative movement in India is an effective step in this regard and the co-operative credit societies are playing an important role in solving the financial problems of small persons, those are called poors.

Co-operation refers to the voluntary associations which are formed on the basis of equality and for some common purposes. The basic principle of co-operation is "each for all and all for each". In the words of H. Calvert, "co-operation is a form of organisation wherein persons voluntarily associated together as human beings on the basis of equality for the promotion of their economic interest"[1]. The idea of co-operative movement in India seems to have come to existence from the Deccan riots of the early part of the 9th century, where debtors revolted against the extortionist practices of the money-lenders. During the period the co-operative movement was in existence in European countries and had made some progress. As such, the first initiative of the co-operative movement started by the government for a reform in the economy.

The Deccan Riots Commission Report of 1825, the Famine Commission Report of 1880 and Sir Frederic Nicholson Report of 1895 and similar other reports were examined the unjust character of the credit system of this country. It has been then, well realised the need for the supply of adequate credit to agriculturist on terms which they could abide by. Therefore, the Taccavi Act of 1871, 1876 and 1879 and agriculturists loan Act of 1884 were enacted to advance short-terms loans to agriculturists for their operations.[2] But the Taccavi loans were inadequate and could be obtained only after a lot of hurdles. To combat all these co-operative credit was considered as an appropriate alternative.

The co-operative movement in India is the result of the enquires and recommendations given by Sir Frederic Nicholson, Mr. Dupernex and Sir Edward Maclagan. So that the Co-operative Society Act was passed for the first time in 1904. The Act permitted the formation of two type of co-operative credit societies. In rural areas the co-operative credit societies were to be formed in the Rinffersen model while in the urban areas the co-operative societies were on the Sehulze Delitzseh model.[3]

The feature of the Rinffeisen type societies are:

(a) Unlimited liabilities of its members.

(b) Limited area of operation i.e. the membership of co-operatives from a limited area.

(c) Limited share Capital.

(d) Loans are granted for productive purpose only.

(e) No dividend is distributed to members.

(f) Honorary Management.

The features of Schulze Delitzseh type societies are:

(a) Limited liability of the members.

(b) Large area of operational membership.

(c) Paid management.

(d) Distribution of dividends to members.

The working of the Act of 1904 suffered from defects and could not fulfill the purposes. The Act only recognised credit societies and made no provision for central agencies for improved supervision. There was inadequate supply of capital at the disposal of the credit societies. Due to small business, their income was low and they could not efford to avail the services of skilled and trained staff. Also, they advanced loans for all sorts of purposes which were seldom linked to the production programme of the members and that the liabilities of the members was unlimited. The classification into rural and urban societies was also unscientific and inconvenient. These loopholes in the Act, hindered the proper growth of the movement and which were remedied to a great extent, by the enactment of co-operative societies Act of 1912.

The Act of 1912 did remove the deficiencies of the previous Act. It was for the first time, the Act permitted the organisation of non-credit societies in India. The publication of the report of Maclagan Committee on co-operation in 1915 was an important landmark in the history of the co-operative movement. In accordance with the Maclagan Committee recommendations, the Montform Reform of 1919 made co-operation a provincial transferred subject. In 1912 the Bombay Government passed a separate co-operative society Act which was followed by similar enactments in other provinces.

The above co-operative societies Act brought into existence a federal co-operative structure with higher level financing institutions to provide guardianship and financial and technical support to the lower level organisations so as to enable them to meet the credit requirements of millions of scattered farmers and artisans.

During the great depression of 1929-33, the co-operative movement received a rude shock. Agricultural prices fell sharply and cultivators, hard pressed by the heavy burden of debt, showed practically no interest in the co-operative movements.

In 1937, the newly established agricultural credit department of the Reserve Bank of India stressed the importance of the multipurpose co-operative societies. During the Second World War the co-operative movement gained considerable momentum due to the rise in the prices of agricultural products.

The main objective of the co-operation is to bring about changes of a fundamental nature in the country from the village level. Since the economic structure of the country has its roots in villages, co-operation was expected to evolve a scheme co-operative community organisation which touches upon all aspects of life.[4] The concept of one village, one society is the main objective of the co-operative movement. The Madras Committee on co-operation (1939-40) urged for the re-organisation of the rural society on a wider basis by grouping small societies together. The National Government after coming into power in 1947 began to take steps for expansion and revitalisation of the movement.[5]

Co-operative Movement after Independence

After the independence, the co-operative movement came to be considered as kingpin of development planning. The objective and the efforts to secure a large increase in agricultural production planned and initiated as a part of the planning for economic development made the role of co-operative credit more positive and crucial not only as a substitute for money-lenders but as dependable source for financing agricultural production and development.

The All India Rural Credit Survey Committee (1951-52) stressed to strengthen and develop co-operatives in order to meet the entire credit needs of the cultivators. During the making of this recommendation, the committee was quite conscious of the structural and other deficiencies in the functioning of co-operatives. Nonetheless they did not visualise any other alternative institutional agency and desired that the co-operatives should alone be developed as the sole institutional agency for agricultural finance.[6] The All India Rural Credit Survey Committee (1954) appointed by R.B.I. reveals that the co-operative and Government lending to the agricultural sector accounted for only thee percent of the total agricultural credit and the share of commercial banks was less than one per cent.[7] The Governments both state and central— played in this respect only marginal role. This committee recommended co-operative credit societies as the most appropriate agency for supply for credit to the rural sector. The Central Government and the R.B.I. made special efforts to strengthen the co-operatives.

The second Indian co-operative congress in March 1955 and the co-operative ministers conference of 1955 discussed the various problems and productiveness of the co-operation. The integrated scheme of rural credit for making co-operative system a success was implemented. As a result of implementation of the measure suggested by the AIRCSC under integrated scheme of rural credit, the proportion of co-operative in total borrowings of farmers had increased from 3.1 per cent in 1951-52 to 15.5 per cent in 1961-62.[8] The Banking Commission (1972) has also stressed the suitability of co-operative agency at the rural base. According to the Commission, "The local participation, democratic management and responsiveness to local needs urge the characteristic of co-operative organisations to make them ideal type of institutions to be sought after".

The Structure Pattern of Co-operative Organisation

The co-operative credit institution are broadly of two categories; i.e. Agricultural credit institutions and Non-agricultural credit institutions. The Agricultural credit institutions are against of two types; i.e. the short-term credit institutions and long-term institutions.The short term wing is federal in character, based on three-tier pattern with the apex bank at the state level, central co-operative banks at the district level and co-operative credit societies at the grass-root level (in villages generally).

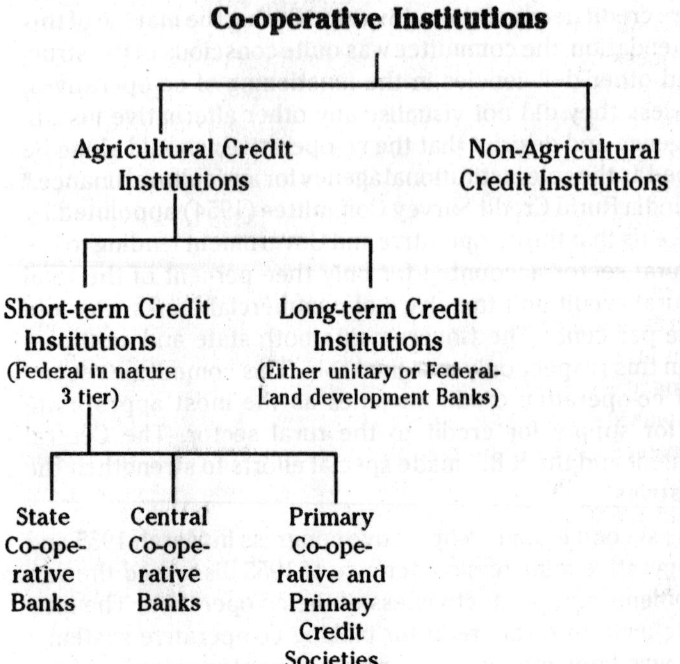

The above chart represents the structural patterns of the co-operative credit organisations of the present time. The long term credit structure is either unitary or federal in character with the state land development Banks (SLBs) as the apex institution at the state level and primary land Development Banks (PLDBs) or branches of SLDBs at the taluk or block level.

Agricultural Credit Institutions (Short terms co-op. credits)

a) State Co-operative Banks

The state co-operative banks (SCB) are the apex organisations in the three-tier co-operative credit structure of any State. As an apex organisation, the SCB has to play a key role in the formation and implementation of credit policies, establishment of effective report between the credit structure on one hand and money market, RBI and NABARD on the other. It has to provide effective leadership to the co-operative movement. The functions of the SCB may be summarised as follows: (i) to develop co-operative credit in the state and to function generally as an integrated state organisation for the provision of credit for agricultural marketing and processing to agriculturists and their societies and to ensure efficient performance of the functions relating to banking unions and other co-operative societies in its area of operation (ii) to issue loans and advances to co-operative societies (iii) to undertake general banking business (iv) to act as an agent for the state Government or local authorities, public trust or an institution established under any state or central Act.

The deposit growth of the state co-operative banks (SCBs) decelerated sharply to 2.1 per cent during 1994-95 as compared with an increase of 29.9 per cent recorded in 1993-94. Loans out standing at Rs. 10,492 crores showed an increase of 7.1 per cent which was substantially lower to the rise of 17.0 per cent in 1993-94. However, there was a significant improvement in the overdue position. Overdues as a percentage to demand declined by three per cent points to 14.0 during 1994-95.[9]

The Table 14.1 indicates the details of the state co-operative bank (SCB) as all India level the provisional data for the years 1992-93, 1993-94 and 1914-95.

From the Table 14.1 the progress and achievements of SCBs can easily be understood out of the stated periods.

Central Co-operative Banks

The Central Co-operative Banks (CCBs) operate as the Central financing agencies at the intermediate level between the primary agricultural co-operatives (PACs) at the village level and at the state co-operative Banks at the apex level. The area of operation for a central co-operation bank is usually confined to a district. The CCBs have undertaken the responsibilities of organising and directing the agricultural credit for production, processing and marketing of crops in an orderly manner. Besides they have to implement and supervise effectively the credit operations. Their functions can be summarised as (i) to mobilise local resources/deposits in rural areas, (ii) provide banking facilities and incul-

Table 14.1 :
(Amounts in Crores of Rupees)

S. No.	*Particulars*	*1992–93*	*1993–94*	*1994–95*
1.	Numbers	28	28	28
2.	Owned Funds	1,348	1,528	1,635
3.	Deposits	8,701	11,305	11,547
4.	Borrowings from NABARD and RBI	4,513	4,749	5,150
5.	Working Capital	15,560	18,919	18,719
6.	Loans issued	10,123	14,107	16,271
7.	Loan outstanding	8,378	9,801	10,492
8.	Loan overdue (as on June 30)	926	1,520	1,162
9.	Loans outstanding			
	i) to % of overdues	11.1	15.5	11.0
	ii) Demand to the % of overdue	15.0	17.0	14.0

Source : RBI Bulletin, 1997 (March), Appendix Table III I.P. –129.

cate banking habits among the members (iii) organise and direct the operations of PACs and other co-operative institutions and provide them required financial assistance (iv) inspect and supervise the working of their affiliated institutions periodically with a view to maintain their efficiency (v) provide necessary guidance and advice on financial and administrative matters.

The deposits of CCBs grew by 14.6 per cent in 1994-95 which was of course lower than the rise of 19.9 per cent recorded in 1993-94. Loans outstanding at the end of March 1995 placed at Rs. 18,240 crore were higher by 2.7 per cent than Rs. 17,757 crore (18.9 per cent) a year ago. The overdue of loan in respect of demand declined form 33 per cent to 31 per cent during the second period.[10]

The Table 14.2 represents a detail about the provisional data informations on CCBsof the country.

There are two CCBs in the Ganjam district of Orissa. They are (i) Berhampur Central Bank Ltd. and (ii) Aska Co-operative Central Bank Ltd. As on March 31, 1996 the BCC bank has collected the

Table 14.2 :
(Amounts in Crores of Rupees)

S. No.	*Particulars*	*1992–93*	*1993–94*	*1994–95*
1.	Numbers	352	361	361
2.	Owned Funds	2,345	2,559	2,783
3.	Deposits	13,555	16,251	18,616
4.	Borrowings from NABARD/ RBI Apex Banks & Comm. Banks	6,777	7,223	7,921
5.	Working Capital	23,719	27,586	30,543
6.	Loans issued	14,155	17,744	22,373
7.	Loan outstanding	14,940	17,757	18,240
8.	Loan overdue (as on June 30)	3,738	3,874	3,482
9.	% of Overdues due to			
	i) Loans outstanding	25.0	21.8	22.0
	ii) Demand	40.0	33.0	31.0

Source : RBI Bulletin, 1997 (March), p. 129.

deposit for Rs. 2755.19 lakhs, while its advance was Rs. 1713.66 lakhs. The C.D. ratio was 62 per cent. Out of the total advances of BCC the percentage of priority sector advance was 79 per cent and the direct finance to the agricultural sector constitute 52 per cent of the total advance and the 100 per cent of its advances constitute the advances to the weaker section of the district 11.

On the other hand, the ACC bank of Ganjam district has collected the deposits of Rs. 1340.75 lakhs and advanced Rs. 1141.78 lakhs during the said period. Its C.D. ratio was 85 per cent and the advance to the priority sector was 73 per cent , the direct finance to the agricutural sector was 46 per cent and the advance to the weaker section contitute 71 per cent of the total advance 12.

The district has 183 branches of the commercial banks, 15 branches of the BCC banks and 13 branches of ACC Bank. It has also 4 branches of Orissa state Co-operative Agricultural Rural Development banks (OSCARD) during the period of 1997-98 Annual Credit Plan.

The percentage of achievement in implementation of the ACP during 1995-96 in favour of the BCC Bank in total is 145 per cent over the targets of its own and similarly, the achievement of the ACC Bank remained at 53 per cent over the target of the same bank.

The CCBs get their working capital from own funds, deposits, borrowings and from other sources. In the own funds, the major portion consists of share capital contributed by Co-operative societies and the state Governments. The rest is made up of reserves. Deposits are largely round from individuals and from co-operative societies. Some deposits are found from the local bodies and from other institutions. Deposits mobilisation by the Central Co-operatives vary from one state to the other. The deposit mobilisation of State Co-operative Banks of Gujrat, Punjab, Maharastra and Himachal Pradesh is very high and on the other hand are low in Assam, West Bengal and Orissa. Borrowings and refinances are mainly found from the sources of RBI and NABARD.

The Primary Co-operative banks and The Primary Co-operative Societies

The field level co-operative institutions which provide credit to individual borrowers consists of (i) Primary Agricultural Credit societies or the primary co-operative banks providing both short-term and medium term credit to their members. At the grass-root level, large sized multi-purpose societies (LAMPS) and Farmers service societies (FSS) have been set up to provide the package of services required. These are base level institutions like the primary co-operative agricultural Credit societies. The functions of PAC may be summerised as (i) to issue loans for development of farm (short-term and medium-term) (ii) to act as an agent for the sale of farm produce (iii) to supply inputs for crop production; viz. seeds, fertilisers, pesticides, fungicides and for the development of animal husbandry activities, viz cattle field etc. (iv) to supply consumer good (v) to provide service and encourage subsidiary occupations and (vii) to encourage thrift.

The number of primary co-operative Banks (PCBs) stood at 1,525, including 91 salary earner's bank and 66 Mahila banks as at the end of June 1996. Of the 1,525 PCBs, 2 salary earner's banks and 54 other Primary (urban) Co-operative banks were under liquidation as on June 30, 1996. 13

During 1995-96 (April-March) the deposits of PCBs recorded higher growth rate of 20.2 per cent as against 19.9 per cent recorded during 1994-95. However, the growth of credit at 21.0 per cent in 1995-96 was marginally lower than 21.5 percent in 1994-95.

The following Table 14.3 (see at p. 216) and 14.4 represents the provisional data based informations on PCBs and of the primary co-operative agricultural societies of the country respectively.

The Table 14.4 represents the provisional informations on the Primary Agricultural Co-operative Societies (PACs) of India.

Table 14.2 : Primary Credit Societies
(Amounts in Crores of Rupees)

S. No.	*Particulars*	*1992–93*	*1993–94*	*1994–95*
1.	(PACs) Numbers in (000's)	84	91	90
2.	Membership in (000's)	88,539	89,067	88,047
3.	Owned Funds	2,032	2,462	2,584
4.	Deposits	1,863	2,307	2,520
5.	Borrowings	7,896	8,487	9,596
6.	Working Capital	12,666	15,207	16,304
7.	Total Loans issued	6,793	7,301	9,373
8.	Total Loan outstanding (as on June 30)	8,116	10,190	11,404
9.	Total Loan overdue % of Overdues to			
	i) Loans outstanding	40.1	38.0	35.0
	ii) Demand	43.0	41.0	36.0

Source : RBI Bulletin, 1997 (March), p. 130.

The branch expansion policy of PCBs has been liberalised with effect from January 8, 1996. Well managed and financially sound banks satisfying prudential norms are permitted to open branches at the centres of their choice. They are, however, required to formally obtain licence from R.B.I. The PCBs were allowed to extend their area of operation to the entire district in which they are registered inclusive of rural areas without prior approval from the RBI. PCBs with deposits above Rs. 50 crores

Table 14.3 : Primary Co-operative Banks of India

(Amounts in Crores of Rupees)

S. No.	Items	As on March 31			End–June		Variations During: Financial Year		Variations During: April–June	
		1994	*1995*	*1996*	*1995*	*1996*	*1994-95*	*1995-96*	*1994-95*	*1995-96*
1	2	3	4	5	6	7	8	9	10	11
							(4–3)	(5–4)	(6–4)	(7–5)
1.	Numbers	1,400	1,431	1,501	1,449	1,525	31	70	18	24
2.	Owned funds	2,723	3,312	3,848	3,371	4,151	589 (21.6)	536 (16.2)	59 (1.8)	303 (7.9)
3.	Deposits	16,769	20,101	24,165	20,577	25,584	3,332 (19.9)	4,064 (20.2)	476 (2.4)	1,419 (5.9)
4.	Borrowings	496	577	758	610	585	81 (16.3)	181 (31.4)	33 (5.7)	–173 (–22.8)
5.	Loans Outstanding	12,172	14,795	17,908	14,730	18,197	2,623 (21.5)	3,113 (21.0)	–65 (–0.4)	289 (1.6)

Source : RBI Bulletin March, 1997 p. 62. (Figure in brackets are Percentage variations)

were granted freedom to extend their area of operation beyond the respective states of their registration provided they are financially sound and have met the priority sector targets, alongwith prudential accounting norms.[15]

In the Ganjam district of Orissa there were 824 different types of co-operative societies in existence by the end of 1992. This includes the co-operative Urban Bank of Berhampur and the consumer co-operative stores, co-operative marketing societies etc.[16]

The investment under agricultural sector through co-operatives for 1989 to 1991 for undivided Ganjam district of Orissa were as follows.

Table 14.5

(Rupees in Lakhs)

Year	*No. of Accts.*	*Amounts*
Kharif Programme		
1989	31314	641.86
1990	14315	214.12
1991	4881	103.69
Rabi Programme		
1988–89	11909	185.84
1989–90	700	14.58
1990–91	4628	77.83

Source : Deputy Registrar, Co-operative Societies, Berhampur Division (Enquiry).

The investment programme received a serious setback on account of the implementation of the debt-relief scheme during 1990. The financial agencies like NABARD and Orissa State Cooperative Bank restricted their flow of refinance due to the debt-relief and for the low recoveries of loans during 1990-91.[17]

The primary agricultural societies have enrolled 3.02 lakh agricultural families comprising 0.35 lakhs of Scheduled Caste families. The coverage of agricultural families under co-operative filed works out to 76 per cent .[18]

The Berhampur Co-operative Bank, which is at the level of a primary co-operative society, is one of the oldest co-operative banks of India as it was established on November 13,1906. It has made an advance of Rs. 346.46 lakhs during March 1992 out of which 66.88 per cent is advanced to the priority sector. The percentage of weaker section advance to the priority sector is 66.04 per cent [19]

To ameliorate the economic condition of tribals and to meet the special requirements other people belonging to the weaker sections residing in forest and hill tracts of the district, six LAMPs have been organised which are working for last one-and-half decades. The main objectives of LAMPs are to wean away tribals from PODU cultivations i.e. shifting, cultivation and to save the tribals form the clutches of the middleman by encouraging them to take up agricultural operation on a permanent basis. The objectives of LAMPs are to motivate the tribals to take up improved agricultural practices, offering them reasonable prices for their agricultural products and keeping this interviews, the LAMPs give agricultural loans.

The Land Development Banks

The long term credit structure is either unitary or federal in character with State Land Development Banks (SLDBs) as the apex institution at the state level and Primary Land Development Banks (PLDBs) or branches of SLDBs at the taluk/block level.

The deposits of State/Central Land Development Banks of India record a high growth of 40 per cent during 1994-95 as compared with an increase of 23.1 per cent in the previous year. Loans outstanding at Rs. 5.646 crore higher by 4.5 per cent as compared with the rise of 14.5 per cent in 1993-94. The proportion of overdues to demand witnessed an increased with the ratio rising the one percentage point to 53.0 per cent during this period.[20]

The members of PLDBs at the end of March 1995 stood at 7.31 in India. The membership of PLDBs increased by 1.39 lakhs to 73.6 lakhs during the year 1994-95. Loans outstanding at Rs. 1,699 crore recorded a rise of 11.3 per cent in 1994-95 as compared with 4.4 per cent increase in the proceeding year. There was a deterioration in the overdue position; overdues as a ratio to demand significantly by 12 percentage points to 57.0 per cent in 1994-95 from 45.0 per cent during 1993-94.[21]

The Table 14.6 and 14.7 represents the data based informations in respects of the state/central Land Development Banks and of the primary Land Development Banks of the country as a whole respectively.

Table 14.6 : State/Central Land Development Banks of the Country (SLDBs) (provisional)

(Amounts in Crores of Rupees)

S. No.	*Particulars*	*1992–93*	*1993–94*	*1994–95*
1.	Numbers	19	20	20
2.	Owned Funds	727	857	938
3.	Deposits	65	80	112
4.	Borrowings	5,373	4,811	6,087
5.	Working Capital	6,265	7,888	8,454
6.	Loans issued (long term)	1,231	1,352	1,540
7.	Loans outstanding	4,719	5,405	5,646
8.	Loan overdue (as on June 30)	923	1,014	845
9.	% of overdues due to			
	i) Loans outstanding	19.6	18.8	15.0
	ii) Demand	53.0	52.0	53.0

Source : RBI Bulletin, 1997 (March), p. 129.

The Table 14.7 is providing the data based information of the Primary Land Development Banks of the country upto the year 1994-95.

The long term agricultural loan provided by the five LDBs of the Ganjam district of Orissa upto 1990-91 is shown in Table 14.8.

The co-operative banks and their societies provide short-terms, medium-term and long-term loans to the rural people mainly for agricultural, agro based and for allied sectors. In some cases, they also provide consumption loans to a limited extent.

Co-operative movement in India is a people's movement for ameliorating the economic conditions through thrift and mutual help. They are borrowers of their own organisations having a

Table 14.7 : PLDBs of India (Provisional data)

(Amounts in Crores of Rupees)

S. No.	*Particulars*	*1992–93*	*1993–94*	*1994–95*
1.	Numbers	726	727	731
2.	Membership (in 000's)	6,503	7,221	7,360
3.	Owned Funds	308	349	372
4.	Borrowings	2,382	2,621	2,816
5.	Working Capital	2,958	3,379	3,676
6.	Loans issued (long term)	435	664	705
7.	Loan outstanding	1,463	1,527	1,699
8.	Loan overdue	382	396	437
9.	% of overdues			
	i) Loan outstanding	26.1	26.0	26.0
	ii) Demand	44.2	45.0	57.0

Source : RBI Bulletin, 1997 (March), p. 130.

Table 14.8 : The Finance Provided by Five LDBs in Ganjam District of Orissa

Years	*Amount (Rs. in lakhs)*
1988–89	88.09
1989–90	13.05
1990–91	32.01

Source : Deputy Registrar, Co-operative Societies, Berhampur (Cm) Enquiry

democratic set-up. It is obvious that the co-operative credit movement has made considerable progress in the rural sector especially in agricultural sector. But the performance did not come upto the expectation. This is due to the fact that the co-operative credit system suffers from certain serious weakness, some of them have been discussed here below.

A large number of PACs are suffering from membership coverage and still smaller number of borrowing members, lack of supervision over the end use of credit, lack of complementary services, absence of tie-up with development plans and programmes and lastly but most emphatically the poor recovery performance. Almost 10 to 15 per cent of the PAC are dormant.

Credit co-operatives, at each stage of the three-tier, have demonstrated having dependance on external sources of finance, among which the more important are borrowings. As on 30th June 1985, the proportion of borrowings in the total working capital of the co-operative banks was 16.3 per cent. Further a sizable proportion of even share capital of the co-operative comes from the Government. Thus in case of resources, co-operatives are heavily dependent on the Government and other refinancing agencies. The aforesaid are all India averages, the position is still worse in a majority of the states.

Because of their strong socio-economic position and their stronghold of the rural economy, large landowners have managed to corner a very sizable proportion of the loans disbursed by the co-operative credit institutions. For instance, in 1982 small and marginal farmers i.e. farmers having holdings of more than five acres, received only 31.2 per cent of the total loans advanced by the PACs while owners having holdings of less than five acres, received 65.4 per cent. The share of agricultural labourers, rural artisans etc., have always been negligible. Thus the benefits of co-operative credit have not been adequately passed on to the weaker sections of the rural society. Prior to the establishment of Regional Rural Banks, the rural poor continued to depend on the non-institutional sources of credit.

It has been observed that adequate control over the end use of the credit has not been exercised. Quite often than not, the proceeds of the loans are used for unproductive purposes.

There are considerable regional disparities in the amounts of loans disbursed by co-operative. In 1982-83, the States of Andhra Pradesh, Gujarat, Haryana, Kerala, Madhya Pradesh, Maharashtra, Punjab and Rajasthan together accounted for about 80 per cent of the total credit disbursed by the co-operative societies in the country as a whole.

The PACs have suffered from incompetence, ignorance and non-performing management. Most of the PACs are weak both financially and managerially and suffer from inadequate business, heavy overdues and faulty and inefficient management. As at the end of June 1985, in the case of PACs, the overdues constituted as high as 40.9 per cent of the loans outstanding. In the matter of central co-operatives one-third of the loans outstanding were overdues. Heavy incidence of overdues has led to the cessation of the process of credit recycling thus crippling these institutions of their capacity to grant loans.

Some of the co-operative credit institutions in the State like Gujarat, Maharashtra and Punjab have faced the problem of ungainful utilisation of funds. In the absence of adequate avenues for development of resources within their territorial jurisdictions, they are forced to keep their surplus resources in the form of deposits with commercial banks. This situation, paradoxically, prevails side by side with the co-operative banks in other states which are hard-pressed for want of adequate resources for meeting their legitimate requirements.

The co-operatives in this country have been receiving Government support and patronage from the very beginning. However, following the recommendations of the All India Rural Credit Survey, the co-operatives have been given since mid-fifties large-scale financial support in various form by the Government in the name of the states partnership. This means, in practical terms the ruling party's and the government bureaucrats control over the co-operatives. This development has led to the following consequences.

i) Politicisation of the movement.

ii) Officialisation of the management.

iii) Lack of accountability and

iv) End of democratic control

However, after the advent of new technology, in banking line the credit needs of agricultural sector increased beyond the capacity of co-operatives. The commercial banks were inducted into the field of agriculture in particular and in general to the rural sector. But still the role of co-operatives for providing loans for agricultural purposes and its roles in the rural sector in India can not be overlooked. The co-operative banks are the banks for small persons of the small area i.e. of the villages. In view of the growing need for credit for diversified developmental and productive activities in the rural areas, CRAFICARD suggested that "in planning the future of reorganised societies, the aim should be to transform them into a single contact point in the village, for all types of credits and not merely for agriculture in the narrow sense. In other words, they should also have the capacity to serve other rural producers such as artisans, craftsmen and agricultural labourers in respect of their economic activities. They must offer a package of services to the clientele, for example, input supplies and marketing help. They have to be servicing agencies either by directly undertaking the services required by the producers or by forging effective link with other agencies such as marketing societies and fertiliser suppliers who render such services". It has also been emphasised that "these societies should transform themselves into single contact point to provide a package of integrated services to the members." In this way there will be no danger to the viability of the PACs and PCBs. They can give their best services to the poor people for the production and development of the nation and they can be called a small man's organisation.

References

1. Paul, R.R. "Co-operative Banking in India". *Money Banking and International Trade*, (1956), Kalyani Publishers, p-91-B.
2. Mimiography Singh, Virendra Bahadur Dept. of Economics. Allahabad University (1976).
3. Dosujh C.L., Co-operative-Progress and Short-commings Indian Economy, Pitambar Publishing Company, New Delhi, (1987), p-82.
4. Government of India, Planning Commission, 3rd Five Year Plan (1961) p-20.
5. Mimiography - *Op-cit*.
6. Dr. Balister Need for Revamping the Rural Co-operaives. "Yojana", January 15, 1994. Vol. 37; No. 24 p-21.
7. Ojha, P.D. (Deputy Governor) R.B.I. "Agricultural Credit Institution: India, their structure and role in development. R.B.I. Bulletin Vol-XL. No. 2 Feb 1986, p-150.
8. Dr. Balister *Op-cit*. p-21.
9. R.B.I. Bulletin - 1997, March, p-66.

10. Ibid-66.
11. Lead Bank Sources.
12. Ibid.
13. R.B.I. Bulletin. *Op-cit*, p-61.
14. Ibid. pp-61,62.
15. Ibid. p. 62.
16. Lead Bank Sources
17. Mahapatra, G.P. Chapter 3, Rural Banks for Rural Development, Discovery Publishing House, New Delhi, 1997, p-58.
18. Ibid.
19. Ibid.
20. R.B.I. Bulleting *Op-cit*, p.67.
21. Ibid.

15

Rural Development through Dairy Co-operatives

Dr. S. N. Tripathy*

In our country, agriculture and allied activities like dairy constitute the integral part of the rural economy. A dairy farming can be adopted as a subsidiary occupation to agriculture. It has considerable scope to mitigate rural under-employment and seasonal unemployment. Since milk constitute the most vital component of diet for human beings, it can solve the problem of malnutrition. In a country like India, where the distribution of land is very much skewed, the distribution of milch animals to landless and other weaker sections will confer increased incomes, employment and minimise the inequalities between the rich and poor. The gross value of output from animal husbandry and dairy development is about Rs. 70,000 crores which is 25 per cent of the total agricultural output.

As mechanisation of farm activities resulting in reducing in labour engagement and left rural women unemployed during most part of the year, dairying is the most basic rural industry generating employment avenues and thereby, accommodate the rural women. The Economic and Socio Commission of the World Food Congress emphasised that "The ultimate solution of the problem of hunger and malnutrition in the developing countries lies in increasing the purchasing power of the mass of the population through general economic development" (FAO, 1969)[1], Thus, the

* Department of Economics, Aska Science College, Aska (Orissa)

key to reducing poverty is diverting agricultural labourers into other productive activities which are having more marginal returns from all productive activities. In fact, the poverty alleviation programmes like IRDP, ERRP, JRY etc. making provisions of assets for poor, deprived, down-trodden and weaker sections of the society find a revealed expression through the supply Jersey cows as a regular source of income.

Co-operatives

The establishment of co-operatives has been regarded as one of the vital instruments for socio-economic change and for human development. Keeping the vital role of co-operatives in mind the first Five Year Plan aptly remained, "In a regime of planned development, co-operative is an instrument, with which relating some of the advantages of decentralisation and local initiative will serve willingly and readily the overall purposes and directives of the plan." The co-operative form of organisation can no longer be treated as only a special with the private sector. It is an indispensable instrument of planned economic action in a democracy. All India Rural Credit Survey (1954) recommended to have large-sized societies to ensure viability to the society.

In the present context of the new economic environment of the country, co-operatives may still be the only institutional structure that will protect the interest and enhance the livelihood of the resource-poor rural population particularly in under-developed regions (Saha, 1995).[2]

In the context of dairy co-operative and rural development, the National Commission on Agriculture (1972) in their interim report on milk production recommended that the benefits of increasing demand of milk in large cities, towns and industrial areas should go to small and marginal farmers and landless labourers.

In India, under the impact of development plans, milk production has increased to 60 million tonnes. The milk production has exhibited continuously an increasing trend in the wake of Operation Flood project, the world's largest integrated dairy development programme. During 1993-94, this programme organised 69,000 dairy co-operative societies involving 9 million farmers. It links rural milk producers with urban consumers and eliminates the middlemen and their commission. Operation Flood aims at collecting milk and milk products, processing and sale of milk through organisation of milk co-operatives.[3]

OMFED

The Orissa State Co-operative Milk Producers Federation (OMFED) as an apex institution has been playing a vital role in procurement of milk through its affiliated eight Co-operative Milk Unions and 456 Primary Milk Supply Co-operative societies and selling the milk and milk products at reasonable prices in cities like Cuttack, Bhubaneswar, Berhampur and Rourkella and other towns.[4] It is revealed from the Table 15.1 that the OMFED has recorded a spectacular performance with regard to its sales of milk and milk products. The OMFED marketed Rs. 180 lakhs during 1984-85, which increased to Rs. 14.79 crores in 1989-90, and subsequently to Rs. 27.20 crores in 1993-94. In percentage term, this increase in sales had been at an annual average of 156 per cent during the period 1984-85 to 1993-94.

The co-operatives milk unions located one each at Balasore, Bolangir, Dhenkanal, Sambalpur, Kalahandi, Ganjam, Baripada

Table 15.1 : Progress of Milk Supply Co-operatives in Orissa

(Rupees in Lakhs)

Sr. No.	*Particulars*	*End of 6th Plan 1984–85*	*End of 7th Plan 1989–90*	*1993–94*
1.	Number of Societies:			
	i) OMFED	1	1	1
	ii) Union	7	8	8
	iii) Primaries	291	461	456
2.	Primaries (000)	26	30	28
3.	Share capital (Primareis)	24	26	21
4.	Working capital (Primaries)	233	245	253
5.	Sales of milk and milk producers			
	i) OMFED	180	1479	2720
	ii) Union	64	105	202
	iii) Primaries	75	100	216

Sources : Data compiled from various issues of Co-operative Movement in Orissa : A Profile.

and Phulbani and 456 Primary Milk Co-operative Societies marketing milk and milk products worth Rs. 2.02 crores and Rs. 2.16 crores respectively through OMFED (Table 15.1).

In the light of above analysis, a few suggestions may be advanced for milk co-operatives. Productivity of milk depends on availability of nutrition fodder at cheap costs which is indispensable for small farmers who undertake milk production over a large area on traditional basis. Small farmers are in the grip of acute shortage of fodder as the milk animals cannot solely depend on crop residuals or on open grazing. Therefore, for raising fodder arrangements through co-operatives should be ensured.

Integrated co-operative arrangement are also indispensable for collection of milk at convenient points, its grading, preservation in storage and transport, processing and ultimately distribution.

Further, improving the quality of animals through cross-breading programme and introduction of new technology in milk processing units can maximise productivity and minimise the cost of production.

Finally, it is anticipated that the National Dairy Development Board, will take development, operation and steps for effective co-ordination among the various institutions involved in the development of dairying.

References

1. Food and Agricultural Organisation of the United Nations (1969), *Manual on Food and Nutrition Policy*, FAO, Rome.
2. Saha, T (1995), Liberalisation and Indian Agriculture: New Role of Farmers Co. operative, *Indian Journal of Agricultural Economics*: Vol. 50(3), p. 491.
3. Ruddar Dutt and K.P.M. Sundaram, *Indian Economy* (1997), S.Chand and Company Ltd., New Delhi.
4. *Cooperative Movement in Orissa : A Profile 1993-94*, Issued by Registrar Co-operative Societies, Orissa, Bhubaneswar.

16

Housing Finance in India : An Overview of Housing Co-operatives

Dr. Bhagabat Patro*
and
Umesh Chandra Panigrahi**

Shelter is recognised as basic human necessity next to food and clothing. The natural desire of every individual is to own a home for providing shelter to himself and his family. Unfortunately, in our country, despite all the efforts made by the Government, ownership of a house remains a distant dream, for a large segment of the population.

The Problem

According, to the estimate of National Building Organisation, the total backlog of housing was estimated at 31 million dwelling units in 1991. Of this, the backlog in rural areas was about 20.6 millions units and the backlog in urban areas are about 10.4 million units. However, the actual backlog of housing shortage is much higher because of the replacement requirement of the existing housing stock, which was not included in the above estimation.

Overcrowding and congestion are some of the disturbing features in the housing condition of the country. The number of persons per dwelling units has increased from 5.60 in 1951 to 5.83

* Dr. Patra is Reader in Economics, Berhampur University (Orissa)
** Sri Panigraphi is Lecturer in Economics, Gopalpur College (Orissa)

in 1961, 6.06 in 1981 and 6.47 in 1991. Again, more than one-third of the country's housing stock is considered to be kutcha units made of non-durable materials. About 70 per cent of the census houses in the rural areas have walls of non-durable materials. Similarly, about 50 per cent of the houses in rural areas have roofs made of non-durable materials. On the whole, the number of houses built in permanent building materials in the country are not more than 30 per cent. This qualitative and quantitative shortage in housing has further aggravated the problem of provisioning the basic amenities like drinking water, sanitation, latrine and electricity. About 67 per cent of population depends on unhygienic sources of water supply like river, ponds, wells etc. Similarly 92 per cent of households in rural areas and 33 per cent in urban areas do not have toiled facilities.

On the whole, the housing problem in our country is of a very severe magnitude and tremendous efforts have to be made to secure adequate and reasonable housing for all. However, it is clear that one of the major constraints for the realisation of this social justice is the insufficient investment in the housing sector. Growth of population, breakdown of the joint family system and inadequate availability of infrastructure are some of other factors responsible for the housing problems. Investment in housing as a proportion to the aggregate plan investment has declined from 34 per cent in the First plan to a mere 12 per cent in the 8th plan (Table 16.1). An examination of the resource allocations for housing sector under Five Year plan indicates that investment in housing in absolute term increased from Rs. 115000/- crores in the First Plan to Rs. 61000 crores in 8th Plan. Of this, the investment made by public sector in housing has increased from Rs. 250 crores in the First Five Year Plan to Rs. 8228/- crores in the Eighth Five Year Plan. (Table 16.2) The investment by private sector increased from Rs. 900 cores to Rs. 69746/- crores in the same period. The proportion of investment in housing by the private sector to the total investment in housing has maintained a dominate position in all the Five Year Plans. The share of the private sector has registered a steady growth over successive plans from more than 75 per cent in the First Plan to more than 91 per cent in the Eighth Five Year Plan.

Structure of Housing Finance in India

Investment in the housing sector comes mainly from two

Table 16.1 : Investment in the Housing Sector

Five Year Plan	*Investment in Housing (Rs. in crore)*	*Total Investment in the Economy (Rs. in crore)*	*Percentage to total Investment*
First	1,150	3,370	34
Second	1,300	6,750	19
Third	1,550	10,400	15
Fourth	2,800	22,635	12
Fifth	4,436	47,561	09
Sixth	19,491	1,72,210	12
Seventh	31,458	3,14,580	10
Eighth	77,976	6,10,000	12

Source : Government of India, The Planning Commission, First Plan to Eighth Plan, New Delhi.

Table 16.2 : Public-Private Sector Investment on Housing

Five Year Plan	*Public Sector*	*Private Sector*	*Public Sector*	*Private Sector*
	(Rs. in Crores)		*(Percentage to total Investment)*	
First	250	900	22	78
Second	300	1000	23	77
Third	425	1125	27	73
Fourth	625	2175	22	78
Fifth	1044	3636	22	78
Sixth	1491	11500	11.5	88.5
Seventh	2458	29000	07	93

Source : Government of India, Ministry of Urban Development, National Housing Policy, 1994.

sources—formal sector and informal sector. The formal Sector, according to Rangarajan Committee (1987), includes budgetary allocation of Central and State Govts. Assistance from financial institutions and agencies such as Life Insurance Corporation (LIC), General Insurance Corporation (GIC), Unit Trust of India (UTI),

Commercial banks, Provident Funds, Housing & Urban Development Corporation (HUDCO), Specialised housing finance institutions and co-operative Housing Financing Societies.

The informal sector, on the other hand, covers households, public and private sector employers extending housing loans to their employees, Private builders providing houses on hire-purchase basis, etc.,

Formal Sector Housing Finance

Formal Sector Housing Finance is flowing to the economy in two major ways: (a) Direct allocation of credit and (b) Mobilisation of resources by accepting deposits and through secularisation. In India, allocation of credit from public financial institutions have been a major source of funding the housing sector. Self-reliant resource mobilisation efforts through capital market is emerging in a new vigour in the recent years to provide financial resources to housing sector.

Central & State Governments are allocating their resources in their respective budgets to implement different social housing schemes. These schemes are implemented for the benefit of economically weaker sections of the society in both urban and rural areas and also for staff housing of Central and State Government employees.

Life Insurance Corporation of India (LIC) and General Insurance Corporation of India (GIC) are the two main primary sources of funding the housing sector and lending money to house building institutions. The LIC also extends housing loans directly to individuals and public sector companies in addition to its own employees. It has a mandate to provide 25 per cent of its annual accretions to the housing sector. In 1989, LIC created a specialised institutions named LIC Housing Finance Ltd., to play greater role in providing finance to housing sector. The LIC has advanced an aggregate of about Rs. 10967 crores for housing for up to March, 1997. The GIC and its subsidiaries advanced 35 per cent of its annual investable funds as loans to the State Governments for rural and EWS Housing, to their housing subsidiaries and to HUDCO.

Prior to 1989, the commercial banks were allocating 0.5 per cent of their total credit for housing. This was revised by Reserve Bank of India. The commercial banks are now required to allocate

1.5 per cent of the annual incremental deposits towards lending to the housing sector. Further, the Bank of India guidelines also asserted that 30 per cent of the allocation should be used for direct lending of which half should be given to rural or semi-urban areas; further 30 per cent of the allocation is to be used for indirect lending and the balance 40 per cent is to be deployed in the Government guaranteed bonds and debentures of HUDCO and NHB. It is estimated that in the 8th Five Year Plan, the contribution of commercial banks is around Rs. 2600 crores for housing sector.

The housing finance companies are of recent origin and involved in providing finance to both individuals and state agencies. The prominent Housing Finance Companies are H.D.F.C., H.U.D.C.O., State Banks Home Finance Ltd., Punjab National Bank Housing Finance Ltd., Can-Fine Homes Finances Ltd., L.I.C. Housing Finance Ltd., Etc.

H.U.D.C.O. is the public sector body operating at national level since 1970 and finances housing projects undertaken by the State Housing Agencies. H.U.D.C.O. also provides financial assistance to co-operative Housing Societies, Private and public sector bodies for undertaking construction of staff housing. H.U.D.C.O.'s lending terms are based on afordability criteria guided by family incomes. Therefore, it adopts differential pattern of housing. HUDCO has allocated 55 per cent of its sanction for E.W.S. and L.I.G. housing projects and balance 45 per cent for middle income group, high-income group, rental and commercial housing projects.

Housing Development Finance Corporation (HDFC) started its functioning since 1978. HDFC provides loan to individuals for house construction and secure its loan by mortgages on property. It also provides loans to co-operative societies and bridge loans for financing construction activities. Its main sources of funds are deposits raised from public and loans from institutions like L.I.C., scheduled banks, G.I.C. and sale of bonds.

The National Housing Banks (NHB) was established as subsidiary of RBI on July 9, 1988 under the National Housing Bank Act, 1987. The aim behind its establishment were : to act as the apex agency to promote housing finance institutions, mobilising the resources for housing sector, provide financial, technical and administrative assistance to housing finance institutions, regulate their working and to co-ordinate with all the agencies connected with housing. Thus, NHB has adopted a multi-agency approach with focus on promoting an efficient and responsive housing finance system.

Provident of pension funds are mandatory savings of the organised sector employees, which are to be invested in Government securities for development programmes. The loans availed by the members from provident fund constitutes a major source of housing finance. Since the quantum of funds available from this source is immense, the issue of loans from it for housing needs is to be explored further.

Unit Trust of India (UTI) has also been supporting housing activities indirectly by way of providing loan to HUDCO and through subscription to bonds and debentures of housing finance Companies. The UTI funds, generally fulfill the needs of high-yielding projects which require heavy investable funds.

Informal Sector Housing Finance

After 50 years of independence informal sector also plays an important role in providing finance to housing sector. The major contribution of the informal sector consists of the households savings by individuals themselves, loans from relatives, provisions of housing loans to employees in both public and private corporate sectors, Sale of houses on hire-purchase basis by the private builders, private money lenders and so on.

II

Cooperative Housing Financing

Co-operative housing has been considered as a well recognised tool for improving the housing situation in India. The concept of non-profit making housing and community as a provider of housing is the basic philosophy of co-operative housing. With taking the moral responsibility, the first cooperative housing society in the country was set up in 1909 in the State of Mysore (now Karnataka) and was known as the Bangalore Building Co-operative Society. Bombay State (Now Maharashtra) in 1913 also set up a housing society known as the Bombay Cooperative Housing Association. It did a pioneering job in propagating the philosophy of co-operative housing by publishing leaflets on various housing problems and the advantages of co-operative housing. In Madras, the Madras Housing Co-operative Society was registered in 1914. However, it became active only in 1923 when the Government started financing it.

Economic depreciation and Second World War significantly affected the growth of the co-operative movements in the housing sector. Thus, in the real sense, the progressive era of housing co-operative began only after independence. The number of registered co-operative housing societies in the country was 792 in 1950. It rose to 80,000 in 1994. The total membership of these societies has also increased from 0.12 million in 1950 to 5 million in 1994 and their working capital has gone up from Rs. 52 million to Rs. 30,000 million in the same period. These societies have been instrumental in the construction of 1.2 million houses in the country till 1994.

The housing movement has, however, not made uniform progress in all the states. The states of Gujarat and Maharashtra claimed a major share of the total i.e. 65 per cent of the total societies in India. In states like Assam, Jammu & Kashmir, the housing movement is almost negligible while in West Bengal and Bihar the progress has also not been satisfactory. A state-wise analysis of the house construction by housing cooperatives in 1993-94 also revealed that states of Karnataka, Tamil Nadu, Gujarat and Maharasthra accounted for 70 per cent of the total houses constructed.

Statistical information shows that the co-operative housing sector has served the poorer sections of the population in a significant way. As much as 52 per cent of total loans sanctioned by the apex cooperative housing societies has benefited the poorer sections and about 72 per cent of the total houses constructed were for low-income groups and economically weaker sections. The apex societies in Assam, Goa, Haryana, Jammu & Kashmir, Maharashtra, Meghalaya, Orissa, Manipur, Pondicheri, Punjab, Rajasthan, Tamil Nadu and West Bengal have introduced rural housing schemes. At present 2000 primary housing cooperative are functioning in rural areas in India.

The co-operative housing Sectnr has evolved a well defined organisational hierarchy comprising of primary housing co-operatives, district federations, state level federations, and the National Co-operative Housing Federation of India.

Primary Housing Co-operatives

A housing Co-operative Society is a legally incorporated organisation of a group of people who desire to develop their houses with collective efforts. After registering with the Registrar of Co-operative Societies under the concerned state co-operative Societies Act, a primary housing co-operative society will undertake housing business on behalf of its members for housing developments.

These primary societies are either engaged in construction of houses or providing finance to their members for house construction against mortgage. The construction societies are again of two types—one which is engaged in the business of construction on an on-going basis and the other is formed basically for construction of houses for their members after which societies exist only for maintenance services for the dwelling units constructed.

District-Level Federation

The district level co-operative housing federations are developed to assist primary housing co-operative of a given district. Such federations exist only in the state of Maharashtra, Gujarat and Uttar Pradesh.

State-Level Federation

The apex co-operative finance societies play a significant role in providing financial assistance to primary and district level co-operative housing societies in their respective jurisdiction. They provide guidance on technical matters, help them in procuring building materials and assist them in general co-ordination and supervision of activities. There are 25 such federations in the country.

National Co-operative Housing Federation of India

The National Co-operative Housing Federation of India (NCHF) was set up in 1969 on the recommendation of the working group on Housing Co-operatives appointed by the Government of India in 1964. It acts as the Chief spokesman of housing Co-operatives at the national level which provide guidance and advise and co-ordinate the activities of the housing co-operatives. It conducts seminars, orientation programmes and symposia to disseminate the new concepts in construction of low cost housing technology in particular among the housing co-operatives.

Housing Co-operative in Orissa

Co-operative housing movement in Orissa is not much satisfactory. However, it has slow and steady growth over the years. Orissa has an apex housing co-operative society since independence. Primary co-operative societies are organised at the grass root level. These societies are at present reorganised into six Urban Co-operative Housing Societies and 57 Sub-divisional housing cooperative societies. Apart from these also 22 primary House Building Societies specially organised by the staff of S.B.I., R.B.I., and other commercial banks. Thus, there are 85 primary housing cooperatives providing their services at present in Orissa. (Table 16.3).

The Primary Hosing Co-operative has increased their membership from a mere 20 in 1950-51 to 50,000 in 1994. They had started their business with Rs.. 4 lakh as working capital in 1950-51 which has increased to Rs. 27.57 crores during 1994. The total number of houses constructed by these societies were 13,509 by the end of 1994.

The condition of housing co-operatives were far from satisfactory. It is found that more then 45 per cent of housing societies are working under loss and another 20 per cent are on no-loss-no-profit basis in the state. (Table16.4). Further, even though remaining 30 per cent of housing societies are making marginal profits, a majority have not earned the profit consecutively.

Source of Finance of the Housing Co-operatives

The main source of finance of the housing co-operatives consists of (a) Share capital (b) Statutory reserves, (c) Borrowings from i) Government, (ii) Central co-operative banks and (iii) other agencies. At present they can raise loans and accept deposits from private sources. Nevertheless the main source of finance has been the LIC. The total contribution of the LIC up to March 31, 1995 is Rs. 2216 crores to the Co-operative Housing Sector.

HUDCO has been sanctioning co-operative housing schemes to apex co-operative housing federation as well as primary housing societies since 1974. It has sanctioned Rs. 719.54 crores for

Table 16.3 : House Building Co-operative Movement in Orissa

	1950-51	*1st Plan*	*2nd Plan*	*3rd Plan*	*4th Plan*	*5th Plan*	*6th Plan*	*7th Plan*	*1990-91*	*1991-92*	*1992-93*	*1993-94*	*1994-95*
No. of (Apex) C.S.	–	1	1	1	1	1	1	1	1	1	1	1	1
No. of Primary C.S.	10	46	299	622	459	427	111	80	94	97	85	86	80
Membership (Apex)	–	–	196	421	449	427	63	78	81	65	65	65	65
Membership (Pry.) (in '000s)	0.02	2	12	21	24	24	27	39	43	46	50	50	58
Working Capital (Apex) (in lakhs)	–	–	129	172	204	171	556	2451	3134	3430	3430	3430	3430
Working Capital (Pry.) (Rs. in lakh)	04	91	104	169	175	161	497	2242	2567	2860	3342	2757	3305
Loan Advance (Apex) (Rs. in Lakh)	1	1	53	12	7	182	183	259	387	356	–	–	–
Loan Advance (Pry.) (Rs. in Lakh)	2	2	34	14	1	3	165	352	308	331	416	437	704
House Construction (Pry.)	–	128	1345	2355	449	524	1022	332	1629	1903	531	400	2891
Profit (Apex) (in Lakh)	–	–	1	1	1	1	4	–	–	21	–	–	–
Profit (Pry.) (in '000s)	–	01	1	1	2	3	24	5	15	13	25	10	20

Source : Cooperative Movement in Orissa. A Profile 1994–95, Registrar of Co-operative Societies, Orissa, BBSR.

Table 16.4 : Position of Primary Housing Cooperatives in Orissa

	1990–91	*1991–92*	*1992–93*	*1993–94*	*1994–95*
Profit :					
No.	52	45	32	27	27
Amount:(in Lakh)	9	13	25	10	20
Loss :					
No.	23	30	36	38	43
Amount (In Lakh)	11	14	60	28	69
No-Loss—No-Profit :					
No.	6	10	17	21	10

construction of 481537 dwelling units upto 1994, both at apex as well as primary level, in the urban and rural areas of India. Around 10 per cent of the working funds of HUDCO are now invested for the benefit of co-operative housing needs. The National Housing Bank also provides loans to the housing co-operatives under its refinance scheme. It has provided Rs. 177 crores to the co-operative housing sector till present.

Housing co-operatives provide housing building loans to its members for construction, renovation and extension of house. Recently, a new scheme known as self-financing scheme has been adopted to provide loans for purchase of flats, apartments sponsored by development authorities, Housing Board and Private Estate Developers. Loans are provided on easy term with less interests both in urban and rural areas. Maximum loan available is Rs. 2,00,000/- in urban and Rs. 70,000/- in rural areas.

Housing Co-operative in the Ninth Five Year Plan

Inadequate financial resources have always been an impediment for fulfilling the housing requirements in the country. Taking the above facts in view, the Planning Commission requested for an amount of Rs. 3000 crores for the housing co-operative during 9th Five Year Plan, the details of which are given in Table 16.5. An equal amount of Rs. 3,000 crores is also be contributed by the housing co-operatives. Thus the total amount of Rs. 6000/- crores would be available to the housing co-operatives during the 9th Five Year Plan period for construction of 12.5 lakh units of new house.

Table 16.5 : Housing Co-operatives in 9th Plan

Year	*Loan Requirement from Govt. Agencies (Rs. in crores)*	*Contribution by Housing Cooperatives (Rs. in crore)*	*No. of houses to be constructed*
1997–98	400.00	400.00	2,00,000
1998–99	500.00	500.00	2,25,000
1999–2000	600.00	600.00	2,50,000
2000–2001	700.00	700.00	2,75,000
2001–2002	800.00	800.00	3,00,000
Total	**3000.00**	**3000.00**	**12,50,000**

Source: Alagh, Yoginder, K. R. Sharma, Prem. S., Ninth Plan Perspective Role of Co-operatives in various segment of co-operatives movement.

Planning Commission, to strengthen co-operative housing sector, suggested the Government to allot 30 per cent of the acquired land to housing co-operatives on a priority basis. It also advised to State Authorities to provide low cost building materials and cost-effective construction technologies to the housing co-operative for construction of houses for their members.

Conclusions

An examination of statistical figures reveals that the housing finance rooted through the co-operative sector is negligible, even though they have a very strong institutional presence. This proves that the potential of co-operative sector has not been tapped adequately to the advantages of rural poor. The co-operative housing to sector has some decisive advantage over it. The other counterparts are : lower rate of interest, quick processing of the applications, greater integration among the population belonging a particular co-operative group and lastly, development of a cultural unit in the co-operatives. These advantages justify emphatic policy intervention of the central and state Government in boosting co-operative *Housing Sector.*

References

1. Bijalani., H.C. & Rao, P.S.N.: "Community Living, State Intervention and Housing Coopertives".

—Umasankar, P.K. & Misra, Girish, K. (Editors) 1993, "Public-private Responsiblility in Urban Housing." Reliance Publishing House & IIPA, New Delhi.

2. Banarjee, Jayadeva. & Aggarwal, Dinesh. (1985) "Housing Co-operatives in West Bengal: Law, Practice & Procedure". Eastern Law House, Calcutta.
3. Mathur, B.S.: Co-operative Movement in India, 1972.
4. Khurana, M.L.: (1995); Co-operative Housing in India: The role of H.U.D.C.O. The Co-operative story of HUDCO 1970-1995(Ed) HUDCO, New Delhi, 1995.
5. Sharma, S.C.: "Housing & Urban Development during Five Year Plans".
6. Tripathy Patanjali: "In pursuit of providing shelter to All", India Express, May 3, 1997.
7. Mahadeva, M: "Housing Finance System in India: An overview" Nagarlok, Volume: XXXVIII, July- Sept, 1996.
8. Alagh, Yoginder, K. & Sharma, Prem. S. : Ninth Plan perspective: Role of Co-operatives in various segments of Co-operative Movement. Co-operative Planning Commission, New Delhi.
9. Housing Finance Institutions Directory, 1996 N.B.O., Government of India, Nirman Bhawan, New Delhi.
10. Hand Book of Housing Statistic, Part-I, 1996. NBO, Government of India, Nirman, Bhawan, New Delhi.
11. Co-operative Movement in Orissa: A Profile 1990-91, — 1994-95. Registrar of Co-operative Societies, Orissa, Bhubaneswar.

Table 11.2

Years	Working Capital (in lakhs)	Share Capital (in lakhs)	No. of looms	Emp. (000)	Prod. (Lakh sqm.)	Sales (in lakhs)	VCP (in lakhs)	Value of Clothes remain unsold (in lakhs)
1990-91	5793.09	192.7	104290	209	516	2933.7	4587.2	1653.8
1991-92	4316.41	391.3	103513	207	361	3552.3	5099.22	1547.6
1992-93	N.A.	N.A.	104951	210	418	N.A.	N.A.	N.A.
1993-94	8565.80	326.9	105662	211	382	4645.4	5326.03	680.03

Source : Annual Audit Reports from the Office of the Registrar of Co-operatives, Orissa.